Treasures from the Princeton Theologians

Edward N. Gross

Treasures From the Princeton Theologians

ISBN: Softcover 978-1-955581-07-3

Copyright © 2021 by Edward N. Gross

All rights reserved. No part of this book may be reproduced or transmitted in any form or by any means, electronic or mechanical, including photocopying, recording, or by any information storage and retrieval system, without permission in writing from the publisher.

Cover Art by Bonnie Heppe Fisher.

Parson's Porch Books is an imprint of Parson's Porch *&* Company (PP*&*C) in Cleveland, Tennessee. PP*&*C is an innovative organization which raises money by publishing books of noted authors, representing all genres. Its face and voice is **David Russell Tullock** (dtullock@parsonsporch.com).

Parson's Porch *&* Company *turns books into bread & milk* by sharing its profits with the poor.

www.parsonsporch.com

Treasures from the Princeton Theologians

List of Works Quoted

AA-PS	Practical Sermons by Archibald Alexander (Presbyterian Board of Publications)
AA-TRE	Thoughts on Religious Experience by Archibald Alexander (Presbyterian Board of Publications)
AA-PT	Practical Truths by Archibald Alexander (American Tract Society)
CH-STA	Systematic Theology by Charles Hodge, Abridged - (edited by Edward N Gross, Baker Book House)
CH-CP	Conference Papers by Charles Hodge (Charles Scribner's Sons)
CH-WL	Way of Life by Charles Hodge (American Sunday School Union)
CH-CE	Commentary on Ephesians by Charles Hodge, James Nisbet & Co.
AAH-CF	Commentary on the Confession of Faith by AA Hodge (Presbyterian Board of Publication)
AAH-OT	Outlines of Theology by AA Hodge, (T Nelson and Sons)
BBW-SSW	Selected Shorter Works by BB Warfield (vol 1, edited by John Meeter, Presbyterian & Reformed)
BBW-SW	The Savior of the World by BB Warfield (Hodder and Stoughton)

These works are a small number of the many works from which great assistance could be secured by Christians today. They have been selected as they represent a good number of both in print and out of print works which ought to intrigue all readers to examine the Princetonians much more thoroughly.

Dedication

I dedicate this anthology to Debby's and my grandchildren

De'Amour Mutloatse

Zaniya Williams

Dieu'Avie Mutloatse

Myles Williams

Zoey Williams

Blaze Schutte

Maxwell Williams

with the prayer that each one may believe in and follow Jesus as a fruitful disciple.

Contents

List of Works Quoted 5
Dedication 7
A Tribute to Benjamin Breckinridge Warfield 23
Preface 31
How Old Princeton Has Helped Me 31
    ACTIVITY 35
    ADOPTION 35
    AFFLICTION 35
    AGGRESSIVE NATURE OF CHRISTIANITY 36
    AMBITION 36
    ANGELS 36
    ANTINOMIANISM 38
    APOLOGETICS 38
    APOSTACY 39
    APOSTLES 39
    ARMOR OF GOD 40
    ASSURANCE 41
    ATHEISM 41
    ATONEMENT 42
    AUGUSTINIANISM 43
    BACKSLIDING 43
    BALANCE 44
    BAPTISM 44
    BEAUTY 45
    BEHAVIOR 45
    BENEDICTION 46
    BIBLE 46

BLOOD	46
BODY	46
BONDAGE	47
BROTHERLY LOVE	47
CALL OF GOD	47
CALVINISM	49
CARNALLY MINDED.	49
CATHOLICITY	50
CHARACTER	50
CHARITY	51
CHASTISEMENT	51
CHILDREN	51
CHRISTIAN	52
CHRISTIANITY	53
CHRISTMAS	54
CHURCH	55
CHURCH AND STATE	56
CIRCUMCISION	57
COMMON GRACE	57
COMMUNION OF SAINTS	58
COMMUNAL SHARING OF GOODS	58
CONFESSION OF CHRIST	59
CONSCIENCE	59
CONSCIENTIOUS	60
CONTENDING FOR THE FAITH	60
CONTENTMENT	60
CONTROVERSY	60

CONVICTION OF SIN	60
CONVICTIONS	61
COVENANT OF GRACE	61
COVENANT OF WORKS	61
CREATION	62
CROSS	63
CROWN	64
CRUCIFIXION	64
DEATH	65
DECEITFULNESS OF SIN	66
DECREES OF GOD	66
DEFENSE OF THE FAITH	67
DEGRADATION	67
DEMONS	67
DEPRAVITY	69
DESIGN	70
DESPAIR	70
DISCIPLES	70
DISCIPLINE	70
DISEASE	71
DISPENSATIONS	71
DISTRACTIONS	72
DIVORCE	72
DOCTRINE	72
DREAMS	73
DRESS	74
DUTY	74

EDUCATION	74
ELECT	75
ELECTION	75
ENEMIES	76
EPISTLES	77
ERROR	77
ESCHATOLOGY	78
ETERNAL LIFE	78
ETERNAL STATE	78
EVANGELISM	79
EVIDENCE	80
EXORCISM	80
EXPIATION	80
EXPERIENCE	80
FAITH	81
FAITHFULNESS	84
FALL OF MAN	84
FALSE TEACHERS	85
FASTING	86
FEELINGS	86
FELLOWSHIP	86
FIGHT OF FAITH	87
FOOLS	87
FORGIVENESS	88
FREE-WILL	88
FRUIT OF THE SPIRIT	89
FRUITFULNESS	89

FUTURE PUNISHMENT	89
GIFTS	90
GIVING	91
GLORIFYING GOD	91
GLORY OF GOD	92
GOD	93
GOSPEL	100
GRACE	101
GREAT COMMISSION	102
GROWTH IN GRACE	103
GUILT	103
HAPPINESS	103
HARSHNESS	104
HEART	104
HEAVEN	105
HELL (See Future Punishment)	105
HERESY	105
HISTORY	106
HOLINESS	107
HOLY SPIRIT	107
HOPE	110
HUMILITY	110
HYPOCRISY	111
IDOLATRY	111
IGNORANCE	112
IMAGE OF GOD	112
IMMORALITY	112

IMPUTATION	112
INCARNATION	113
INDECISION	113
INFANTS	113
INFIDELITY (Skepticism)	114
INHERITANCE	114
INSIGNIFICANCE	114
INSPIRATION	115
INTERCESSION	116
INTERPRETATION OF SCRIPTURE	117
INTOLERANCE	118
JEHOVAH	118
JESUS CHRIST	119
JOY	125
JUDGING OTHERS	126
JUSTIFICATION	127
KINDNESS	128
KINGDOM OF GOD	128
KNOWLEDGE	129
LABOR	130
THE LAMB OF GOD	131
LANGUAGE	131
THE LAMB OF GOD	131
LIBERTY	133
LIFE	134
LIGHT	134
THE LORD'S SUPPER	134

THE LOST	135
LOVE	135
MARRIAGE	137
MATERIALISM	137
MEANS OF GRACE	137
MEDIATOR	137
MEDITATION	138
MERCY	138
MESSIAH	138
MINISTERS	139
CHRISTIAN MINISTRY	140
MIRACLES	141
MISSIONARIES	142
MONEY	143
MONOTHEISM	143
MORALITY	143
MORTIFICATION (Dying to Sin)	144
MYSTICISM	144
NATIONS	145
NATURAL MAN	145
NATURAL THEOLOGY	146
OATHS	148
OBITUARIES	148
OBEDIENCE	148
OBLIGATION	149
OLD AGE	149
ORIGINAL RIGHTEOUSNESS	149

ORIGINAL SIN	149
ORTHODOXY	150
PANTHEISM	150
PARADISE	150
PAUL & ISAIAH	151
PEACE	151
PELAGIANISM	151
PERFECTION	152
PERSEVERANCE	152
PHARISEEISM	153
PHILOSOPHY	153
PHYSICIANS	154
POLYGAMY	154
THE POOR	154
POVERTY	155
POWER	155
PRAISE	156
PRAYER	156
-United	158
PRAYERLESSNESS	159
PREACHING	159
PREDESTINATION	159
PRESERVATION	160
PRIDE	160
PRIESTHOOD OF BELIEVERS	160
PROCRASTINATION	161
PROFESSION OF FAITH	161

PROGRESSIVE REVELATION	161
PROMISES OF GOD	162
PROPERTY	162
PROPHECY	163
PROPHETS	163
PROTESTANTISM	163
PROVIDENCE OF GOD	163
QUALIFICATIONS FOR THE CHRISTIAN MINISTRY	164
RATIONALISM	164
REASON	165
RECONCILIATION	166
REDEMPTION	166
THE REFORMATION	168
REGENERATION	168
RELIGION	169
REPENTANCE	169
REPROOF	170
REPUTATION	171
RESPONSIBILITY	171
RESTITUTION	171
RESTORATION	172
RESURRECTION	172
REVELATION	173
REVIVAL OF RELIGION	173
REWARD	174
RULERS	174
SABBATH	174

SACRAMENTS	175
SALVATION	176
SANCTIFICATION	177
SATAN	178
THE SAVIOR	180
SCRIPTURE	180
SECURITY OF BELIEVERS	183
SEDUCTION	183
SELF CONTROL	184
SELF DECEPTION	184
SELF DEPENDENCE	184
SELF DENIAL	185
SELF EXAMINATION	185
SELFISHNESS	185
SELF SACRIFICE	186
SEMI-PELAGIANISM	186
SENSUALITY	187
SEPARATION FROM THE WORLD	187
SERVANTS OF CHRIST	187
SERVICE	188
SHEEP	188
SIN	188
SINGING	191
SINGLEMINDEDNESS	191
SINNERS	191
SOLDIERS OF CHRIST	192
SONSHIP	192

SORROW	193
THE SOUL'S WORTH	193
SPEECH	193
SPIRIT	193
SPIRITUALITY	194
STABILITY	194
STRENGTH	194
STUDENTS OF THEOLOGY	194
SUBMISSION TO GOD	195
SUFFERING	196
TAKING OFFENSE	196
TALENTS	196
TEMPERAMENT	197
TEMPLE OF GOD	197
TEMPTATION	197
TEN COMMANDMENTS	198
TESTIMONIES	198
THEOLOGIANS	198
THEOLOGY	199
THEORIES	200
THINGS INDIFFERENT	201
TIME	201
TONGUE	201
TOTAL ABSTINENCE	202
TRANSLATION OF THE SCRIPTURES	202
TRIBULATION	202
TRINITY	203

TROUBLE	204
TRUTH	205
UNION WITH CHRIST	207
UNITY OF BELIEVERS	207
UNITY OF MANKIND	207
VISIONS	208
VOCATION	208
VOWS	209
WALKING WITH GOD	209
WAR	210
WARFARE, SPIRITUAL	210
WATCHMEN	212
WATER	212
WEALTH	212
WILL	212
WISDOM	212
WITNESSING FOR CHRIST	213
WORDS	213
THE WORD OF GOD	214
THE WORK OF THE LORD	215
WORKS (GOOD)	215
WORLD	216
WORLDLINESS	216
WORSHIP	216
WRESTLING	217
WRITING	217
YOUTH	217

ZEAL..218
Appendix One...219
Thoughts on Archibald Alexander, Charles Hodge, and AA Hodge....... 219
by the late Dr. David C. Calhoun

A Tribute to Benjamin Breckinridge Warfield
on the 100th Anniversary of His Death

(1851-1921)

On this centennial anniversary of the death of BB Warfield, we want to praise God for his life and work as the fourth Old Princeton theologian. It was in the year that Princeton's first great theologian, Archibald Alexander, died (1851), that Benjamin Breckenridge Warfield was born at his family's estate near Lexington, Kentucky.

Being a precocious Presbyterian child, Warfield memorized the Shorter Catechism by six years of age, and at sixteen, professed his faith and became a member of Second Presbyterian Church in Lexington, KY.

Church historian and Princeton expert, David C Calhoun wrote, "He entered Princeton College in 1868 as a sophomore. His greatest academic interests were in mathematics and physics, in which he obtained perfect marks. He graduated in 1871 at the age of nineteen, having won highest honors, prizes for essay and debate, and a fellowship in science for further studies in Europe."[1]

Warfield would later reflect on his college years from 1868-1871: "Religion was a very real and a very persuasive force among us.... It was said in our time that no class in Princeton College ever passed through its four years without experiencing a religious revival. Our class formed no exception. Our revival came near the end of our junior year. Scarcely anyone in the class was left unchanged...."[2]

A visiting Scottish minister, William Arnot, pastor of Free High Church, Edinburgh, visited Princeton with a colleague and wrote, "It is a greater college than I expected.... We attended... the students' own prayer meeting – three hundred in the chapel; both of us addressed them; tender and impressive meeting."[3]

Following his graduation, Warfield surprised his parents, in an 1872 letter from Europe, by announcing that he desired to enter studies for the Christian ministry. "Years later Charles Barrett, a close college friend and companion

---

[1] David Calhoun, Princeton Seminary, Banner of Truth Trust, vol 2, pp 118-119.
[2] David Calhoun, Princeton Seminary, BTT, vol 2, p22.
[3] David Calhoun, Princeton Seminary, BTT, vol 2, p22.

in Europe, who was also beginning seminary study, remembered their first Sunday evening at the seminary: … 'What was it that decided you to enter the ministry? I can see his face, the tender look that came into his face. He was very near to me just at that moment, now forty-three years ago…. I can hear the very tone of his voice. He turned to me and said, Because I think that in the work of the ministry I can do the most to repay the Lord for what he has done for me.'"[4]

After serving churches in Concord, KY, and Dayton, OH, Warfield married Annie Pearce Kinkaid, the daughter of a prominent Lexington lawyer who, among other notable legal accomplishments, had won a case defending Abraham Lincoln. Declining a call to serve further in the Dayton church, Benjamin and Annie went to Europe for a honeymoon and his further studies at the University of Leipzig. This was an eventful time for them both.

Warfield studied under Old Testament scholar Franz Delitszch and made many lifelong friends. But Annie suffered some form of nervous disorder while hiking with her husband in the Harz Mountains during a thunderstorm. Though active during their pre-Princeton days (pre-1887), this condition slowly progressed until, much later in Princeton, she became an "invalid," demanding much care from Dr. Warfield. Though they did travel some, her worsening condition further limited their travel and Warfield often chose "to be near her in her relatively frail nervous condition rather than accepting engagements away."[5]

Calhoun adds, "In 1887 Benjamin Breckenridge Warfield was called from Western Seminary to Princeton to succeed Archibald Alexander Hodge as the Charles Hodge Professor of Didactic and Polemic Theology. The thirty-six-year-old Warfield had established a solid reputation as a careful biblical scholar….

"In his inaugural address, Warfield said, 'Though the power of Charles Hodge may not be upon me, the theology of Charles Hodge is within me… and this is the theology… I have… in my heart to teach …. Oh, that the mantle of my Elijah might fall upon my shoulders; at least the message that was given him is set within my lips.'"[6]

---

[4] David C Calhoun, Princeton Seminary, vol 2, Banner of Truth Trust, p 117
[5] Fred Zaspel, Banner of Truth, issue 595, Apr 2013, pp 22-26 for a fuller account of the life of Anne K Warfield.
[6] David C Calhoun, Princeton Seminary, vol 2, BTT, pp113-114

Warfield's address was on the topic of "Verbal Inspiration" and his summary stated,

> "If the sacred writers clearly claim verbal inspiration and every phenomena supports that claim, and all critical objections break down by their own weight, how can we escape admitting its truth? What further proof do we need? ...Let us bless God, then, for His inspired word! And may He grant that we may always cherish, love, and venerate it, and conform all our life and thinking to it! So may we find safety for our feet, and peaceful security to our souls."[7]

Dr. Calhoun continues, "The best-known teacher at Princeton Seminary at the turn of the century was B. B. Warfield. Fifty years old in 1902, Dr Warfield was in his prime. Student O.T. Allis described Warfield as 'a tall, dignified, and impressive figure, [with] ruddy cheeks, hair parted in the middle, sparkling eyes, and a graying full beard.' With 'singular grace and courtesy of demeanor,' he 'bore the marks of a gentleman to his fingertips.'"[8]

George L. Robinson, a 1903 graduate from Princeton Seminary and further student in Germany, reminisced,

> "Dr Warfield was the best teacher I ever had either in America or Germany. I took notes under him assiduously; and the notes I took I have used more than those of all other professors together. He taught us with rare clarity and persuasiveness. He combined quizzing and lecturing in a most marvelous way. He kept a man on his feet from twenty to thirty minutes, interrogating him and in Socratic style informing him."[9]

Throughout his life, while, in his writings, he related, patiently debated, and kindly defeated many sub-biblical claims and aberrant views, Warfield defended "the three pillars" on which he believed the structure of Christianity rested: the supernatural, the incarnation, and redemption."[10]

Calhoun summarized, Warfield's "scholarly emphases shifted during the decades of his life. As a New Testament professor in the 1880s he dealt mostly with textual criticism... revelation and inspiration. The historical

---

[7] In Calhoun, Princeton Seminary, Banner of Truth Trust, vol 2, p119
[8] D Calhoun, Princeton Seminary, BTT, vol 2, p 204
[9] In Calhoun, Princeton Seminary, BTT, vol. 2, p 205
[10] David Calhoun, Princeton Seminary, BTT, vol 2, p 246

origins captured his attention during the 1890s. From 1900-1910 he focused on Christology, and from 1910-1921 he wrote on the application of redemption and the doctrine of sanctification. After his death about half of Dr Warfield's written works were selected by Ethelbert Warfield, Caspar Wistar Hodge, and William Armstrong and published in ten substantial volumes by the American division of Oxford University Press."[11]

Dr. J. Gresham Machen "believed that despite his constant care for his wife, Dr. Warfield had 'done about as much work as ten ordinary men.'"[12] Calhoun reflects, "By a profound study and extensive reading in English, German, French and Dutch, BB Warfield, to a degree that has rarely been equaled, excelled in the whole field of theological learning – exegetical, historical, and doctrinal"[13]

I think that, given the global contemporary concerns about race, prejudice, and racial reconciliation, it will be particularly interesting to our readers to note how he related to this important social issue. David Calhoun wrote,

> "Dr. Warfield had a particular sympathy and concern for African Americans. Warfield, wrote that since Christians know 'that God has made of one blood all the nations of the earth,' their task is to 'serve as the hand of the Most High in elevating the lowly and rescuing the oppressed.' He questioned whether it was 'good public policy (apart from all question of religion and the kingdom of God) to continue a social system that allowed a class of people to have heaped upon it year after year, petty injustices and insults, to beget undying hatred in its heart and to perpetuate all the evils of race alienation into an indefinite future, if not even to treasure up for ourselves wrath against the day of wrath?'"[14]

Dr. Calhoun continues, "As a Southerner – 'in birth, training, and affiliations' …Warfield admitted sorrowfully that 'the Southern people are not thoroughly awake either to the necessity of, or to their duty in this matter.' In a brief poem entitled **Wanted – A Samaritan**, Warfield, thinking and wresting about racial inequality, wrote,

---

[11] Calhoun, Princeton Seminary Banner of Truth Trust, vol. 2, p 321
[12] Calhoun, Princeton Seminary, BTT, vol. 2, p. 316
[13] In Calhoun, Princeton Seminary, BTT, vol. 2, p 320
[14] David Calhoun, Princeton Seminary, BTT, vol. 2, p 326

Prone in the road he lay,
Wounded and sore bested;
Priests, Levites, passed that way,
And turned aside the head.
They were not hardened men
In human service slack:
His need was great, but then,
His face, you see, was black."[15]

In 1913, while Warfield was acting President of the seminary for just one year, he offended some "by vigorously supporting the seminary's decision to allow a black student to live in Alexander Hall…. In 1922 President Lowell of Harvard refused to allow black students to live in Harvard's dorms. From its early period, Princeton Seminary admitted African-American students and later provided them with the opportunity to take graduate courses at the college. When in 1876 some college students protested to (President) James McCosh about a black student enrolled in his course, McCosh suggested that they were perfectly free to drop the course. But even McCosh was not able to change the undergraduate admissions policy. Princeton University did not have an African American graduate until 1947."[16]

Warfield scholar, Dr. Fred Zaspel, wrote a brilliant, helpful, and well-researched article in *Themelios* entitled, **"Reversing the Gospel: Warfield on Race and Racism"** (pp 25-32). In it, he states,

> "Benjamin Breckinridge Warfield (1851–1921) of Old Princeton earned international reputation as the vigorous defender of the historic Christian faith-particularly in its Reformed expression- and it was in the traditional categories of biblical and theological studies that his publishing energies were almost exclusively spent. Social causes crop up only very seldom in his works, but one social cause stands out as one holding his particular interest: the cause of the American blacks. His literary output here was not extensive, to be sure, but it was pointed, revealing a deep sense of urgency about the issue. And though Warfield seldom became involved in any organized efforts outside the seminary, this was the exception ….
>
> "To Warfield, the "wicked caste" society that America then was constituted a moral and theological evil that, if not reversed, would

---

[15] David Calhoun, Princeton Seminary, Banner of Truth Trust, vol 2, p 326
[16] David Calhoun, Princeton Seminary, BTT, vol 2, pp 505-506

bring only further harm to our nation. The theological foundation of Warfield's opposition to racism was two-fold: 1) the unity of humans created in Adam in God's image, and 2) the unifying entailments of the gospel of Christ.[17]

Zaspel shows how "both of Warfield's parents had come from families of outspoken abolitionists and with important connections to the cause of emancipation."[18] Dr. Zaspel further noted,

> "However, the post-civil war-even post-reconstruction-society was still deeply segregated, even if the slaves had been freed. Race antagonism was not gone, and in this decidedly segregated society blacks were given little room for self- or social advancement. The plight of the freedmen and their children as Warfield presents it-as 'virtually subjects and not citizens, peasants instead of freedmen,' though seven million of America's then fifty million souls-is disturbingly revealing. 'Wicked caste' was not at all overstating the case, Warfield insisted, and when he took up this cause he must have seemed a voice virtually alone. In 1885 Warfield became a member of the Presbyterian Board of Missions to Freedmen and worked for their betterment. As noted above, Warfield was not given to social activism, and he was not disposed to serve on committees. But this was the exception, and his passion for the cause is evident. In 1887 and 1888 he published articles decrying the accepted situation and pleading for Christians to consider more seriously the doctrine they profess to believe."[19]

BB Warfield was beloved and revered by his students. As a preacher, he was not shy to express his heart and passion. He wanted them to grow strong in Christ and by His Spirit. So, "he suggested a dozen devotional classics that he looked upon as 'indispensable':

> Augustine's *Confessions; The Imitation of Christ;* Rutherford's *Letters;* John Bunyan's *Pilgrim's Progress* and William Law's *Serious Call* to name a few. "To these ... I should add two or three others which have peculiar interest to us as Princetonians, Jonathan Edwards'

---

[17] Fred Zaspel, Themelios, p 25
[18] Zaspel, Themelios, p27
[19] Fred Zaspel, Themelios, p

Religious Affections, Archibald Alexander's *Thoughts on Religious Experience* and Charles Hodge's *Way of Life.*"[20]

On Christmas Eve of 1920 Dr Warfield suffered a heart attack. He returned to teach an afternoon class on 1 John 3, A student present noted, "the discourse quickly gathered about the sixteenth verse as a center – 'Hereby perceive we the love of God, because he laid down his life for us; and we ought to lay down our lives for the brethren.' All the eloquence of Dr Warfield's Christian heart, all the wisdom of his ripened scholarship focused on the interpretation of that text. The laying down of His life in our stead was a great thing, but the wonder of the text is that He being all that He was, the Lord of glory, laid down His life for us, being what we are, mere creatures of His hand, guilty sinners deserving His wrath. 'The more fully we realize his glory and his gift and our sinfulness,' Dr Warfield continued, 'the deeper becomes our wonder at His grace and our wish to glorify His name.'"[21]

Following THAT lecture, he returned home, long without the presence of his beloved Anne who died six years prior, and that evening went home to be with the Jesus he so loved.

So lived and died, by any measure, a very great man. A giant intellect and massive heart. "John DeWitt said that he had known intimately the three great Reformed theologians of America in the preceding generation – Charles Hodge, William Shedd, and Henry B Smith – and that he was certain not only that Warfield knew a great deal more than any one of them, but that he knew more than all three of them together!"[22]

Calhoun captures the sentiment at Warfield's passing and well beyond, "The Princetonians – Warfield's colleagues and his students – respected Dr. Warfield as a master thinker and teacher and loved him as a humble Christian who helped them live more Christ-like lives. Twenty years after he studied at Princeton, F. T. McGill wrote that BB Warfield 'possessed the most perfect combination of faculties of mind and heart that I have ever known in any person…. If Dr Warfield was great in intellectuality, he was just as great in goodness. Over a long period of years this man stands out in my mind as the most Christ-like man I have ever known.'"[23]

---

[20] David Calhoun, Princeton Seminary, Banner of Truth Trust, vol 2, p 324
[21] David Calhoun, Princeton Seminary, BTT, vol 2, p 317
[22] In David Calhoun, Princeton Seminary vol 2, p 320, BTT
[23] Calhoun, Princeton Seminary, BTT, vol 2, p 325

It is a true honor, on this 100th year anniversary of his death, to present both this biographical sketch and quotations of Dr. Benjamin B. Warfield, together with the other Old Princeton theologians. May it help secure for them the attention and respect that their lives and ministries deserve. And may this anthology become an often-resorted-to treasure for many throughout the 21st century and until Jesus returns.

David C Calhoun, Fred Zaspel and Edward N Gross, Contributors

(June 2021)

Preface

How Old Princeton Has Helped Me

"And through his (Abel) faith, though he died, he still speaks" (Heb. 11:4b).

I became a Christian during a tumultuous family time in my childhood home. My dad and mom were contemplating divorce (1966) when mom went to a gospel preaching church, taking my brother John and me. That night, Feb 27, 1966, we were all converted (at different services). Though we did not know it, "the old had passed away; behold, the new had come." Dad bowed his knee to Jesus later that year. The marriage and family were saved, with my parents later becoming medical missionaries in Africa.

We all began devouring the Bible. We noted the truth of what Jesus promised in both our lives and many others. "And the one who falls on this stone will be broken to pieces; and when it falls on anyone, it will crush him" (Matt. 22:44). By His sovereign and amazing grace, we were led to fall upon Him and not He upon us! Our lives were thoroughly broken, healed, and restored by His saving power.

Love, obedience, joy, and fruitfulness-with persecution, all became a part of my life. Bible reading and memorization, with concordance in hand, were in these early years my consuming focus. When I discovered Cruden's Complete Concordance, which replaced the short concordance in the back of my Bible, it was as if I had hit a gold mine! I was so focused on the Scriptures that I could not tell you what I first read of Christian writings outside of the Bible.

But when I entered college in 1972, this all changed. I was attending a Western Civilization lecture, taught by Dr. Rembert B Carter, when he spoke on the importance of research in "original documents." I do not know how or why, but a fire was lit in my soul. And, as a result, I determined NOT to focus on what men said of men, getting information from second-hand sources; but, what the people said, themselves, in their own words. In the documents that history had preserved for us.

This drove me to learn Greek and Hebrew so that I could study the Bible in the original languages of its writers. And it led me to read and cherish writings of people of the past who had been mightily used of God.

Eventually I worked my way through the Apostolic fathers, Apologists, Church fathers, Reformers, Puritans, Covenanters, Revivalists, up to the Princeton Theologians. And when I landed on the Princetonians, my heart and mind found a special home. I found in them and their writings, the combination of scholarship and spirituality I longed for. And I have never put them down, though I have needed help from more contemporary scholars and witnesses who have interacted with the Scriptures, together with issues and church developments we face, which the Princetonians could not foresee and did not address. Indeed, I do not consider any written human statements as grasping either the apex or entirety of expression concerning biblical truth. We must not stop with any "school of thought," as if the Holy Spirit cannot give greater illumination to a subject.

The Princetonian's biographies and writings were riveting to me. Spanning from Alexander's birth in 1772 to Warfield's death in 1921, these four men were molded by the events both of a developing nation and a quickly growing Church. They ministered throughout a significant part of the history of the United States of America, experiencing something of the Post-Colonial era, Revolution, Independence, Expansion, Revivals, Industrial growth, Civil War, Reconstruction, right up to WW1. And they wrote about these things as well as theology. They wrote profoundly and deeply on issues of national, personal, and theological importance. In my time of seeking sound biblical guidance, they became some of my greatest teachers.

When I joined my parents in Kenya after graduating from college (1975), I was amazed with the fruitfulness of my preaching in and outside of churches there. So much so, that I questioned the wisdom of "wasting" valuable time pursuing a Masters of Divinity degree at seminary. My dad and others quickly convinced me of the need of further biblical grounding, so I enrolled at a seminary which had emerged from Old Princeton.

In time, I joined them in Kenya as Principal of the Bible College of East Africa, with my darling wife, Deborah, and two young children. Events and opportunities led to our returning to the USA for me to pursue doctoral studies (at Trinity Evangelical Divinity School). With the help of Old Princeton's emphasis on both academic and spiritual excellence, I decided to enroll in the newly emerging Doctor of Missiology degree program. This was a more practical than theoretical degree program which allowed me great flexibility in pursuing both missions and Old Princeton.

After much discussion, the faculty mentors approved my selection for a major project: "Power Encounter in Selected Writings of the Princeton Theologians." This focus allowed me to tackle the relevant missiological themes within the subject of "spiritual warfare," while digging deeply into the writings of Princeton's major theologians, who wrestled with all the issues of missions, miracles, and revivals, having experienced, and examined them.

I emerged in 1988 with developing convictions greatly assisted by both the historic writings of those great Reformed minds and the contemporary reflections of world-class mission experts from all over the globe. By God's grace, my thesis was popularized and published by Baker Book House as: Miracles, Demons and Spiritual Warfare-An urgent call for discernment. Simultaneously, I concluded abridging Charles Hodge's Systematic Theology from its three volumes into one volume.

Fast forwarding to today, I am ever humbled by the gracious blend of Princetonian and missiological counsel which have helped develop my thinking and guide my steps. I have sat at the feet of spiritual giants, all who have been devoted to the Holy Scriptures and the Christ revealed therein. And I have been blessed by the lives and teachings of many more who, like the Princetonians, have wrestled with the issues of life and Church with the Bible in their hands and the Spirit in their hearts.

Today miracles abound, still largely in non-western contexts. True supernatural events which would pass the scrutiny of Princetonian investigation, and, I am sure, elicit their approval. Disciple making movements worldwide are flourishing, many being rapidly expanded by Acts-like outpourings and fillings of the Holy Spirit. For such renewals, the Princetonians prayed, having all experienced revivals in their own times and lives. But they always examined claims of the miraculous with a careful eye to retaining God's peerless glory. For any miracle, to them and to us, is nothing but the finger of God at work in this world. And thus, can and should be, examined, tested, and verified to be both biblically consistent and Kingdom-advancing. And when found to be authentic, as so many are, they produce from our hearts much praise and glory to their loving and all-powerful Author.

So, most of my recent work and writings have been targeted on New Testament Discipleship, Disciple Making Movements, and church renewal during these days of spiritual tumult--with much time being devoted to prayer. As such, my dear wife Deb and I labor under the organization,

Compassion for Life, with this personal calling: "we follow Jesus and make disciples of love who will advance His Kingdom by multiplication and missional unity."

The Princetonians were devoted to both defending the Faith and the unity of the Church. One aspect of their calling was to debate every departure from the Historic Christian Faith, while they heartily advanced the brotherhood of all believers—even of those holding significant theological conclusions differing from their own. If the differences did not impinge upon the gospel of God's grace in the salvation offered through Jesus Christ alone, they could and did enjoy fellowship with other believers.

Old Princeton has helped me navigate the deep waters of ministry in this quickly changing world. But their help is not like one fearfully holding my hand and forbidding me to go here or there. Just as they wrestled with the world and its thought during their days, so we have moved on and do the same. Our day demands a like devotion to Christ and His Word, while we embrace truth from every quarter. For the God of the Word is the Author of truth. I believe the reprinting of their writings, on this the centennial of Warfield's death, will help us all keep in step with the Spirit and go forward in Jesus' name and for His glory.

Ed Gross – June 2021

ACTIVITY

There is no mistake more terrible than to suppose that activity in Christian work can take the place of Christian affections. Activity, of course, is good: surely in the cause of the Lord we should run and not be weary. But not when it is substituted for inner religious strength. (BBW-SSW)

ADOPTION

This adoption proceeds according to the eternal purpose of the Father, upon the merits of the Son, and by the efficient agency of the Holy Ghost. By it God the Father is made our Father. The incarnate God-man is made our elder brother, and we are made— (1) like him; (2) intimately associated with him in community of life, standing, relations, and privileges; (3) joint heirs with him of his glory. The Holy Ghost is our indweller, teacher, guide, advocate, comforter, and sanctifier. All believers, being subjects of the same adoption, are brethren. (AAH-OT)

The spirit of adoption. 1. It is a spirit of reverential love, of admiration, of gratitude and delight. 2. A spirit of confidence, founded on this relation and on the assurance of God's love and care. 3. A spirit of zeal for his glory, jealousy for his honor, and desire to see that honor promoted. 4. A spirit of obedience and resignation. A willingness that his will and not our own should be done. (CH-CP)

AFFLICTION

Sometimes the children of God grow faster when in the fiery furnace than elsewhere. As metals are purified by being cast into the fire, so saints have their dross consumed and their evidence brightened, by being cast into the furnace of affliction. (AA-TRE)

For your more rapid growth in grace, some of you will be cast into the furnace of affliction. Sickness, bereavement, bad conduct of children and relatives, loss of property or of reputation, may come upon you unexpectedly and press heavily on you. In these trying circumstances, exercise patience and fortitude. Be more solicitous to have the affliction sanctified than removed. Glorify God while in the fire of adversity. That faith which is most tried is commonly most pure and precious. (AA-TRE).

AGGRESSIVE NATURE OF CHRISTIANITY

Christianity is thus aggressive. It cannot be replaced by the individual man without the consciousness on his part of the obligation to uphold and extend it. A Christian, from the nature of the case, is fired with zeal for the glory of Christ, and with love for his fellowmen. His Christianity makes him an advocate of the truth and a proselyter. (CH-CP)

AMBITION (Sinful)

That ambition is evil in its nature, and therefore degrading in its influence, is evident, because Christ always reproved this desire of pre-eminence. He always taught that those who desired to be first should be last and least. This He did on various occasions; as when the two disciples, James, and John, came to him to ask that they might sit at his right hand and at his left; and when there was a contention among them, who should be greatest. (CH-CP)

ANGELS

-Importance of

So much is said in the Scriptures of angels, and such important functions in the providence of God over the world, and especially in the experience of His people and of His Church, are ascribed to them that the doctrine of the Bible concerning them should not be overlooked. (CH-STA)

-Work of

The Scriptures teach that the holy angels are employed (1) in the worship of God, (2) in executing the will of God, and (3) especially in ministering to the heirs of salvation. They are represented as surrounding Christ and as ever ready to perform any service in the advancement of His kingdom that may be assigned to them. (CH-STA)

Some have divided the angels into ASSISTING and MINISTERING: the first are supposed to be always engaged in acts of worship, while the last are always employed in other services. But it would be much more reasonable to suppose that they all, in turn, take their part in both these services. (AA-TRE)

-Power of

The power of angels is dependent and derived. It must be exercised in accordance with the laws of the material and spiritual world. Moreover, their intervention is not optional, but permitted or commanded by God at His pleasure; and, so far as the external world is concerned, it would seem to be only occasional and exceptional. These limitations are of the greatest practical importance. We are not to regard angels as intervening between us and God, or to attribute to them the effects which the Bible everywhere refers to the providential agency of God. (CH-STA)

The extent of their agency is limited and yet from their exalted nature the effects which they can produce may far exceed our comprehension. An angel slew all the first-born of the Egyptians in a single night; the thunder and lightning attending the giving of the law on Mt. Sinai were produced by angelic agency. (CH-STA)

-And Men's Minds

If the angels may communicate one with another, there is no reason why they may not, in like manner, communicate with our spirits. In the Scriptures, therefore, the angels are represented as not only affording general guidance and protection, but also as giving inward strength and consolation. If an angel strengthened our Lord Himself after His agony in the garden, His people also may experience the support of angels; and if evil angels tempt to sin, good angels may allure to holiness. (CH-STA)

- Rejoicing at New Birth

There is no more important event which occurs in our world than the new birth of an immortal soul. The celestial inhabitants, the messengers of God, take a lively interest still in events in which a gay and ungodly world feel no concern. For "there is joy in the presence of the angels of God over one sinner that repenteth." How they know certainly when a soul is born to God, we need not inquire; for they have faculties and sources of knowledge unknown to us. We know that "they are all ministering spirits, sent forth to minister for them who shall be heirs of salvation"; but how they carry on their ministry we cannot tell. (AA-TRE)

A Reason for Consolation

The Scriptural doctrine of the ministry of angels is full of consolation for the people of God. They may rejoice in the assurance that these holy beings encamp round about them, defending them day and night from unseen enemies and unapprehended dangers. At the same time, they must not come between us and God. We are not to look to them nor to invoke their aid. (CH- STA)

ANTINOMIANISM

"Antinomianism," as the word imports, is the doctrine that Christ has in such a sense fulfilled all the claims of the moral law on behalf of all believers, that they are released from all obligations to fulfil its precepts as a standard of character and action. This horrible doctrine, slanderously charged against Paul is repudiated by him—Roman 3:8 and 6:1. (AAH-OT)

APOLOGETICS

What particulars are embraced under the head of Apologetics? This department falls under two heads: (1) Is there a God. (2) Has He spoken; and includes 1st. The proof of the being of God. 2nd. The Development of Natural Theology. 3rd. The evidence of Christianity. (AAH-OT)

-Concerning Objections

There are two important practical principles which follow from the fact just mentioned. First, our inability to free any well-authenticated truth from objections or difficulties is not sufficient or a rational ground for rejecting it. And secondly, any objection against a religious doctrine is to be regarded as sufficiently answered if it can be shown to bear with equal force against an undeniable fact. If the objection is not a rational reason for denying the fact, it is not a rational reason for rejecting the doctrine. This is the method which the sacred writers adopt in vindicating truth. (CH-STA)

-And the Resurrection

From the empty grave of Jesus, the enemies of the cross turn away in unconcealable dismay. Christ has risen from the dead! After two thousand years of the most determined assault upon the evidence which establishes it, that fact stands. And if it stands, Christianity too must stand as the one supernatural religion. The resurrection of Christ is the fundamental apologetical fact of Christianity. (BBW-TSW)

-And the Bible

We should despair of the conversion of no one; and we should use all our efforts to prevail on sceptical men to read the Bible. The Bible has converted more infidels than all the books of "evidence" which exist. (AA-TRE)

APOSTACY

The whole apostacy of Judaism into formality and ritualism was simply the result of carrying out the idea that the outward was more important than the inward; that rites and ceremonies, observance of fasts and festivals were more important than the weightier matters of the law. (CH-CP)

APOSTLES

-Qualifications of

Who then were the Apostles? They were a definite number of men selected by Christ to be his witnesses, to testify to his doctrines, to the facts of his life, to his death and specially to his resurrection. To qualify them for this office of authoritative witnesses, it was necessary (1) That they should have independent and plenary knowledge of the gospel. (2) That they should be inspired, i.e., that they should be infallible in all their instructions. (3) That they should be authenticated as the messengers of Christ, by adherence to the true gospel, by success in preaching (Paul said to the Corinthians that they were the seal of his apostleship, Cor. 9: 2); and by signs and wonders and divers miracles and gifts of the Holy Ghost. Such were the gifts, qualifications, and credentials of the original Apostles; and those who claimed the office without possessing these gifts and credentials, were pronounced false apostles and messengers of Satan. (CH-STA)

-Teachings of

The doctrines which the apostles taught were not the truths of reason but matters of revelation to be received not on rational or philosophical grounds, but on the authority of God. The apostles were not philosophers, but witnesses; they did not argue using the words of man's wisdom, but simply declared the counsels of God. Faith in their doctrines, then, was not to rest on the wisdom of men, but on the powerful testimony of God. (CH-STA)

After the day of Pentecost, the apostles claimed to be the infallible organs of God in all their teachings. They required men to receive what they taught not as the word of man but as the Word of God (1 Thess. 2:13); they declared, as Paul does (1 Cor. 14:37), that the things which they wrote were the commandments of the Lord. They made the salvation of men to depend on faith in the doctrines which they taught. Paul pronounces anathema even an angel from heaven who should preach any other gospel than that which he had taught (Gal. 1: 8). John says, "He that knoweth God heareth us; he that is not of God heareth not us" (1 John 4:6). (CH-STA)

-Permanence of

The office of the Apostles as described in the New Testament, was, from its nature incapable of being transmitted and has not in fact been perpetuated. (CH-STA)

-Same as Missionaries?

In like manner the word "apostle" is sometimes used in its etymological sense "a messenger", sometimes in a religious sense, as we use the word "missionary"; and sometimes in its strict official sense, in which it is confined to the immediate messengers of Christ. Nothing can be plainer from the New Testament than that neither Silas nor Timothy, nor any other person, is ever spoken of as the official equal of the twelve Apostles. These constitute a class by themselves. They stand out in the New Testament as they do in all Church history, as the authoritative founders of the Christian Church, without peers or colleagues. (CH-STA)

ARMOR OF GOD

The armor of God means that armor which God has provided and which he gives. We are thus taught from the outset, that as the strength which we need is not from ourselves, so neither are the means of offence or defence. Nor are they means of man's devising. This is a truth which has been overlooked in all ages of the church, to the lamentable injury of the people of God. Instead of relying upon the arms which God has provided, men have always been disposed to trust to those which they provide for themselves, or which have been prescribed by others. (CH-CE)

If our adversary was a man and possessed nothing beyond human strength, ingenuity and cunning, we might defend ourselves by human means. But as we must contend with Satan, we need the armour of God. (CH-CE)

Panoply [the whole armor] includes both the defensive and offensive armour of the soldier. The believer has not only to defend himself, but also to attack his spiritual enemies; and the latter is as necessary to his safety as the former.

It will not do for him to act only on the defensive, he must endeavor to subdue as well as to resist. (CH-CE)

-One Offensive Weapon

The only offensive weapon of the Christian is "the sword of the Spirit". (which) means the sword which the Spirit gives. It is that which God has spoken, his word, the Bible. This is sharper than any two-edged sword. It is the wisdom of God and the power of God. It has a self-evidencing light. It commends itself to the reason and conscience. It has the power not only of truth, but of divine truth. In opposition to all error, to all false philosophy, to all false principles or morals, to all sophistries of vice, to all the suggestions of the devil, the sole, simple and sufficient answer is the word of God. This puts to flight all the powers of darkness. The Christian finds this to be true in his individual experience. It dissipates his doubts; it drives away his fears; it delivers him from the power of Satan. It is also the experience of the church collective. All her triumphs over sin and error have been affected by the word of God. So long as she uses this and relies on it she goes on conquering; but when anything else, be it reason, science, tradition, or the commandments of men, is allowed to take its place or to share its office, then the church, or the Christian, is at the mercy of the adversary. (CH-CE)

ASSURANCE

In general (assurance) is the full conviction or persuasion that we are the children of God and the heirs of eternal life. This (assurance) may be Antinomian, when that conviction is founded on a false view of salvation, supposing that the elect are sure of eternal life irrespective of their character, and that a man may know his election by other evidence than that derived from holiness of heart and life. (CH-CP)

ATHEISM

Atheism, according to its etymology, signifies a denial of the being of God. It was applied by the ancient Greeks to Socrates and other philosophers, to indicate that they failed to conform to the popular religion. In the same sense it was applied to the early Christians. Since the usage of the term Theism has been fixed in all modern languages, atheism necessarily stands for the denial of the existence of a personal Creator and Moral Governor. (AAH-OT)

-A "crime" against God

Atheism is everywhere regarded as a crime because the evidence of the existence of God are everywhere present, above us, around us, and within us. They are addressed to the moral constitution, as well as to the speculative understanding. They cannot be resisted without the same violence to moral obligations that is involved in calling virtue vice, and vice virtue. Hence, the Scriptures always speak of unbelief as a sin against God, and the special grounds of the condemnation of the world. (CH-WL)

ATONEMENT

-Value of

Augustinians admit the value (of Christ's atonement) to be infinite, for it is determined by the dignity of the sacrifice. As no limit can be placed on the dignity of the eternal Son of God who offered Himself for our sins, so no limit can be assigned to the meritorious value of His work. It is a gross misrepresentation of the Augustinian doctrine to say that it teaches that Christ suffered so much for so many, and that He would have suffered more had a greater number of people been included in the purpose of salvation. What was sufficient for one was sufficient for all. Nothing less than the Light and heat of the sun is sufficient for any one plant or animal. But what is necessary for each is abundantly sufficient for the infinite number and variety of plants and animals which fill the earth. All that Christ did and suffered would have been necessary had only one human soul been the object of redemption, and nothing different, and nothing more would have been required had every child of Adam been saved through His blood. (CH-STA)

-Design of

Augustinians readily admit, however, that the death of Christ had a relation to the whole human family as well. It is the ground on which salvation is offered to every creature under heaven who hears the gospel. Moreover, it secures to the whole race at large, and to all classes of men, innumerable blessings both providential and religious.

In view of the effects which the death of Christ produces on the relation of all mankind to God, it has in all ages been customary with Augustinians to say that Christ died sufficiently for all, but efficaciously only for the elect. There is a sense, therefore, in which He died for all, and there is a sense in which He died for the elect alone. (CH-STA)

It is here (John 3: 16), as well as elsewhere taught, that it was the design of God to render the salvation of all men possible, by the gift of his Son. There was nothing in the nature, or the value, or the design of his work to render it available for any one class of men only. (CH-CP)

AUGUSTINIANISM

If the office of the theologian, as is so generally admitted, be to take the facts of Scripture as the man of science does those of nature, and found upon them his doctrines, instead of deducing his doctrines from the principles. of his philosophy, it seems impossible to resist the conclusion that the doctrine of Augustine is the doctrine of the Bible. According to that doctrine God is an absolute sovereign. He does what seems good in His sight. He sends the truth to one nation but not to another. He gives that truth saving power in one mind but not in another. It is of Him, and not of us, that any man is in Christ Jesus and is an heir of eternal life. (CH-STA)

God is infinitely exalted above all His creatures. His glory is the end of all things, and his good pleasure the highest reason for whatever comes to pass. Augustinianism is the only system which accords with this depiction of the character of God and His relation to His creatures. (CH-STA)

BACKSLIDING

There is in nature no more inconsistent thing than a backsliding Christian. Look at one side of his character and he seems to have sincere penitential feelings, and his heart to be right in its purposes and aims; but look at the other side, and he seems to be "carnal, sold under sin". (AA-TRE).

The backsliding believer can only be distinguished from the final apostate by the fact of his recovery. At least, when Christians have slidden far back, no satisfactory evidence of the genuineness of their piety can be exhibited, nor can they have any which ought to satisfy their own minds. (AA-TRE)

No one has any right to presume that if he backslides, death may not overtake him in that unprepared condition. Backsliding then is a fearful evil; may we all be enabled to avoid it; or if fallen in it, to be recovered speedily from so dangerous a state! (AA-TRE)

BALANCE

There are ways in which believers dishonor Christ and make a false representation of him and of his religion. It is done by those who carry any right principle to excess. (a.) By the Puritans regarding the Sabbath, to things indifferent in worship, to days of religious observance. (b.) By the Quakers regarding dress and conformity to the world. (c.) By those who deny the Church any liberty in her organization. (CA-CP)

BAPTISM

-Its Significance

As a sign, baptism signifies the great truths that the soul is cleansed from the guilt of sin by the sprinkling of the blood of Christ and purified from the pollution of sin by the renewing of the Holy Ghost. (CH-STA)

-Its Mode

Surely it is only a curious question how exactly baptism is to be administered. Our concern is in its significance, not in the mode of its performance. The New Testament leaves us in no doubt as to its meaning. But we may search the New Testament in vain if we are seeking minute instructions how we are to perform it. It is a washing of the body with water to symbolize the absolute cleansing of the soul in the blood of Jesus Christ. We must not lose this symbolism. But it does not follow that to preserve it we must enact a complete bath in the way we administer the rite. Any application of water which will symbolize this cleansing will serve as such a sign and seal. (BBW-SSW)

-Its Proper Subjects

All those, and those only, who are members of the visible church, are to be baptized. These are, 1st, they who make a credible profession of their faith in Christ; 2d, the children of one or both believing parents. (AAH-OT)

-Qualifications for Adults

About the qualifications for adult baptism there has ever been a general agreement: (1) There must be a knowledge of at least the fundamental doctrines of the gospel. Some may unduly enlarge and some unduly restrict the number of such doctrines, but no Church advocates the baptism of the ignorant. Since baptism involves a profession of faith, it must involve a profession of faith in certain doctrines; and those doctrines must be known to be professed. (2) All churches are agreed in demanding of adults who are candidates for baptism a profession of their faith in Christ and the gospel of His salvation. (3) They agree in requiring of those who are baptized the renunciation of the world, the flesh, and the devil. This involves a turning from sin and a turning to God. (CH-STA)

BEAUTY

-Of Holiness

When it is said that holiness is beautiful, it is meant that it gives a peculiar pleasure, and that of the highest kind, which from analogy is called beauty. This beauty is revealed most clearly in the Lord Jesus Christ. He is represented as most beautiful. The Scriptures are filled with the descriptions of the beauty of holiness as manifested in Jesus Christ. The Church is represented as ravished with his beauty. All beauty is a gift. It never can be bought. It is a peculiar form of the manifestation of God in us. The beauty of holiness in us is the manifestation of God in us. (CH-CP)

BEHAVIOR

-Based on Inward Truth

All good conduct must proceed from good principles, but good principles cannot exist without a knowledge of the truth. "Truth is in order to holiness", and between truth and holiness there is an indissoluble connection. (AA-TRE)

The only way to secure an outward deportment which is desired is to cultivate the inward disposition of which such deportment is the natural expression. (CH-CP)

-Of Christians

Those for whom Christ died are, in their new creaturehood, are to live no longer for themselves but for Him who died and rose again for them. The revolution in standing is marked by a revolution in living. (BBW-TSW)

The outward conduct becoming (our) relation to God (is). 1. A life regulated by his commands and devoted to his service. A life of holiness. 2. A life elevated above the world, not immersed in its pleasures and not devoted to its possessions. A life which has its end and consummation in heaven. 3. A life of inward intercourse and fellowship with God. 4. A life of joy and cheerful anticipation of the time when we shall see him as he is, when shall occur the manifestation of the sons of God. (CH-CP)

Men do not act sufficiently from principle, but too much from custom, from fashion, and from habit. Thus, many actions are performed without any inquiry into their moral character. (AA-TRE)

BENEDICTION

-Apostolic

In the apostolic benediction a prayer is addressed to Christ for His grace, to the Father for His love, and to the Spirit for His fellowship (2 Cor. 13:14). The personality and divinity of each are solemnly recognized every time that this benediction is pronounced and received. (CH-STA)

BIBLE (See Scriptures, also)

The Bible is a perfectly plain and a perfectly practical book. The purpose of its gift to the world was not at all that scholars might have a field in which they might try the depth of their insight and expend their best efforts in seeking and securing truth. It was given to plain and practical men, as a prescription to cure them of the disease of sin; to busy and careless men as a trumpet call which they could not choose but hear. Its prime purpose was simply to tell sinful men what a God they had, and what they practically needed to do to serve that God and save their souls. (BBW-SSW)

BLOOD

-Of Christ

It is essential to peace with God that the soul should see that justice is satisfied. This is the reason why the death of Christ, why His blood, is so inexpressibly precious in the eyes of His people. All the experience of the saints is a protest against the principle that expiation is unnecessary, that sin can be pardoned without a satisfaction of justice. (CH-STA)

BODY

-Of Christians

The body belongs to Christ, is the subject of redemption, and the temple of the Spirit. It is a profanation, therefore, to make our members the instruments of unrighteousness. (CH-CP)

BONDAGE

The nature of (our) liberty is determined by the nature of the bondage from which we are delivered. 1. It was a bondage in the law, to the obligations to fulfill all its precepts as a condition of salvation. 2. It was a bondage to sin. This power exists. It is a real controlling influence which determines the character and conduct. It cannot be broken or overthrown by any effort of our own. 3. It was a bondage to Satan. This subjection is real. Satan does rule over men. They are his captives. He controls them at will, so far as God permits. 4. It is a bondage of their reason and conscience to human authority. 5. It is a bondage to human despotism. (CH-CP)

BROTHERLY LOVE

In the Christian sense of the terms, brotherly love is the love which should exist among Christians as brethren in Christ. If a man does not love his Christian brethren, he does not love Christ; is none of his. This love is the cement, the life, the blessedness of the Church, and of any society on earth. Its perfection is heaven. In proportion as it is wanting in a man, or a community, or a church, in that proportion do they approach the character and condition of the lost. (CH-CP)

Cultivate and exercise brotherly love more than you have been accustomed to do. Christ is displeased with many of His professed followers because they are so cold and indifferent to His members on earth, and because they do so little to comfort and encourage them; and with some, because they are a stumbling block to the weak of the flock, their conversation and conduct not edifying, but the contrary. (AA-TRE)

CALL OF GOD

-Call to Salvation

This act of the Spirit by which men are brought into saving union with Christ is expressed by the word vocation (or calling): "partakers of the heavenly calling" (Heb. 3: 1); "walk worthy of the vocation wherewith ye are called" (Eph. 4:1). Such then is the established usage of Scripture. It is by a divine call that sinners are made partakers of the benefits of redemption. And the influence of the Spirit by which they are translated from the kingdom of darkness into the kingdom of God's dear Son is a vocation or effectual calling. (CH-STA)

Common grace, or that influence of the Spirit, which is granted to all men, is often effectually resisted. But since the special work of regeneration is the effect of almighty power, it can no more be resisted than the act of creation. The effect follows immediately on the will of God, as when He said, "Let there be light," and light was. (CH-STA)

-Call to Christian Service

The Spirit also calls men to office in the Church and endows them with the qualifications necessary for the successful discharge of its duties. The role of the Church in this matter is simply to ascertain and authenticate the call of the Spirit. (CH-STA)

The work of foreign missions is not a distinct part of the general work of the Church. The commission under which the Church acts has equal reference to all parts of the field. The work of the missionary is therefore not different from the work of a minister. A man who enlists as a soldier, does not enlist for any one field. He is to go wherever he is sent. (CH-CP)

How does God reveal his will to ministers, as to where they should labor? He does it first, by his inward dealings with them, and secondly, by his outward dispensations. First, as to his inward dealings. 1st. He furnishes them with gifts requisite to some special field of labor. 2d. He addresses their understandings. He presents to them the wants of the different parts of the great field; the facilities for usefulness; the demand for laborers. 3d. He addresses their conscience. 4th. He addresses their hearts, awakens an interest in particular portions of the field, and infuses into them an earnest desire for the work.

Secondly, as to his outward dispensations. 1st. He removes obstacles out of the way, such as want of health, obligations to dependent parents, and other hindrances of like nature. 2d. He sends messages to them by friends. 3d. He sometimes stirs up the church to call them here or there. (CH-CP)

-Duty of Candidates Called of God

1. To feel that they are bound to go wherever God may call them; that it is not for them to choose. 2. To feel perfectly submissive, and say, Lord what wilt thou have me to do. 3. To investigate the subject; not to dismiss it, but to examine conscientiously. 4. To use all the means to come to an intelligent decision, and to keep their minds open to conviction. (CH-CP)

CALVINISM

It is very odd how difficult it seems for some persons to understand just what Calvinism is. And yet the matter itself presents no difficulty whatever. It is capable of being put into a single sentence; and that, on level with every religious man's comprehension. For Calvinism is just religion in its purity. We have only, therefore, to conceive of religion in its purity, and that is Calvinism. (BBW-SSW)

The Calvinist is the man who is determined to preserve the attitude he takes in prayer in all his thinking, in all his feeling, in all his doing. He is the man who is determined that religion in its purity shall come to its full rights in his thinking, and feeling, and living. Other men are Calvinists on their knees; the Calvinist is the man who is determined that his intellect, and heart, and will shall remain on their knees continually. Calvinism is, therefore, that type of thought in which there comes to its rights the truly religious attitude of utter dependence on God and humble trust in his mercy alone for salvation. (BBW-SSW)

The fundamental postulate of what we know as the Calvinistic system is that God is a person, and, as a person, acts in all things positively. No body of Christians possess a clearer or more pervading appreciation of all that enters into the idea of God's character as righteous and holy and good, faithful and loving and gracious than those that bear the name of Calvinists. (BBW-SSW)

CARNALLY MINDED

To be carnally minded is death. It not only leads to death but is death. That is, death consists in the degradation, the corruption, and the misery which are involved in this state of mind. To be spiritually minded is life and peace. That is, the life and blessedness of the soul consist in the elevation, the holiness and happiness involved in being spiritually minded. (CH-CP)

CATHOLICITY (Universality of Christ's Church)

It is a great sin against Christ and against his body, if we refuse to recognize as a fellow-Christian or refuse Christian fellowship to any true Christian because he differs from us in anything whatsoever. This union is Catholic, not only as uniting Christians of all denominations, but of all ages, rich and poor, learned, and unlearned, barbarian, Scythians, bond and free. These distinctions are real. They are not to be ignored, but they are all superficial, outward, and transient. Underneath them all is this majestic bond of union, which unites all these classes as one body in Christ Jesus. (CH-CP)

CHARACTER

-Better than Gifts

The design of this chapter (1 Cor. 13) is to show the superiority of graces to gifts. The apostle teaches that a man may have the highest intellectual abilities, the largest stores of knowledge, and the greatest amounts of power, and yet be a reprobate. Therefore, the knowledge of the truth; the ability to present and enforce it, will avail us nothing, without inward piety. (CH-CP)

-And our Destiny

What was (the Parable of the Rich Man and Lazarus) meant to teach? Not that the rich because rich go to hell, and that the poor because poor go to heaven. This would contradict the great principle of the Bible, that character and not external circumstances determine our destiny before God. (CH-CP)

-Its Power over Others

A large part of the power of one man over others lies in his character or excellence. Everything which increases our excellence increases our power, and everything which increases the respect and confidence which others entertain toward us, increases our influence over them for good. (CH-CP)

-Importance of Knowing its Weak Points

To preserve consistency, it is necessary to be well acquainted with the weak points in our own character, to know something of the strength of our own passions, and to guard beforehand against the occasions and temptations which would be likely to cause us to act inconsistently with our Christian profession. (AA-TRE)

CHARITY

The greatest charity in the world is the communication of divine truth to the ignorant. (AA-PS)

CHASTISEMENT

God holds a rod for his own children, and when the warnings and exhortations of the Word, and the secret whispers of the Spirit are neglected, some painful providence is sent-some calamity, which has so much natural connection with the sin, as to indicate that it is intended as a chastisement for it. These strokes are often very cutting and severe, but they must be so to render them effectual. (AA-TRE)

CHILDREN

-Jesus and

What Jesus did for children we may perhaps sum up as follows. He illustrated the ideal of childhood in his own life as a child. He manifested the tenderness of his affection for children by conferring blessings upon them in every stage of their development as he was occasionally brought into contact with them. He asserted for children a recognized place in his kingdom and dealt faithfully and lovingly with each age as it presented itself to him in the course of his work. He chose the condition of childhood as a type of the fundamental character of the recipients of the kingdom of God. He adopted the relation of childhood as the most vivid earthly image of the relation of God's people to him who was not ashamed to be called their Father which is in heaven, and thus reflected back upon this relation a glory by which it has been transfigured ever since. (BBW-SSW)

-Depravity of

As soon as a child is capable of moral action, it gives the evidence of a perverted moral character. Not only do we see the manifestations of anger, malice, selfishness, envy, pride, and other evil dispositions, but the whole development of the soul is toward the world. The soul of a child turns by an inward law from God to the creature, from the things that are unseen and eternal to the things that are seen and temporal. In its earliest manifestations it is worldly, of the earth, earthy. As this is the testimony of universal experience, so also it is the doctrine of the Bible: (Job 11:12; Ps. 58:3; Prov. 22:15). (CH-STA)

-Prayer for

Let pious (spiritually-minded) parents learn never to give over praying for their unconverted children, however hopeless the case may seem to be, for God will in faithfulness hear their supplications, and answer them sooner or later in one way or another. (AA-PT)

-Rules for

It is a good rule, even in the government of children, not to legislate too much. Vex them not with trivial and unnecessary rules. Train them to govern themselves as much as possible. That child who is obedient only when the eye of the parent is on it, has not been effectively managed. Allow children liberty in such things as are innocent, and to which they are inclined by the instinct of nature. (AA-TRE)

-The Great Sin of

There is no one thing on which mothers should insist more uniformly and peremptorily than that their children should tell the truth, the whole truth, and nothing but the truth. Lying above all other things may be said to be the vice of children. Keep a vigilant eye on this matter and pass not slightly over an offence of this kind. Manifest by every proper means your utter detestation of lying, in all its kinds and degrees. (AA-TRE)

CHRISTIAN

-Its Definition

A Christian is, 1. One who believes that Jesus is the Son of God. 2. That he is the Prophet, or infallible teacher. 3. That he is the High Priest, who by offering himself a sacrifice for sins, has reconciled us to Go. 4. That he is our faithful and absolute sovereign, whose will we are bound to obey, in whom we must trust for protection, and to whose service we must be devoted. A Christian, then, is one over whom these truths exert a controlling influence, both as to his inward and outward life. (CH-CP)

-Its Depiction

And the Apostle asserts that they who are Christ's, and they only, are delivered from the dominion of evil, and are under the control of the Spirit. No one therefore who is not free, of whom this is not true has a right to regard himself as a Christian. (CH-CP)

(Mark) the folly of those who profess to be Christians and hope that they are so if they are the servants of sin. That is, if they are not delivered from its reigning power. They must not only desire and strive against it, but they must more and more overcome it. (CH-CP)

-The Best

He is the best Christian who prays most. (AA-PT)

The best Christians are in general those who not merely from restless activity of natural disposition, but from love to Christ and zeal for His glory, labor most and suffer most in His service. (CH-STA)

CHRISTIANITY

-Its Definition

The best way to determine what Christianity is, is to ask what makes a man a Christian in the true and proper sense of the term. A Christian is one who knows and receives as true what Christ has revealed in his word, whose inward state (religious consciousness) is determined by that knowledge, and whose life is devoted to the obedience and service of Christ. Christianity is therefore a system of doctrine, it is an inward life, and it is a rule of action. (CH-CP)

-Its Doctrines

It is a matter of complete indifference how much debated the constitutive doctrines of Christianity are, or how "controversial" they may be. Everything important is debated, and everything that is precious will certainly be dragged into controversy. If we are to hold nothing that is questioned, we shall hold to nothing at all. What is important with respect to the doctrines which we lay at the basis of our church organizations, is not that they shall be incapable of being debated, but that they are sound, "wholesome," for the soul's health, the indispensable foundations for a life of service here to the God whose very name is holy and of communion with him and of rejoicing in him forever. (BBW-SSW)

-Its Historicity

Christianity is a historical religion, all whose doctrines are facts. He who assaults the trustworthiness of the record of the intervention of God for the redemption of the world, is simply assaulting the heart of Christianity. If there is to be no historical content in our religion, in a word, Christianity is but another form of that religious aspiration common to all men, clothed in forms which are a product of the chance conditions of those men who have created it. The issue is in short—Is Christianity of God, or made by man? — is it a magnificent dream or is it a divine reality? (BBW-SSW)

-Its Uniqueness

Christianity is the one revealed religion. While the tenets of other religions are the product of human thought, the doctrines of Christianity are communications from God. Christianity thus stands fundamentally in contrast with all other religions. (BBW-SSW)

-Its Offense

The offense of Christianity has always been the cross; as of old, so still today, Christ crucified is to Jews a stumbling-block and to Greeks foolishness. It would be easy to remove the offense by abolishing the cross. But that would be to abolish Christianity. Christianity is the cross; and he who makes the cross of Christ of no effect eviscerates Christianity. (BBW-SSW)

-Its Power

What Christianity brings to the world is not the bare command to love God and our neighbor. The world needs no such command; nature itself teaches the duty. What the world needs is the power to perform this duty, with respect to which it is impotent. And this power Christianity brings it in the redemption of the Son of God and the renewal of the Holy Ghost. Christianity is not merely a program of conduct; it is the power of a new life. (BBW-SSW)

-And Sinners

For Christianity addresses itself only to sinners. Its Founder himself declared that he did not come to call the righteous but sinners; and its chief expounder declared with energetic emphasis that Christ Jesus came into the world to save sinners. Christianity makes no appeal to men who do not feel the burden of sin. (BBW-SSW)

CHRISTMAS

The observance of Christmas is not commanded. Therefore, it is not obligatory. The true Protestant principle is that what is not commanded cannot be enjoined (demanded). The importance of this principle as a protection from the burden of human authority (is evident). Much may be said for it and much against it. It was not celebrated before the fourth century. Origen mentions only three festivals as generally observed, Good Friday, Easter, and Pentecost. Augustine places Christmas in the secondary class of festivals. Chrysostom says in his time it was new. It had, he said, been introduced within ten years. (CH-CP)

CHURCH

-Its Relationship to Christ

The Church is described as the body of Christ, as his fold, as his kingdom, his family, his temple; all of which is intended to express its relation to him as his dwelling, as his possession, as the object of his delight, and as filled with his Spirit and presence. (CH-CP)

We are (Christ's) body, the members of his body. Nothing is so intimately a man's own as his body. It has a common life with him. It has a common consciousness with him. The pains and pleasures of the body are our own pains and pleasures. It has a common interest and destiny with him. So, if we are Christ's body, we are bound to him in all these ways. (CH-CP)

-Local and Visible

Christians are required to associate for public worship, for the administration of the sacraments, for the maintenance and propagation of the truth. They therefore form themselves into churches and collectively constitute the visible kingdom of Christ on the earth, consisting of all who profess the true religion, together with their children. (CH-STA)

-Its Government

Our Lord Jesus Christ, as mediatorial King, has appointed a government for his Church; and—. Hence the Church is a Theocratic kingdom. All authority and power descends, and does not ascend. Pastors and elders teach and rule in the name of God, and not of man. Hence all the power of church officers, either in their several or collective capacity, is ministerial and declarative. They have only to define what Christ has taught, to carry that teaching to all men, and to execute the laws he has given, and to administer the penalties he has designated, according to his will and in his name. (AAH-CF)

-And Israel

The commonwealth of Israel was the Church. It is so called in Scripture (Acts 7: 38). The Hebrews were called out from all nations of the earth to be the peculiar people of God. They constituted His kingdom, and to them were committed His oracles. To the Israelites pertained "the adoption, and the glory, and the covenants, and the giving of the law, and the service of God, and the promises" (Rom. 9:4). Nothing more can be said of the Church under the new dispensation. (CH-STA)

The Church under the new dispensation is identical with that under the old. It is not a new Church, but one and the same. It is the same olive tree (Rom. 11: 16-17). It is founded on the same covenant, the covenant made with Abraham. The conclusion is that God has ever had but one Church in the world. (CH-STA)

The terms of admission into the Church before the advent were the same that are required for admission into the Christian Church. Those terms were a credible profession of faith in the true religion, a promise of obedience, and submission to the appointed rite of initiation. (CH-STA)

CHURCH AND STATE

This Theocratic government of the Church which Christ has established is entirely independent of civil government. The persons subject to the jurisdiction of the government of the Church are also subject to the jurisdiction of the government of the State; but the ends, the laws, the methods, and the sanctions of the two are so different, that the one never can any more interfere with the other than waves of colour can interfere with vibrations of sound. (AAH-CF)

The kingdom of Christ is not a democracy, nor an aristocracy, but truly a kingdom of which Christ is absolute sovereign. Accordingly, the State has no authority to make laws to determine the faith, to regulate the worship, or to administer the discipline of the Church. It can neither appoint nor depose its officers. Nor does any civil officer in virtue of his office have any authority in the kingdom of Christ. Nor is Church power vested ultimately in the people or in the clergy. Rather, it is derived from Christ and is to be exercised by others in His name and according to the rules laid down in His Word. (CH-STA)

Being designed to embrace all other kingdoms, the kingdom of Christ can exist under all forms of civil government without interfering with any. This is what Christ had in view when He declared that His kingdom was not of this world; His claim to be a king was not incompatible with the legitimate authority of the civil magistrate or of the Roman emperor. His kingdom belonged to another sphere. It took cognizance of things which lie beyond the province of secular power, and it left untouched all that belongs peculiarly to civil rulers. Therefore, every form or claim of the Church which is incompatible with the legitimate authority of the State is inconsistent with the nature of Christ's kingdom as declared by Himself. (CH-STA)

Legitimate in the earth-

As Christ is the only head of the Church, it follows that its allegiance is to Him, and that whenever those outside the Church undertake to regulate its affairs or to curtail its liberties, its members are bound to obey Him rather than men. They are bound to resist such usurpations and to stand fast wherewith Christ has made them free. They are under equal obligation to resist all undue assumption of authority by those within the Church, whether it be by the brotherhood, or by individual officers, or by Church councils or courts. The allegiance of the people terminates on Christ. They are bound to obey others only so far as obedience to them is obedience to Him. (CH-STA)

CIRCUMCISION

Circumcision in the Old Testament is presented in two different aspects. First, it was the symbol of regeneration, of inward purity of heart. And, secondly, it was the sign and seal of a covenant. It designated and sealed those who were the people of God. It distinguished them from other men and assured them of their interest in the blessings of the covenant. (CH-CP)

COMMON GRACE

In addition to the grace of salvation to the elect, the Bible speaks of a divine grace to every man. Whatever God does in nature, in the material world, and in the minds of men, He does through the Spirit. The Holy Spirit as the Spirit of truth, of holiness, and of life in all its forms is present with every human mind, enforcing truth, restraining from evil, exciting to good, and imparting wisdom or strength when, where, and in what measure seemeth to Him good. In this sphere also He divides "every man severally as he will" (1 Cor. 12: 11). This is what in theology is called common grace. (CH-STA)

The Spirit of God is present with every human mind, restraining from evil and exciting to good, and that to His presence and influence we are indebted for all the order, decorum, and virtue, as well as for religion and its ordinances, which exist in the world. Consequently, the greatest calamity that can befall an individual, a church, or a people is that God should take His Holy Spirit from them. (CH-STA)

COMMUNION OF SAINTS

The communion of saints consists in the fact that they have this in common: They sustain a common relation to Christ. The more intimate the union with Christ, the more intimate the communion of saints. The more conscious we are of our union with Christ, the more conscious we shall be of our communion with his people. As the union between Christ and his people is a vital one, more intimate than any other, so the bond which unites saints is the most intimate of all bonds. (Consider) the lamentable defects of Christians in this respect, not only of churches but of individual Christians. They do not love each other as they ought. They do not sympathize with and assist each other as they ought but feel and act towards their fellow Christians very much as they do towards other men. The Bible makes Christian communion essential. If we do not feel our union with believers, and sympathize with them, we are not united to Christ. (CH-CP)

COMMUNAL SHARING OF GOODS

How are the Scriptures to be understood when they describe the experience and conduct of early Christians? 1. It is a description founded in genuine religious experience. 2. It is a description founded on facts. The early Christians did feel and act as they are described in the Acts of the Apostles. 3. This experience being actual is not ideal or normal. It was on course modified by their peculiar circumstances, and by their imperfections of knowledge, experience and feeling. Consequently, it is not an authoritative example to us. That they continued to attend the temple, that they celebrated the eucharist daily in connection with an ordinary meal, that they had all things in common, may have been actual, and the effect of genuine religious feeling; but it does not follow that these things were right then, or obligatory now. They were youthful excesses, which experience, and the teaching of the Spirit led them to modify. (CH-CP)

CONFESSION OF CHRIST

To confess Christ is to acknowledge him to be what he really is and declares himself to be. To be the Son of God. To Be God manifest in the flesh. To be the Saviour of the world. To be the Lord. It is not enough that we cherish the conviction in our hearts, or confess it to ourselves or to God, to friends who agree with us. It must be done publicly, or before men, friends, and foes; amid good report and evil report; when it brings reproach and danger, as well as when it incurs no risk. It must be with the mouth. It is not enough that men may infer from our conduct that we are Christians. We must audibly declare it. It must be sincere. Not everyone that saith, Lord, Lord shall enter the kingdom of heaven. It is only when the outward act is a revelation of the heart that it has any value. (CH-CP)

The relation in which we stand to Christ as our king, renders a public acknowledgment of his authority necessary. In the kingdoms of this world, no one is admitted to the privileges of citizenship without a profession of allegiance. And in the kingdom of Christ, those who do not acknowledge his authority, reject him. By refusing to confess him as Lord, they declare that they are not his people. (CH-WL)

CONSCIENCE

Of this mysterious power conscience, the obvious characteristics are, 1. That it is independent of the understanding and of the will. No man can force himself by a volition to approve what he sees to be wrong. 2. It is authoritative. It asserts the right to rule, to control our hearts and lives. And this authority we cannot deny. 3. It does not speak in its own name. The authority which it exerts is not its own. The vengeance which it threatens is not its own displeasure. It is the representative of God. It brings the soul before His bar. (CH-CP)

The greatest happiness flows from an approving conscience, and the greatest misery from a wounded conscience. (CH-CP)

Keep a good conscience. If wickedness had no other punishment than the stings of conscience which follow evil actions, it would be reason enough to induce every considerate man to avoid that which is of so much pain. No misery of which the human mind is susceptible is so intolerable and so irremediable as remorse of conscience. (AA-TRE)

CONSCIENTIOUS

Learn to be conscientious; that is, obey the dictates of your conscience uniformly. Many are conscientious in some things and not in others; they listen to the monitor within when it directs to important duties; but in smaller matters they often disregard the voice of conscience and follow present inclination. Such cannot grow in grace. (AA-TRE)

CONTENDING FOR THE FAITH

The way to contend for the truth is, First, to confess it, to proclaim it. The power is in the truth. Second, to answer misrepresentations and gainsayers. This should be done with meekness, speaking the truth in love, remembering that Paul may plant and Apollos water, but it is God who gives the increase. (CH-CP)

CONTENTMENT

(Contentment) is as a Christian grace one of the fruits of the Spirit. Nothing short of his power can so mortify our natural desire for enjoyment and pre-eminence, as to make us cheerfully to acquiesce in being poor, suffering, of little account and of little esteem. (CH-CP)

This state of mind (contentment) arises out of the assurance that not only are our circumstances determined by his wisdom but by his love. If it were better for us to be richer, happier, more eminent, or powerful, he would make us so. It would be to act as children who cry for poison, to be craving after forms of good which God denies. (CH-CP)

CONTROVERSY

Avoid curious and abstruse speculations respecting things unrevealed, and do not indulge a spirit of controversy. Many lose the benefit of the good impression which the truth is calculated to make, because they do not view it simply in its own nature, but as related to some dispute, or as bearing on some other point. (AA-TRE)

CONVICTION OF SIN

The necessity of this conviction of sin arises out of the fact that the gospel is a plan for the salvation of sinners. It is designed for sinners. If we are not sinners, we do not need the gospel. If we do not feel that we are sinners, we do not feel our need of the gospel and will not embrace it. If we do not feel ourselves guilty, we will not look to Christ for pardon. If we do not feel ourselves to be polluted, we will not look for nor desire cleansing. We must therefore be convinced of sin to be saved. (CH-CP)

CONVICTIONS

Convictions are the root on which the tree of vital Christianity grows. No convictions, no Christianity. Scanty convictions, hunger-bitten Christianity. Profound convictions, solid and substantial religion. Let no man fancy it can be otherwise. Ignorance is not the mother of religion, but of irreligion. knowledge of God is eternal life, and to know God means that we know him aright. (BBW-SSW)

COVENANT OF GRACE

The plan of salvation is presented in the form of a covenant. This is evident, first, from the frequent use of the word covenant in reference to the divine scheme of redemption. Secondly, and more decisively from the fact that the elements of a covenant are included in its plan. There are parties, mutual promises or stipulations, and conditions. Thus, it is in fact a covenant, whatever it may be called. As this is the Scriptural mode of representation, it is of great importance that it be retained in theology. (CH-STA)

(The covenant of grace) is of grace (1) because it originated in the mysterious love of God for sinners who deserved only His wrath and curse; (2) because it promises salvation not on the condition of works or anything meritorious on our part, but as an unmerited gift; and (3) because its benefits are secured and applied not in the exercise of the natural powers of the sinner, but by the supernatural influence Of the Holy Spirit, granted as an unmerited gift. (CH-STA)

COVENANT OF WORKS

God made to Adam a promise which depended on man's satisfying a condition, and He also attached to disobedience a certain penalty. This is what in Scriptural language is meant by a covenant, and this is all that is meant by the term as here used. (CH-STA)

God then did enter a covenant with Adam. That covenant is sometimes called a covenant of life because life was promised as the reward of obedience. Sometimes it is called the covenant of works because works were the condition on which the fulfillment of that promise depended, and because it is thus distinguished from the new covenant, which promises life on condition of faith. (CH-STA)

It lies in a covenant that there must be two or more parties. A covenant is not of one. The parties to the original covenant were God and Adam. Adam, however, acted not in his individual capacity but as the head and representative of his whole race. (CH-STA)

CREATION

The Scriptural doctrine therefore is: (1) the universe is not eternal—it began to be (2) it was not formed out of any preexistence or substance, but was created out of nothing; and (3) the creation was not necessary—God was free to create or not to create, to create the universe as it is, or any other order and system of things, according to the good pleasure of His will (CH-STA)

-How Long to Create?

According to the more obvious interpretation of the first chapter of Genesis this work was accomplished in six days. This therefore is the common belief of Christians. It is a belief founded on a given interpretation of the Mosaic record; this interpretation, however, must be controlled not only by the laws of language, but by facts. This is at present an open question. The facts necessary for its decision have not yet been duly authenticated. The believer may calmly await the result. (CH-STA)

-Purpose of Creation

Men have long endeavored to find a satisfactory answer to the question, why did God create the world? What end was it designed to accomplish? The only satisfactory method of determining the answer is appealing to the Scriptures. There it is explicitly taught that the glory of God, the manifestation of His perfections, is the last end of all his works. This in the Bible is declared to be the end of the universe, of the external world or works of nature, of the plan of redemption, of the whole course of history, of the mode in which God administers His providence and dispenses His grace, and of particular events. It is the end which all rational creatures are commanded to keep constantly in view, and it comprehends and secures all other right ends. (CH-STA)

-Redemption of

Even the lower creation, by virtue of the relation in which it stands to man, partakes in his redemption. If the very ground was cursed for man's sake that the place of his abode might sympathetically partake in his punishment, no less shall it share in his restoration. Man's sighs are not the only expression of the evil that curses human life in its sinful development. The whole creation groans and travails together with him. But it shares also in the hope of the coming deliverance. For there shall be a new heaven, we are told, and a new earth. (BBW-TSW)

-Man's Superiority

"How much better," our Savior exclaims, "is a man than a sheep!" But why, we may ask, is a man better than a sheep? Precisely what is it in man which distinguishes him from all other creatures which inhabit the world with him, and raises him above them all? There are two outstanding endowments of human nature which separate it fundamentally from all other earthly natures, and from the foundations of its immeasurable superiority to them. Man is endowed as no other creature is, with an irresistible sense of dependence and an ineradicable sense of obligation. It is because man is conscious of his dependence that he is a religious being. And it is because he is conscious of his obligation that he is a moral being. And it is precisely in these two characteristics—that he is a religious and that he is a moral being—that his superiority to other earthly creatures consists. (BBW-SSW)

CROSS

-Of Christ

The cross of Christ is the focus in which the most intense rays alike of divine grace and justice meet together, in which they are perfectly reconciled. his is the highest reach of justice, and at the same times and for the same reason the highest reach of grace the universe can ever see. (AAH-CF)

To glory in the cross is, 1. To rejoice in it, Christ crucified, the only ground of salvation. 2. To make it the sole ground of confidence. 3. To look for honor to no other source. 4. To make it the sole instrument of success in preaching. (CH-CP)

-Bearing One's Own

The cross is the emblem of suffering. To bear the cross is to endure suffering. Each man has his own cross. One has sickness, feebleness of body; another, poverty; another want (lack) of success; another, reproach; another, insignificance. In any case we must bear our burden cheerfully, looking unto Christ as our example, our helper and our reward. (CH-CP)

CROWN

Whosoever will not take Christ with His cross shall never sit with Him on His throne. "No cross, no crown", holds out an important truth in few words. (AA-TRE)

I charge you, then, brethren, companions of the blessed life, remember the crown rights of your Lord and Savior! Let his honor be precious in you sight! I have charged you in the words of Paul to let no man rob you of your crown: I charge you now in yet more insistent tones, to let no man your Savior of his crown. In Him and in Him alone is redemption. In His hands He holds, as sovereign Lord of salvation, all the issues of life. Say in your heart and shout abroad with your lips, that all men may know it assuredly, that God has made this Jesus both Lord and Christ, and beside there is no other. (BBW, TSW)

CRUCIFIXION

-Of Christ

The truths which are exhibited in clear and strong light by the crucifixion of Christ, are such as these: 1.The infinite evil of sin, which in order to its pardon required such a sacrifice. 2. The holiness and justice of God, which would not suffer sin to pass without full evidence of the divine disapprobation, and his inflexible purpose to visit it with condign punishment. 3. The wisdom of God, in contriving a method of salvation by which his own glory would be promoted in the eternal salvation of hell-deserving sinners.... 4. But the most wonderful exhibition of the cross is the mercy of God, the love of God to sinners—such love as never could have been conceived of, had it not been manifested by the gift of His own Son. (AA-PT)

-Of the Christian to the World

To be crucified unto the world (is) to die to, to renounce, to be indifferent to, and free from the power of the world. The world loses its power over me, and its attractions for me. (CH-CP)

DEATH

-Defined

Death is the dissolution of the body, the separation of the soul from its earthly tabernacle. The soul does not cease to exist. It does not become unconscious. Its eternal destiny is immediately decided. (CH-CP)

-And the Soul's Destiny

According to the Scriptures and the faith of the Church, the probation of man ends at death. As the tree falls, so it lies. He that is unjust remains unjust, and he that is righteous remains righteous. According to the parable of the rich man and Lazarus, there is no passing after death from one state to another; there is a great gulf between the righteous and the wicked from that time forth. The destiny of the soul is decided at death. (CH-STA)

-Conquered by Christ

The Captain of our salvation conquered death and him that had the power of death, that is the Devil, by dying Himself. By this means he plucked from this monster his deadly sting, by satisfying the demands of God's holy law. "For the sting of death is sin, and the strength of sin is the law." All those, therefore, who are united to Christ meet death as a conquered and disarmed enemy. (AA-TRE)

-Most Unconcerned About

In view of the absolute and undoubted certainty of our departure out of life, it seems passing strange that we should be so unconcerned. If even one of a million escaped death, this might afford some shadow of a reason for our carelessness; but we know that "it is appointed unto men once to die." In this warfare there is no discharge, and yet most men live as if they were immortal. (AA-TRE)

-Christ, Worth Dying for

This single consideration should reconcile us to the thoughts of death; that then we shall be freed from all sin. O how blessed is that state, where we shall see no more darkly through a glass, but face to face; where we shall know no more in part, but as we are known! O bright and delightful vision of the glory of God in the face of Jesus Christ! Surely this is worth dying for. (AA-TRE)

DECEITFULNESS OF SIN

All sin takes its origin from false views of things. In all sin there is some bait- some apparent good—some expectation of pleasure or profit from unlawful indulgence. In all sin the mind is under a delusive influence. Right thoughts and motives are for the moment forgotten or overborne. (AA-PT)

The deceitful heart promises, that if now indulged, it will consent to forsake the beloved sin at some future time—perhaps it promises never to solicit for indulgence again. "This once only" has been the plea which has often decided the eternal destiny of an immortal soul. (AA-PT)

DECREES OF GOD

The doctrine of the Bible is that all events, whether necessary or contingent, good or sinful, are included in the purpose of God, and that their futurition or actual occurrence is rendered absolutely certain. (CH-STA)

-Will Come to Pass

The decrees of God are certainly efficacious, that is, they render certain the occurrence of what He decrees. Whatever God foreordains, must certainly come to pass. The distinction between the efficient (or efficacious) and the permissive decrees of God, although important, has no relation to the certainty of events. All events embraced in the purpose of God are equally certain, whether He has determined to bring them to pass by His own power, or simply to permit their occurrence through the agency of His creatures. It was no less certain from eternity that Satan would tempt our first parents, and that they would fall, than that God would send His Son to die for sinners. The distinction in question has reference only to the relation which events bear to the efficiency of God. Some things He purposes to do, others He decrees to permit to be done. He effects good, He permits evil. He is the author of the one, but not of the other. (CH-STA)

-Eternal

That the decrees of God are eternal follows necessarily from the perfection of the divine Being. He cannot be supposed to have at one time plans or purposes which He had not at another. He sees the end from the beginning; the distinctions of time have no reference to Him who inhabits eternity. (CH-STA)

-And God's Glory

The final cause of all of God's purposes is His own glory. This is frequently declared to be the end of all things. "Thou art worthy," say the heavenly worshippers, Lord, to receive glory and honour, and power: for thou hast created all things, and for thy pleasure they are and were created" (Rev. 4:11). All things are said to be not only of God and through Him, but for Him (Rom. 11: 36). (CH-STA)

DEFENSE OF THE FAITH

The ingathering of the heathen is the special work of the Church. It is a missionary work. It was so understood by the apostles. Their two great duties were the propagation and the defence of the truth. To these they devoted themselves. While they travelled, led hither and thither preaching the gospel through all parts of the Roman world, they labored no less assiduously in defence of the gospel. All the epistles of the New Testament, those of Paul, Peter, John, and James, are directed towards the correction of false doctrine. These two duties of propagating and defending the truth the apostles passed on to their successors. (CH-STA)

The first necessary condition of contention for the faith is the firm conviction that the Bible is the infallible rule of faith, i.e., that whatever the Bible teaches God teaches, and therefore is infallibly true, and consequently no man can reject it without rejecting the testimony of God. If a man allows himself to depart from what he sees the Bible teaches, there is no security for him. He may believe anything. (CH-CP)

DEGRADATION

-Of the Sinner

We approach nearer to the great lesson of the parable (Prodigal Son) when we note that there is certainly imbedded in its teaching that great and inexpressibly moving truth that there is no depth of degradation, return from which will not be welcomed by God. A sinner may be too vile for any and everything else; but he cannot be too vile for salvation. (BBW-TSW)

DEMONS (Evil angels)

-Nature of

In the spiritual world there is only one devil, but there are many demons. These evil spirits are represented as belonging to the same order of beings as the good angels. All the names and titles, expressive of their nature and powers, given to the one, are also given to the others. Their original condition was holy. When they fell or what was the nature of their sin is not revealed. (CH-STA)

-Power of

As to the power and agency of these evil spirits, they are represented as being exceedingly numerous, as everywhere efficient, as having access to our world, and as operating in nature and in the minds of men. The same limitations, of course, belong to their agency as belong to that of the holy angels: (1) they are dependent on God and can act only under His control and by His permission; (2) their operations must be according to the laws of nature; and (3) they cannot interfere with the freedom and responsibility of men. Nevertheless, their power is very great. (CH-STA)

-Possession by

The most marked exhibition of the power of evil spirits over the bodies and minds of men, is afforded by the demoniacs so often mentioned in the evangelical history. By possession is meant the inhabitation of an evil spirit in such a relation to the body and soul as to exert a controlling influence, producing violent agitations and great sufferings, both mental and corporeal. There is no special improbability in the doctrine of demoniacal possessions. Evil spirits do exist. They have access to the minds and bodies of men. Why should we refuse to believe, on the authority of Christ, that they were allowed to have special power over some men? (CH-STA)

We are not to deny what is plainly recorded in the Scriptures as facts on this subject, nor have we any right to assert that Satan and his angels do not now in any cases produce similar effects. On the other hand, we should abstain from reading Satanic or demoniacal influence or possession into any case where the phenomena can be otherwise accounted for. The difference between believing whatever is possible and believing only what is certain is strikingly illustrated in the case of Luther and Calvin. The former was disposed to refer all evil to the spirits of darkness; the latter referred to their agency only what could be proved to be actually their work. (CH-STA)

DEPRAVITY

-Defined

The whole human race, by their apostasy from God, are totally depraved. By total depravity is not meant that all men are equally wicked, nor that any man is as thoroughly corrupt as it is possible for a man to be, nor that men are destitute of all moral virtues. All this is perfectly consistent with the Scriptural doctrine of total depravity, which includes the entire absence of holiness. There is common to all men a total alienation of the soul from God so that no unrenewed man either understands or seeks after God; no such man ever makes God his portion, or God's glory the end of his being. The apostasy from God is total or complete. All men worship and serve the creature rather than the creator. They are all therefore declared in Scripture to be spiritually dead. They are destitute of any principle of spiritual life. (CH-STA)

It should be noted that man's inability since the fall relates only to "the things of the Spirit." He has retained not only the liberty of choice or power of self-determination, but also the ability to perform moral acts, good as well as evil. Those areas where fallen man retains his ability are designated "things external"; those areas where he has lost his ability are designated "the things of God" and "the things connected with salvation." (CH-STA)

-A Spiritual Death

By nature all men are dead in trespasses and sins. Spiritual life was lost to the whole human race by the transgression of Adam. If there were only a spark of life in the human soul, it might be cherished, and by assiduous culture, might grow to maturity. But in man's corrupt nature there dwelleth no good thing. All the thoughts and imaginations of his heart are "only evil continually." (AA-PT)

-Universal

All the children of men, of all ages, nations, and circumstances, and however educated, invariably sin as soon as they become capable of moral action. A universal fact must have a cause universally present. This can only be found in the common depravity of our nature. (AAH-CF)

DESIGN

-God, the Author

The Bible teaches that God is immanent in the world, preserving and controlling all the physical causes, and the immediate author of all organic structure indicative of design (CH-CP)

DESPAIR

Where the Spirit dwells there will be peace and joy. Despair is inconsistent with spiritual life. Doubt and despondency are hostile to it. (CH-CP)

DISCIPLES

-The Need of Young

The new man often remains in a dwarfish state, because he is fed upon husks; or he grows into a distorted shape by means of errors which are inculcated upon him. It is of unspeakable importance that the young disciple has sound, instructive, and practical preaching to attend on. It also is of consequence that the religious people with whom he converses should be discreet, evangelical, and intelligent Christians; and that the books put into his hands should be of the right kind. (AA-TRE)

DISCIPLINE

-Of Christians

Judicious, seasonable discipline is a powerful means of grace, and often would be the effectual means of recovering the backslider, if exercised as it should be. (AA-TRE)

If whenever there is an appearance of declension in a church member, the pastor, or some other officer of the church, would go to the person, and in the spirit and by the authority of Christ would address a serious admonition to him, and then a second and a third, and if these were unheeded, then bring him before the church, backsliding, in most cases, would be arrested before it proceeded far. (AA-TRE)

Never resort to Church discipline for anything which is not forbidden in the word of God. The only ground of discipline is an offense. (CH-CP)

-Of Children

Exercise a salutary discipline towards your children, even with the rod, when it is necessary, but let this species of discipline be the last resort, and used rather seldom. It is far better than a dark room or anything which keeps the child a long time in a bad humor. But carefully avoid chastisement in the heat of passion, for this will do your children more harm than good. (AA-TRE)

DISEASE

-Physical vs. Spiritual

The superstitious heathen travel hundreds of miles to visit some fountain supposed to possess a healing virtue. But when it is announced that a WELL OF SALVATION is opened for the healing of the maladies of the soul, very little interest is felt by most in the tidings. Men are not sensible of their spiritual diseases, and therefore do not seek a cure. (AA-PT)

-Not Always Satanic

Do not attribute the effects of mere disease to the devil; although I do not deny that he has an agency in producing some diseases; especially, by harassing and disturbing the mind to such a degree, that the body suffers with it. But it is very unwise to ascribe every feeling and every word of the melancholy man to Satan; whereas, many of these are natural consequences of bodily disease. (AA-PT or TRE)

DISPENSATIONS

The plan of salvation has, under all dispensations, the patriarchal, the Mosaic, and the Christian, been the same. There are the same promise of deliverance from the evils of the apostasy, the same Redeemer, the same condition required for participation in the blessings of redemption, and the same complete salvation for all who embrace the offers of divine mercy. (CH-STA)

Although the covenant of grace has always been the same, the dispensations of that covenant have changed. The first dispensation extended from Adam to Abraham. The second dispensation extended from Abraham to Moses. The third dispensation of this covenant was from Moses to Christ. All that belonged to the previous periods was taken up and included in it. The gospel dispensation is called new in contrast to the Mosaic economy, which was old and about to vanish away. (CH-STA)

DISTRACTIONS

What we suffer from is the distraction arising from the multiplicity of objects. We purpose to seek Christ as the main end, but there are so many subordinate ends, so many other things which we seek, that we lose all unity and force in our life. A stream divided into many channels, flows shallow and feebly in them all. It is only by collecting all the water into one channel that the current becomes deep and strong. So it is with life. If you would serve Christ with earnestness, you must serve him alone. (CH-CP)

DIVORCE

The divine law as to divorce is, that marriage is a contract for life between one man and one woman, and that it is dissolved only by death (Rom. 7:2); and that the only causes upon which any civil authority can dissolve the union of those whom God has joined together are (a) adultery, (b) willful, causeless, and incurable desertion. (AAH-CF)

The civil law, however, has no authority to grant divorces upon any other grounds than those defined as allowed by the law of God. Whenever they do so, as is constantly done in fact, the civil authorities put themselves into direct conflict with the law of God in the case. Hence all Christians and church courts are bound in such cases to regard the judgment of the civil authority, and to regard and treat unlawful divorces as null and void. And if the parties to a marriage unrighteously dissolved marry again, they are to be regarded and treated by those who fear God as living in those new marriages in the sin of adultery. Matt. 19:8; Acts 4:19; 5:29. (AAH-CF)

DOCTRINE

-And Facts

It is a somewhat difficult matter to distinguish between Christian doctrines and facts. The doctrines of Christianity are doctrines only because they are facts; and the facts of Christianity become its most indispensable doctrines. The Incarnation of the eternal God is necessarily a dogma: no human tongue could bear witness to it as a fact. And yet, if it be not a fact, our faith is vain, we are yet in our sins. On the other hand, the Resurrection of Christ is a fact, an external occurrence within the cognizance of men to be established by their testimony. And yet, it is the cardinal doctrine of our system: on it all other doctrines hang. (BBW-SSW)

-False

Any doctrine, therefore, which contradicts the facts of consciousness or the laws of belief which God has impressed upon our nature must be false. If, therefore, it can be shown that there are certain truths which men as constrained by the constitution of their nature to believe, those truths are to be retained in despite of all the arts of sophistry. (CH-STA)

If what they preach be another gospel, another method of salvation, then what Paul said must befall them. "Though we, or an angel from heaven, preach another gospel unto you than that which we have preached unto you, let him be accursed." It need not, however, be entirely another gospel. If the truth is perverted, sublimated, rendered unintelligible, or unadapted to the end of convincing and converting sinners and edifying the people of God, it will bring us woe in some form and at some time. (CH-CP)

DREAMS

-Sources of

Dreams have been by some divided into natural, divine, and diabolical. (AA-TRE)

-From God

But there is nothing inconsistent with reason or Scripture in supposing that, on some occasions, certain communications, intended for the warning or safety of the individual himself, or of others, may be made in dreams. To doubt of this is to run counter to a vast body of testimony in every age. And if ideas received in dreams produce a salutary effect, in rendering the careless serious, or the sorrowful comfortable. In the view of divine truth, very well; such dreams may be considered PROVIDENTIAL, if not divine. But if any are led by dreams to pursue a course repugnant to the dictates of common sense or the precepts of Scripture, such dreams may rightly be considered diabolical. (AA-TRE)

-And Prayer

Two things are in our power, and these we should do: first, to avoid evil thoughts and such pampering of the body as has a tendency to pollute our dreams; and, secondly, to pray to God to preserve us from evil thoughts even in sleep. Particularly, we should pray to be delivered from the influence of Satan during our sleeping hours. (AA-TRE)

DRESS

The same rule as to particulars of dress and modes of living does not apply to all persons and places. It depends on usage, on rank, or on other adventitious circumstances. There is great danger of becoming pharisaical, and making religion consist in externals. (CH-CP)

DUTY

Living for Christ (was) the unifying principle of (Paul's) outward and active life. Negatively—he did not seek wealth or honor, either as his main, or his subordinate object. He sought simply the glory of Christ. Now this Is what we ought to do. This is what we expect you to do, and especially those who are now going away. Because it is your duty. This is the highest thing you can do. Whatever else you do will in the end be regarded as nothing. (CH-CP)

We are also free, accountable agents. Every Christian duty is therefore a grace; for without him we can do nothing (John 15:5). And equally every Christian grace is a duty; because the grace is given to us to exercise, and it finds Its true result and expression only in the duty. (AAH-CF)

EDUCATION

-Of Youth in Bible Knowledge

True religion prevails in any community, in proportion to the degree In which the young are instructed in the facts and indoctrinated in the truths of the Bible. Where the young are from the beginning imbued with the knowledge of the Bible, there pure Christianity abides; and where they are allowed to grow up in ignorance of divine truth, there true religion languishes and loses more and more its power. Such is the testimony of experience. (CH-STA)

-And the Bible

The triumph of the Bible over these difficulties—a triumph which has been repeated until it has become a matter of course—marks the introduction of the Bible into the world as easily the greatest event that has ever occurred in the history of the diffusion of literature, and just as easily the most powerful educative force which has ever entered humanity. (BBW-SSW)

The Church not only stayed the downward progress of education and increased the number of readers, but, by its demand that the Bible should be read by all ranks and classes and sexes and ages, introduced the principle of universal education into the world and advanced far toward making it a realized fact. The service of the Bible to the Greek and Roman people was therefore, hardly less than that which it rendered to the outlying barbarians, to whom it for the first time gave letters and a written tongue. It made them literate. Thus, the Bible became the mother of truly popular education. Has there ever been a greater revolution wrought in the intellectual history of the race. (BBW-SSW)

ELECT

All the elect believe—John 10:16,-29, 37-39; 17:2, 9, 24. 1. And only the elect believe—John 10:26. And those who believe do so because they are elect—Acts 13:48; 2:47. (AAH-OT)

ELECTION

-A Scriptural Fact

The salvation of men, for example is said to be "according to the eternal purpose which he purposed In Christ Jesus" (Eph. 3: 11). Believers were chosen in Christ before the foundation of the world (Eph. 1: 4). Christ as a sacrifice was "foreordained before the foundation of the world, but was manifest in these last times for you, who by him do believe in God" (1 Pet. 1 :20-21). This is the constant representation of Scripture. (CH-STA)

-And the Gospel

The gospel is for all, election is a special grace in addition to that offer. The non-elect may come if they will. The elect will come. The decree of election puts no barrier before men preventing them from accepting the gospel offer. Any man, elect or non-elect are left to act as they are freely determined by their own hearts. (AAH-OT)

-And Human Freedom

The doctrine of election does not presume that God constrains men inconsistently with their freedom. The non-elect are simply let alone, to do as their own evil hearts prompt. The elect are made willing in the day of God's power. God works in them to WILL as well as to DO of his good pleasure. To be MADE WILLING takes away no man' s liberty. (AAH-OT)

-United with Faith and Holiness

The decree of election does not secure salvation without faith and holiness, but salvation THROUGH faith and holiness, the means being just as much decreed as the end. The Calvinist believes, as well as the Arminian, that every man who does (practices) evil will be damned, elect or non-elect. (AAH-OT)

-A Great Blessing to Ponder

The marvel of marvels is not that God, in his infinite love, has not elected all of this guilty race to be saved, but that he has elected any. If we know what sin is, and what holiness is, and what salvation from sin to holiness is, that is the way we shall feel. That is the reason why meditation on our eternal election produces such blessed fruits in our hearts and lives. That God has saved me, even me, sunk in my sin and misery, by the marvels of his grace, can only fill me with adoring praise. That he has set upon me from all eternity to save me, wretched sinner that I am—how can I express the holy joy that fills my heart at every remembrance of it! This is the foundation of all my comfort, the assurance of all my hope. (BBW-SSW)

ENEMIES

-Of Christians

The enemies of the Christian have been commonly divided into three classes, the world, the flesh, and the devil; but though these may be conceived of, and spoken of separately, they resist the Christian soldier by their combined powers. The devil is the agent, the world furnishes the bait or the object of temptation, and the flesh, or our own corrupt nature, is the subject on which the temptation operates. (AA-TRE)

ENTHUSIASM (Emotional excess)

In judging of religious experience, it is all-important to keep steadily in view the system of divine truth contained in the Holy Scriptures; otherwise, our experience, as is too often the case, will degenerate into enthusiasm. Many ardent professors seem too readily to take it for granted that all religious feelings must be good. They therefore take no care to discriminate between the genuine and the spurious, the pure gold and the tinsel. Their only concern is about the ardor of their feelings; not considering that if they are spurious, the more intense they are, the further they will lead them astray. (AA-TRE)

In these exercises there is not a tincture of enthusiasm. Indeed, holy affections thus produced by the contemplation of truth are the very opposite of enthusiasm, which always substitutes human fancies or impulses for the truths of God, which it uniformly undervalues. In this case we see also how high the exercises of Scriptural piety may rise without degenerating into any extravagance. Many Christians seem not to know or believe that such spiritual discoveries of the beauty of holiness and the glory of the Lord are now attainable: but still there are some, and often those of the humbler class of society, who are privileged with these spiritual discoveries, and prize them above all price. (AA-TRE)

EPISTLES

-Visible

Believers are the epistles of Christ. They are his witnesses. They represent him among men. It is their sole duty to make a fair representation of what he is, and of what his religion is, before the world. This idea is often presented in the Old Testament, and the people were often upbraided because the name of God was blasphemed among the gentiles for their sake. (CH-CP)

ERROR

-Its Fruit

Error never can under any circumstances produce the effects of truth. (AA-TRE)

-And Genuine Faith

What degree of knowledge is absolutely necessary to the existence of piety cannot be accurately determined by man, but we know that genuine faith may consist with much ignorance and error. (AA-TRE)

-Must Be Reproved

Listen respectfully to the opinions of others, but never fail to give your testimony, modestly but firmly, against error. "Let your speech be always with grace, seasoned with salt. Let no corrupt communication proceed out of your mouth, but that which is good to the use of edifying, that it may minister grace unto the hearers." (AA-TRE)

ESCHATOLOGY

-And Missions

The first great event which is to precede the second coming of Christ, is the universal proclamation of the gospel. Christ repeatedly taught that the gospel is to be preached to all nations before His second coming. Thus, in Matthew 24: 14 He says, "This gospel of the kingdom shall be preached in all the world for a witness unto all nations; and then shall the end come", and in Mark 13:10, "The gospel must first be published among all nations." (CH-STA)

The old dispensation was temporary and preparatory; the new is permanent and final. In sending forth the disciples to preach the gospel and in promising them the gift of the Spirit, Jesus assured them that He would be with them in that work unto the end of the world. This dispensation is, therefore, the last before the restoration of all things—the last, that is, in which men will be converted and the elect ingathered. There is no indication in Scripture that the dispensation of the Spirit is to give way to a new and better dispensation for the conversion of the nations. When the gospel is fully preached, then comes the end. (CH-STA)

ETERNAL LIFE

The Scriptures know of only two methods of attaining eternal life: the one demands perfect obedience, and the other demands faith. (CH-STA)

ETERNAL STATE

-Of the Righteous

The future happiness of the saints will entail indefinite enlargement of all their faculties, entire exemption from all sin and sorrow, intercourse and fellowship with the high intelligences of heaven (patriarchs, prophets, apostles, martyrs, and all the redeemed) constant increase in knowledge and in the useful exercise of all their powers, secure and everlasting possession of all possible good, and outward circumstances such as will minister to their increasing blessedness. (CH-STA)

-Of the Wicked

The sufferings of the finally impenitent, according to the Scriptures, involve the loss of all earthly good, exclusion from the presence and favour of God, utter reprobation or the final withdrawal of the Holy Spirit, a consequent unrestrained dominion of sin and sinful passions, the operations of conscience, despair, evil associates, actual inflictions, and perpetuity. (CH-STA)

God is the life of the soul. His favour and fellowship with Him are essential to its holiness and happiness. If His favour be forfeited, the inevitable consequences are the death of the soul, i.e. loss of spiritual life, and unending sinfulness and misery. (CH-STA)

-Unalterable at death

The condition of the soul after death is unalterable. There is an impassable gulf between heaven and hell. We are within a hairs-breadth of heaven or hell every moment, and therefore should live in fear and trembling, and that others are in the same predicament, and therefore we should endeavor to awaken them to a sense of their danger. (CH-CP)

EVANGELISM

Only if we catch the apostles' viewpoint, and can say to our souls with the clearness of conviction which they felt, that there is salvation in Jesus alone, will we be inspired with the zeal that filled them, to evangelize the world. (BBW-TSW)

-Our Failure

In the gift of His Son, the revelation of His Word, the mission of the Spirit, and the institution of the Church, God has made abundant provision for the salvation of the world. That the Church has been so remiss in making known the gospel is her guilt. We must not charge the ignorance and consequent perdition of the heathen upon God. The guilt rests on us. We have kept to ourselves the bread of life and allowed the nations to perish. (CH-STA)

But, it may be asked, may not the Church fail in her duty of extending the knowledge of the gospel? May she not withhold the gospel from the world, and thus bring down the blood of the perishing on her head? Undoubtedly she may, unhappily she has done, and is doing just this. But our faithlessness shall never make of none effect the faithfulness of God. Let us hearken to the philosophy of Mordecai: "For if thou altogether holdest thy peace at this time, then shall relief and deliverance arise from another place, but thou and thy father's house shall perish." God has not committed his honor to another.

His purposes of mercy will never fail because of our unfaithfulness, for his providence is overall. (BBW-SSW)

EVIDENCE

-Of the Indwelling Spirit

As in all other cases, the test laid down by Christ applies here also. That is, by their fruits ye shall know them. A good tree bringeth forth good fruit. The only evidence of the indwelling of the Spirit is the fruit of the Spirit. (CH-CP)

EXORCISM

Exorcists there were and healers enough, who pronounced other names over the afflicted children of men. None of them had power to save. If ever the evils of this life are to be relieved, the forces of disease and decay, of injury and death, to be broken, it will be only by Jesus that it will be done; only His name, by faith in His name, can give that perfect soundness for which we long. (BBW-TSW)

EXPIATION

Men are sinners and that, being sinners, they need of expiation for their guilt, as well as moral purification, if they are to experience salvation. Sacrifices, therefore, were instituted from the beginning to teach the necessity of expiation and to serve as prophetic types of the only effectual expiation, which, in the fulness of time, was to be offered for the sins of men. It is not, then, simply this or that declaration of Scripture, or this or that institution which must be explained away if the justice of God be denied, but the whole form and structure of the religion of the Bible. That religion as the religion for sinners rests on the assumption of the necessity of the expiation. This is its cornerstone; the whole fabric falls into ruin if that scone be removed. (AA-TRE)

EXPERIENCE

-And the Scriptures

And lest we should attribute to the teaching of the Spirit the operations of our own natural affections, we find in the Bible the norm and standard of all genuine religious experience. Scriptures teach not only the truth, but what are the effects of the truth on the heart and conscience, when applied with saving power by the Holy Ghost. (CH-STA)

In our day there is nothing more necessary than to distinguish carefully between true and false experiences in religion; to "try the spirits whether they are of God." And in making this discrimination, there is no other test but the infallible Word of God; let every thought, motive, impulse and emotion be brought to this touchstone. "To the law and the testimony; if they speak not according to these, it is because there is no light in them." (AA-TRE)

Christian experience is ever and must ever be essentially the same, because experience is only the effect produced by Christian doctrine on the soul, by the Holy Spirit. As therefore Christian doctrine is a fixed quantity, always the same and always essentially the same in the apprehension of believers, Christian experience must always be the same. The only true standard of that experience is to be found in the Scriptures. Ours must correspond with that. We must feel as Paul and John felt about sin, Christ and heaven. (CH-CP)

-And One's View of Sin

It is a matter of fact that the religious experience of every man is determined by his view of sin. It is his sense of guilt and pollution which leads him to God for help, and of course the kind of help he seeks and is willing to accept, depends upon his views of his sinfulness. All genuine religious experience consists in the conformity of our convictions and feelings with the truth of God. (CH-CP)

FAITH

-Its Definition

. In the strict and special sense of the word, faith means a belief in things not seen which is based on testimony. (CH-STA)

This is faith—receiving as true what God has testified, and doing so because He has testified it. (CH-STA).

-Its Foundation

This is a point of great practical importance. If faith, or our persuasion of the truths of the Bible, rests on philosophical grounds, then the door is opened for rationalism; if it rests on feeling, then it is open to mysticism. The only sure and satisfying foundation is the testimony of God, who cannot err and who will not deceive. (CH-STA)

Against all undue assumptions of authority, Protestants hold fast to two great principles: (1) the right of private judgment and (2) the exclusivity of the Scriptures as the infallible rule of faith and practice. The object of faith, then, is all the truths revealed in the Word of God. (CH-STA)

-Not Produced by Miracles

No amount of mere external evidence can produce genuine faith. The Israelites, who had seen a long succession of wonders in the land of Egypt, who had passed through the divided waters of the Red Sea, who were daily receiving by miracle food from heaven, who had trembled at the manifestations of the Divine majesty on Mount Sinai, within sight of that mountain made a golden calf their god. The men who saw the miracles of Christ performed almost daily in their presence, cried out, "Crucify him! Crucify him!" Hence our Saviour said that those who hear not "Moses and the prophets, neither will they be persuaded, though one rose from the dead." We may confidently conclude, therefore, that those who now believe not the gospel, would not be persuaded had they seen all the miracles which Christ performed. (CH-WL)

-Saving Faith

The specific act of saving faith which unites us to Christ, and is the sole condition or instrument of justification, involves two essential elements: (1.) Assent to what the Scriptures reveal to us concerning the person, offices, and work of Christ; and (2.) Trust or implicit reliance upon Christ alone, for all that is involved in a complete salvation. (AAH-CF)

-Spurious Faith

While it is of importance to distinguish faith from every ocher grace, yet It is necessary to insist on the fact that that faith which does not produce love and other holy affections is not a genuine faith. (AAH-CF)

-Temporary Faith

Temporary faith is that state of mind often experienced in this world by impenitent hearers of the gospel, induced by the moral evidence of the truth, the common influences of the Holy Ghost, and the power of religious sympathy. Sometimes the excited imagination joyfully appropriates the promises of the gospel -Matt. 13: 20. Sometimes, like Felix, the man believes and trembles. Oftentimes it is at first impossible to distinguish this state of mind from genuine saving faith. But not springing from a divine work of recreation it has no root in the permanent principles of the heart. It is always, therefore,1st, inefficient, neither purifying the heart nor overcoming the world; 2d, temporary. (AAH-CF)

-And Knowledge

What Protestants maintain is that knowledge, i.e., the cognition of the import of the proposition to be believed, is essential to faith; and, consequently, that faith is limited by knowledge. We can believe only what we know, i.e. what we intelligently apprehend. If a proposition be announced to us in an unknown language, we can affirm nothing about it. We can neither believe nor disbelieve it. Should the man who makes the declaration, assert that it is true, if we have confidence in his competency and integrity, we may believe that he is right, but the proposition itself is no part of our faith. According to the Apostle (1 Cor. 14:9-16) knowledge, or the intelligent apprehension of the meaning of what is proposed, is essential to faith. (CH-STA)

It has been said that he who believes the Bible to be the Word of God may properly be said to believe all it teaches, although much of its instruction may be to him unknown. But this is not a correct representation. The man who believes the Bible is prepared to believe on its authority whatever it declares to be true. But he cannot properly be said to believe any more of its contents than he knows. (CH-STA)

-First Act of a Believer

The first conscious exercise of the renewed soul is faith. An apt analogy is the case of a man born blind whose eyes have been opened. His first conscious act is seeing. It is so with the believer. As soon as his eyes are opened by the renewing of the Holy Ghost, he is in a new world. Old things have passed away; all things are become new. Apprehension of "the things of God" as true lies at the foundation of all the exercises of the renewed soul. (CH-STA)

-Living by

Life includes all our activity as rational, moral and religious beings. Living by faith is to have our whole activity, inward and outward, permanently and characteristically determined by faith. (CH-CP)

FAITHFULNESS

-In the Layman and Minister

In saying that a servant is faithful, you say that he is diligent, honest, obedient, in short, that he performs all his duties as a servant. To say that a Christian is faithful, is to say that he receives God's truth, that he is assiduous in all his religious and social duties. So, of a minister; to say that he is faithful, is to say that he is diligent in study; that he dispenses the truth, and nothing but the truth; that he does this in season and out of season; that he conscientiously discharges his obligations as a minister, to the ignorant, to the wicked, to the sick, to the suffering, to the young and to the old. It is also to say that he is devoted to his work; that he gives himself wholly to it; that he does not serve God and mammon, Christ and Belial, himself and his Master, but that his eye is single and his life undivided. (CH-CP)

-Its Permanence

Fidelity in the service of God is not a debt to be paid and forgotten. It is not a service to be rendered at a particular time or place, but one which lasts as long as we live. We are to be faithful unto death. If a man could be faithful for years, and become unfaithful, his former fidelity would count for nothing. (CH-CP)

-And the Holy Spirit

It is, finally, more clear than anything else, that we cannot be faithful, that we cannot discharge this high though simple duty, unless we are at all times filled by the Holy Ghost. (CH-CP)

FALL OF MAN

Man is not in his original and normal state. Apostatizing from God, man fell into a state of darkness and confusion. Reason and conscience are no longer adequate guides as to "the things of God." Of fallen men the apostle says that "when they knew God, they glorified him not as God, neither were thankful; but became vain in their imaginations, and their foolish heart was darkened. Professing themselves to be wise, they became fools, and changed the glory of the uncorruptible God into an image made like to corruptible man, and to birds and four-footed beasts, and creeping things" (Rom. 1: 21-2) (CH-STA)

FALSE TEACHERS

To be thus acceptable to God it is necessary that we should not huckster the word of God. That is,1st. We should not make gain of it, use it for our own advantage, make it a means of our own honor or profit. 2d. We should not adulterate it. It is only the pure gospel that is an odor of a sweet smell, and therefore only those who offer or diffuse the pure gospel. Adulterated truth and those who diffuse it are an offense, and as a smoke in the nostrils of God. (CH-CP)

FAMILY

-The Root of Society

A genuine and thorough reformation must commence in the family, which is the foundation of all social institutions, civil and religious. Here is the root whence springs the whole tree with all its spreading and towering branches. (AA-TRE)

The character of the Church and of the State depends on the character of the family. If religion dies out in the family, it cannot elsewhere be maintained. A man's responsibility to his children, as well as to his God, binds him to make his house a Bethel; if not a Bethel, it will be a dwelling place of evil spirits. (CH-STA)

-Its Need of Worship

Since the family is the most intimate bond of fellowship among men, it is of the utmost importance that it be hallowed by religion. Parents and children are purified and strengthened when the whole household is stated in assembled, morning and evening for the worship of God. There is no substitute for this divinely appointed means of promoting family religion. All persons subject to the watch or care of the Church should be required to maintain in their households this stated worship of God. (CH-STA)

FASTING

Fasting in a religious sense is a voluntary abstinence from food for a religious purpose. It is a natural expression of sorrow, because sorrow destroys the desire for food and the power to digest it. In all ages, therefore, fasting has been connected with religious services in times of humiliation and distress. It was prescribed on certain occasions under the law, voluntarily practiced by good men, and recognized in the New Testament. This abstinence is either total or partial, either for a day or for protracted periods. It is nowhere enjoined in Scripture, and therefore cannot be made obligatory. (CH-CP)

External fasting, without corresponding internal penitence and humiliation, is hypocrisy, and such fasting is severely reproved by the prophet. (AA-PT)

FEELINGS

All unholy feelings are subdued in the presence of God, unsound principles are corrected in the light of divine truth. We become conformed to the things with which we are familiar. (CH-CP)

Everywhere in the Scriptures it is asserted or assumed that the feelings follow the understanding, that the illumination of the mind in the due apprehension of spiritual objects is the necessary preliminary condition of all right feeling and conduct. (CH-STA)

FELLOWSHIP

"Fellowship" is a good word, and a great duty. But our fellowship, according to Paul, must be in the "furtherance of the gospel." And it is precisely the gospel which is left out of the basis of this proposed fellowship. Let us by all means have fellowship: but let our fellowship be first of all with the Father and with his Son Jesus Christ—with whom we can have fellowship, we are told, only if we walk in the light of his revealed salvation. (BBW-SSW)

This union is Catholic, not only as uniting Christians of all denominations, but of all ages rich and poor, learned and unlearned, barbarian, Scythians, bond and free. These distinctions are real. They are not to be ignored, but they are all superficial, outward and transient. Underneath them all is this majestic bond of union, which unites all these classes as one body in Christ Jesus. (CH-CP)

As Christ is the head of His earthly kingdom, so is He its only lawgiver. He prescribes the terms of admission in His kingdom. We are to receive all those whom Christ receives. No degree of knowledge nor confession beyond which is necessary to salvation can be demanded as a condition of our recognizing any one as a Christian brother and treating him as such. For men to reject from their fellowship those whom God has received into His is an intolerable presumption. All those terms of communion which have been set up beyond profession of faith in Christ are usurpations of an authority which belongs to Him alone. (CH-STA)

FIGHT OF FAITH

The Christian life. is called the fight of faith, not because it is a conflict in behalf of a creed, but because faith is the contending principle; it is a fight in which faith is the combatant. The fight, therefore, which we have to endure, is a conflict to preserve the inward life of the soul, which consists in faith. Why is it called a good fight? Because it is the conflict in behalf of what is good; not for riches, honor, dominion, but for holiness. Because it is a conflict which ends in triumph. (CH-CP)

FOOLS

The fact is plain that religion is in the Scriptures often called wisdom, and wickedness, folly. The good are the wise; the wicked are fools. But why is this? Because it implies the selection of the best ends and the use of the best means. The highest end is God's glory; the best means, obedience to his will. It is the height of folly to select any creature good or temporary attainment as the chief end. This all but the righteous do, and therefore all but the righteous are fools. (CH-CP)

FOREKNOWLEDGE

Foreknowledge is an act of the infinite intelligence of God, knowing from all eternity, without change, the certain futurition of all events of every class whatsoever that ever will come to pass. (AAH-OT)

If God be ignorant of how free agents will act, His knowledge must be limited and it must be constantly increasing, a notion which is altogether inconsistent with the true idea of His nature. His government of the world also, in that case, must be precarious for it would be dependent on the unforeseen conduct of men. The Church, therefore, in obedience to the Scriptures has almost with one voice professed faith in God's foreknowledge of the free acts of His creatures. (CH-STA)

FORGIVENESS

-Christ, Our Example of

We are. commanded to be followers or imitators of Christ. In his endurance of injuries. —Never was such ingratitude, disrespect, indifference, malice, contempt and scorn, heaped on any other head; and that head encircled with the radiance of divine perfection and the crown of universal dominion. Yet, 1. There was no resentfulness. He did not call down fire from heaven on his enemies. He did not return evil for evil. He did good for evil and prayed for those who shed his blood. 2. He did not threaten. In this there is a strong contrast between him and many of the martyrs. (CH-CP)

The fact that Christ is so forbearing towards us, will render his true disciples forbearing towards others. Christ, notwithstanding our vileness, and notwithstanding our guilt, treats us as though we were pure and innocent. He not only forgives us offenses infinitely greater and more numerous than any we ever can experience from our fellow-men, but he continues to heap his favors upon us while we are trying his patience to the uttermost. If he forgives us ten thousand talents, should we not forgive our fellow-servant and hundred pence? He who feels that he has been forgiven much, will be disposed to forgive much. (CH-CP)

FREE-WILL

A man is free when his outward acts and volitions are truly and properly his own, determined by nothing outside himself but proceeding from his own views, feelings, and immanent dispositions, so that they are the real, intelligent, and conscious expression of his character or of what is in his mind. (CH-STA)

The will is not determined by any law of necessity, nor is it independent, indifferent, and self-determined, but it is always determined by the preceding state of mind, so that a man is free so long as his activity is determined and controlled by his reason and feelings. (CH-STA).

-Different from free agency

No little ambiguity arises from confounding liberty of the will with liberty of the agent. These forms of expression are not really equivalent. The man may be free when his will is in bondage. It is a correct and established usage of language, expressive of a real fact of consciousness, to speak of an enslaved will in a free agent. He that commits sin is the servant of sin. The will of a man who has been for years a miser is in a state of slavery, yet the man himself is perfectly free. His avarice is himself. It is his own dark, cherished feeling. We maintain that the man is free, but we deny that the will is free in the sense of being independent of reason, conscience, and feeling. In other words, a man cannot be independent of himself, nor can any one of his faculties be independent of all the rest. (CH-STA)

FRUIT OF THE SPIRIT

The Christian graces are inseparable. One cannot exist without the other. There cannot be faith without hope, or repentance without love, or love without meekness. This finds its analogy in physical life. Respiration, arterial action, digestion, cannot be conducted independently of one another. Though this is true, yet one grace may be more prominent than others. (CH-CP)

FRUITFULNESS

The acceptableness of Christ, of the gospel and of ministers in the sight of God, does not depend on the effect produced. It is not only when men are saved by them, that they are agreeable to God, but also when men perish for neglecting the truth. Christ when mocked, scourged and crucified, was as acceptable to God as when enthroned. The gospel is as glorious and excellent when men reject to their own condemnation, as when they believe. And ministers, if faithful, are as well-pleasing to God when unsuccessful as when successful. (CH-CP)

FUTURE PUNISHMENT

-Its Duration

The punishment of the impenitent sinner is necessarily endless, 1st. Because of the necessity of punishment. 2d. Because the ground of necessity is permanent. The soul never ceases to be guilty and sinful, and therefore never ceases to be miserable. (CH-CP)

-Its Extent

It follows that the punishment of the wicked will be inconceivably great. They are shut out from God and from all good. They are given up to all the power of evil, which constantly increases. They must associate only with those like themselves. They have no hope. In the manner in which there are to be degrees in the glory and blessedness of heaven, as our Lord teaches us in the parable of the ten talents, so there will be differences as to degree in the sufferings of the lost some will be beaten with few stripes, some with many. (CH-STA)

-Its Justice

It is plain that endless sin deserves endless punishment, and that is all the Scriptures or the Church teach. One sin deserves the wrath and curse of God. He is under no obligation in justice to provide a redemption. The instant a soul sins it is cut off from the communion and life of God. As long as it continues to sin, it will continue to deserve his wrath and curse. It is obvious that the sinful tempers and conduct indulged in hell will deserve and receive punishment as strictly as those previously indulged in this life. Otherwise, the monstrous principle would be true that the worse a sinner becomes the less is he worthy of blame or punishment. (AAH-OT)

It is obvious that the question of the duration of future punishment can be decided only by divine revelation.

What the infinitely wise and good God may see fit to do with His creatures is not for us worms of the dust to determine. If we believe the Bible to be the Word of God, all we have to do is to ascertain it teaches on this subject and humbly submit. (CH-STA)

GIFTS

-Spiritual

The apostle classifies spiritual gifts on three different principles. 1. Their relation to our own inward character. He teaches that those which involve moral and religious excellence are immeasurably above those which imply intellectual superiority and power. 2. Those which are permanent are more important than those which are temporary. 3. Those which are useful, are, in that point of view, the greater. (CH-CP).

All gifts, however great, valuable in themselves, without love are of no avail. They will not sanctify or save our souls. We should not seek ourselves, our own exaltation, nor covet gifts which tend to chat result, but should seek the good of others and gifts which may edify one another. (CH-CP)

GIVING

It is a shame to think how small a portion of their gains some professors devote to the Lord. Instead of being a tithe, it is hardly equal to the single sheaf first-fruits. If you have nothing to give, labour to get something. Sit up at night and try to make something, for Christ has need of it. Sell a corner of your land and throw the money into the treasury of the Lord. In primitive times many sold houses and lands and laid the whole at the apostles' feet. Do not be afraid of making yourself poor by giving to the Lord or to His poor. His word is better than any bond, and He says, "I will repay it." Cast your bread on the waters, and after many days you will find it again. Send the Bible—send missionaries—send tracts to the perishing heathen. (AA-TRE)

GLORIFYING GOD

The redeemed become the property of the Redeemer. "You are not your own: for ye are bought with a price" (1 Cor. 6:19). This right of property, extending to both soul and body, brings with it the obligation to glorify God in our body and spirit which are his. We are God's in such a sense that the only legitimate end of our being is his glory. If our own we would live for ourselves, but life belongs to Christ. We must live for Christ. (CH-CP)

It is only in loving Christ that we love God, in glorifying Christ that we can glorify God, and in serving Christ that we can serve God. (CH-CP)

We are to so act that intelligent beings, men and angels, shall be led to glorify God. When anything comes to be decided, whether it should be done or left undone, the rule is not (a) Whether it will be agreeable or disagreeable to ourselves. (b) Nor whether it will be agreeable or otherwise to others, i.e., popular! (c) Nor whether it will be expedient or inexpedient. (d) But whether it will be for the glory of God or not, that is, whether it will tend to make men admire and worship God. (CH-CP)

"Whatsoever ye do, do all Co the glory of God" (1 Cor. 10:31). The Bible gives no statement -it gives a command. It teaches, as they said of Jesus, with authority. It comes, not coldly saying, "This is the best thing, on the whole, to do," but calmly declaring, "This is a thing which you SHALL do - on penalties." And it is well to note this sharply. There are no if's and and's about it. It simply says, "DO IT!" The question for us is, are we doing it? Why, for instance, are you going to your business house tomorrow morning? To make money? Good. For what? Consciously in order to glorify God in the wise, true, noble use of it? No? Well, then, are you a Christian? My dear lady friend, to serve what purpose are you planning to give that entertainment tomorrow? Is it in order to glorify God through it? Perhaps you never thought of that. Well, are you a Christian? What God commands is let us face it unflinchingly—that we shall do nothing without taking absolute care to see that we are trying to glorify God in the doing of it. (BBW-SSW)

Two things you should carry with you everywhere, and to the end of life. 1. That the conviction of the love of Christ, the sense of his love, its greatness and freeness, should fill you and govern you. 2. That the single object of life is thus to cause him to be glorified. Do this and you will be blessed, and a blessing, go where you will, and suffer what you may. (CH-CP)

GLORY OF GOD

By the glory of God is meant his divine perfection, his essential and infinite excellence, which renders him the proper object of admiration and adoration. To act for the glory of God, is to act so that his glory should be manifested, brought into view, acknowledged and admired. (CH-CP)

The final cause of all of God's purposes is His own glory. This is frequently declared to be the end of all things. "Thou art worthy," say the heavenly worshippers, O Lord, to receive glory, and honor, and power: for thou hast created all things, and for thy pleasure they are and were created" (Rev. 4:11). All things are said to be not only of God and through Him, but for Him (Rom. 11:36). (CH-STA)

The Bible, Augustine, and Reformed theology give answer to all such questions as the following: Why did create the world? Why did He permit the occurrence of Why was salvation provided for men and not for angels? Why was the knowledge of that salvation so long confined to one people? Why among those who hear the gospel do some receive and others reject it? To all these and similar questions the answer is: Thus, it seemed good in the eyes of God. Whatever He does or permits to be done is done or permitted for the more perfect revelation of His nature and perfections. (CH-STA)

GOD

-His Attributes (Nature)

The divine attributes are the perfections which are predicated of the divine essence in the Scriptures, or visibly exercised by God in his works of creation and providence and redemption. (AAH-OT)

A Christian child says, "God is a Spirit, infinite, eternal, and unchangeable, in his being, wisdom, power, holiness, justice, goodness, and truth" (Westminster Catechism). Men and angels veil their faces in the essence of that answer. It is the highest, greatest, and most fruitful truth ever embodied in human language. (CH-STA)

If in answering the question, "What is God?" we allow ourselves to be determined by the teachings of His Word and the constitution of our own nature, and if we refer to Him, in an infinite degree, every good we find in ourselves, then we can have no hesitation in believing that he is holy, just, and good. But if we turn to philosophical speculations to decide every question concerning the divine nature, we must give up all confidence in our apprehensions of God as an object of knowledge. It is surely most unreasonable to sacrifice to such speculations all religion and all confidence in the intuitive judgments of the human mind, as well as all faith in God and in the Bible. (CH-STA)

When we predicate intelligence, will and power of God, we mean and the Scriptures mean that God really possesses attributes analogous, i.e., of the same kind as the faculties which that word expresses in us. So, when we predicate of him, love, mercy, holiness and goodness, the same is true. In all these cases we must eliminate from the ideas which those words express when used of ourselves, everything, when we apply them to God, which implies any limitation or imperfection. (CH-CP)

God is defined to be a Spirit infinite, eternal and immutable in his being, wisdom, power, holiness, justice, goodness, and truth. In the presence of his immensity all creatures sink into insignificance. In the essence of his power, all else is weakness; and in the presence of his wisdom, all else is ignorance. He is so infinitely exalted above all things that all things are as nothing in comparison with him. His honor, his will, his blessedness is therefore the highest conceivable end of all things. (CH-CP)

-His Absoluteness

"Absolute" when applied to the being of God signifies that he is an eternal self-existent person, who existed before all other beings, and is the intelligent and voluntary cause of whatsoever else has or will exist in the universe, etc., that he sustains, consequently, no necessary relation to anything without (apart from) himself. (AAH-OT)

-His Eternity

God is without beginning of years or end of days—He is and always has been and always will be; and to Him there is neither past nor future; the past and the future are always and equally present to Him. (CH-STA)

-His Existence

The existence of God is an objective fact. It may be shown that it is a fact which cannot be rationally denied. (CH-STA)

-His Government

God's universe has never for one moment escaped from his governing hand. The event to which it is journeying may seem to us sometimes to very far off; but it is purely divine. And it runs to this best conceivable end, through the best conceivable course. To acknowledge that much, we owe to the God who has made it, and who, having made it, upholds and governs it. (BBW-SSW)

-His Grace

(Grace) is represented as the crowning attribute of the divine nature. Its manifestation is declared to be the grand end of the whole scheme of redemption. Paul teaches that predestination, election, and salvation are all intended for the praise of the glory of the grace of God which He exercises towards us in Chr ist Jesus (Eph. 1: 3-6). He raises men from spiritual death and makes them "sit together in heavenly places in Christ Jesus: that in the ages to come he might show the exceeding riches of his grace" (Eph. 2 :6-7). (CH-STA)

-His Immensity

When we attribute this perfection (immensity) to God, we mean that his essence fills all space. The spirit of God, like the spirit of a man, must be an absolute unit, without extension or dimensions. Therefore, the entire indivisible Godhead must, in the totality of his being, be simultaneously present every moment of time at every point of space. (CH-STA)

-His Immutability

God is absolutely immutable in His essence and attributes. He can neither increase nor decrease. He is subject to no process of development or of self-evolution. His knowledge and power can never be greater or less. He can never be wiser or holier or more righteous or more merciful than He ever has been and ever must be. He is no less immutable in His plans and purposes. Infinite in wisdom, there can be no error in their conception; infinite in power, there can be no failure in their accomplishment. (CH-STA)

-His Infiniteness

The infinite, although illimitable and incapable of increase, is not necessarily all. A thing may be infinite in its own nature without precluding the possibility of the existence of things of a different nature. The infinite, therefore, is not all. An infinite spirit is a spirit to whose attributes as a spirit no limit can be set. It no more precludes the existence of other spirits than infinite goodness precludes the existence of finite goodness, or infinite power the existence of finite power. (CH-STA)

God is infinite in being because no limit can be assigned to His perfections and because He is present in all portions of space. A being is said to be present wherever it perceives and acts. As God perceives and acts everywhere, He is everywhere present. This, however, does not preclude the presence of other beings. (CH-STA)

"Infinite" means that which has no limits. When we say God is Infinite in his being, or in his knowledge, or in his power, we mean that his essence and the active proper ties thereof, have no limitations which involve imperfections of any kind whatsoever. (AAH-OT)

-His Justice

The word justice or righteousness means rightness, that which satisfies the demands of rectitude or law. When we regard God as the author of our moral nature, we conceive of Him as holy; when we regard Him in His dealings with His rational creatures, we conceive of Him as righteous. He is a righteous ruler; all His laws are holy, just, and good. In His moral government He faithfully adheres to those laws. He is impartial and uniform in their execution. As a judge He renders unto every man according to his works. He neither condemns the innocent nor clears the guilty, neither does He ever punish with undue severity. (CH-STA)

Notwithstanding all the apparent inequalities in the distribution of His favors, notwithstanding the prosperity of the wicked and the afflictions of the righteous, the conviction is everywhere expressed that God is just, that somehow and somewhere He will vindicate His dealings with men and show that He Is righteous in all His ways and holy in all His works. (CH-STA)

-His Love

The love of a holy God to sinners is the most mysterious attribute of the divine nature. This manifestation of this attribute for the admiration and beatification of all intelligent creatures is declared to be the special design of redemption. God saves sinners, we are told, "that in the ages to come he might show the exceeding riches of his grace in his kindness toward us through Christ Jesus" (Eph. 2:7). (CH-STA)

The importance of the object to be obtained or the strength of the feeling which prompts to its attainment, is to be measured by the means adapted to that end. To give up an angel, or a world, or a myriad of worlds, would indicate that the feeling was strong and the object of vast importance. But to give up his Son, places these things beyond our comprehension. It shows the love to be absolutely infinite—such as admits of no limit or measure. (CH-CP)

Proof that God is love: 1. Negatively, there is no evidence of malignity in him. 2. Creation and providence constantly manifest it. 3. Redemption is the great overwhelming demonstration of it. 4. It Is declared in a thousand forms in the Scriptures, that God is merciful, long-suffering, tender, compassionate; that his love is stronger than a father's, or a mother's, or a husband's. (CH-CP)

-His Mercy

(His mercy) is universal. All rational creatures and especially men are its objects. It is merciful to the just and to the unjust. It takes no regard of character or conduct. This is illustrated in the arrangements of creation, in the dispensations of his providence, in the provisions of his grace, which are adapted to all and sufficient for all. (CH-CP)

(His mercy) is indestructible. A parent never ceases to love his child, and cannot do it. Let the child be ever so ungrateful and wicked, and return to his father's house, he is received with rejoicing as the prodigal. So, with God, his mercy is ever lasting. (CH-CP)

-His Omnipotence

It is by removing all the limitations of power, as It. exists in us, that we rise to the idea of the omnipotence of God. We can do very little. God can do whatever He wills. We, beyond very narrow limits, must use means to accomplish our ends. With God means are unnecessary. He wills and it is done. (CH-STA)

Instead of exalting, it degrades God, to suppose that He can be other than He is, or that He can act contrary to Infinite wisdom and love. When, therefore, it is said that God is omnipotent because He can do whatever He wills, it is to be remembered that His will is determined by His nature. It is certainly no limitation to perfection to say that it cannot be imperfect. (CH-STA)

-His Omnipresence

As all [true] religion consists in communion with God, and as all communication supposes his presence, this doctrine (of God's omnipresence) lies at the foundation of all (true) religion. (CH-CP)

It cannot require any effort in Him, the omnipresent and infinite intelligence, to comprehend and to direct all things however complicated, numerous, or minute. God is as much present everywhere, and with everything, as though He were only in one place and had but one object of attention. (CH-STA)

-His Sovereignty

The sovereignty of God is his absolute light to govern and dispose of the work of his own hands according to his own good pleasure. This sovereignty rests not in his will abstractly, but in his adorable person. Hence it is an infinitely wise, righteous, benevolent, and powerful sovereignty, unlimited by anything outside of his own perfections. The grounds of his sovereignty are—(1.) His infinite superiority. (2.) His absolute ownership of all things, as created by him. (3.) The perpetual and absolute dependence of all things upon him for being, and of all intelligent creatures for blessedness. (AAH-CF)

From these and similar passages of Scripture it is plain (1) that the sovereignty of God Is universal. It extends over all His creatures from the highest to the lowest. (2) It is absolute. There is no limit to be placed to His authority. He doeth His pleasure in the armies of heaven and among the inhabitants of the earth. (3.) It is immutable. It can neither be ignored or rejected. It binds all creatures as inexorably as physical laws bind the material universe. (CH-STA)

The sovereignty of God supposes that the whole plan of creation, providence and redemption, was adopted on the ground of God's good pleasure; that the carrying out of that plan in all its infinitude of details is determined by his absolute will. So that if it be asked why Adam fell; why salvation was provided for man and not angels; why that salvation was revealed at first to Jews and not to Gentiles; why you and not others are made partakers of this redemption; why one man is a noble and another a peasant; one sick and another well; one happy and another miser able; we have nothing to say but: "Even so, Father, for so it seemed good in thy sight." (CH-CP)

The practical importance of this great doctrine is plain because it determines our relation to God which determines our religion. If a man misconceives his relation to God, of course his religion will be perverted. (CH-CP)

(This doctrine of God's sovereignty) is to all other doctrines of Scripture what the granite formation is to the other strata of the earth. It underlies and sustains them, but it crops out only here and there. So, this doctrine should underlie all our preaching, and should definitely presented and asserted only now and then. (CH-CP)

This sovereignty of God is the ground and peace for all His people. They rejoice that the Lord God omnipotent reigneth, and that neither necessity, nor chance, nor the folly of man, nor the malice of Satan controls the sequence of events and all their issues. Infinite wisdom, love, and power belong to Him, our great God and Saviour into whose hands all power in heaven and earth has been committed. (CH-STA)

-His Truthfulness

God is absolutely true. This is a common property of all the divine perfections and actions. His knowledge is absolutely accurate; his wisdom infallible; his goodness and justice perfectly true to the standard of his own nature. In the exercise of all his properties God is always self-consistent. He is also always absolutely true to his creatures in all his communications, sincere in his promises and threatenings, and faithful in their fulfilment. (AAH-CF)

-His Will

The secret will of God is his decretive will, called secret, because although it is sometimes revealed to man in the prophecies and promises of the Bible, yet it is for the most part hidden in God. The revealed will of God is his preceptive will, which is always clearly set forth as the rule of our duty. Deut. 29:29. (AAH-OT)

-Is a Spirit

It is impossible to overestimate the importance of the truth contained in the simple proposition, God is a Spirit. It is involved in that proposition that God is immaterial. None of the properties of matter can be predicated of Him. He is not extended or divisible, or commanded, or visible, or tangible. He has neither bulk nor form. (CH-STA)

If God be a Spirit, it follows of necessity that He is a person—a self-conscious, intelligent, volitional agent. As all this is involved in our consciousness of ourselves as spirit, it must be true of God, God is of a lower order of being than man. (CH-STA)

The Scriptures everywhere represent God as possessing all the attributes of a spirit. On this foundation all (true) religion rests: all intercourse with God, all worship, all prayer, all confidence in God as preserver, benefactor, and Redeemer. The God of the Bible is a person. He spoke to Adam. He revealed Himself to Noah. He entered into covenant with Abraham. (CH-STA)

-And Sin

The purpose of God with respect to the sinful acts of men and wicked angels is in no degree to cause evil, nor to approve it, but only to permit the wicked agent to perform it, and then to overrule it for his own most wise and holy ends. (AAH-CF)

-Our Knowledge of

The knowledge of God is eternal life (John 17:3). It is for creatures the highest good. And the promotion of -that knowledge, the manifestation of the manifold perfections of the infinite God, is the highest end of all His works. (CH-STA)

We form our idea of God, it is said, (1) by the way of causation; that Is, by referring to Him as the great First Cause every virtue manifested by the effects which He produces; (2) by the way of negation; that is, by denying to Him the limitations and imperfections which belong to His creatures; (3) by the way of eminence, in exalting to an infinite degree or without limit the perfections which belong to an infinite Being. (CH-STA)

All men have some knowledge of God. That is, they have the conviction that there is a Being on whom they are dependent and to whom they are responsible. (CH-STA)

GOSPEL

-Nature of

The gospel is a system of grace. All its blessings are gratuitously bestowed; all is so ordered that in every step of the progress of redemption and in its consummation the grace or undeserved love of God is conspicuously displayed. Nothing is given or promised on the ground of merit. Everything is an undeserved favour. (CH-STA)

The gospel is the offer of salvation upon the conditions of the covenant of grace. (CH-STA)

-The Only Way of Salvation

The gospel claims to be the only method of salvation. It takes for granted that men are in a state of sin and condemnation from which they are unable to deliver themselves. It teaches that acceptance of Christ as God and Saviour is the one indispensable condition of salvation, that there is no other name under heaven whereby men can be saved. It provides, therefore, for a Church and a ministry whose great duty it is to make known to men this great salvation. All this takes for granted that without this knowledge men will perish in their sins. (CH-STA)

-Duty of those who Hear

The two great duties which press upon every man who hears the gospel are, 1. To accept Christ as his own Saviour, and 2. To make him known to others as the Savior of men. (CH-CP)

-Universal Need for

The heathen cannot be saved without the gospel. 1. Because the Bible declares the light of nature to be insufficient. 2. Because it has declared faith in Christ to be necessary. 3. Because it is commanded the gospel to be preached to all nations as the means of saving them. We should consecrate ourselves to this work. We waste our lives if they are devoted to any other object. (CH-CP)

-Necessity to Preach

The reason for which woe is denounced on ministers who fail to preach the gospel is that men cannot be saved without it. All men are exposed to eternal death. There is but one way of deliverance from that death, and woe to him who, although officially called and dedicated to the work, fails to make that way known. If any man knows of a certain preventive for cholera, which now threatens our land, he would be a murderer if he did not make it known. So, the blood of souls, the Scriptures assure us, will be required of those watchmen who fail to warn their fellowmen of their danger. (CH-CP)

GRACE

Grace is love exercised towards the unworthy. (CH-STA)

-And Salvation

The religion of the Bible. accords with the consciousness of men. Two truths are universally admitted by unrenewed men; viz.: their own ill-desert and helplessness. The only religion therefore suited to convince sinners must teach salvation by grace. (CH-CP)

(Salvation by grace) is the leading characteristic of the gospel. Everything that detracts from this attribute mars the gospel. Therefore, it is a test of doctrine. (CH-CP)

The end or design of the whole scheme of redemption is the praise of the glory of the grace of God, i.e., its purpose is to exhibit to the admiration of intelligent creatures the glorious attribute of divine grace, or the love of an infinitely holy and just God towards guilty and polluted sinners. (CH-STA)

GREAT COMMISSION

"Go ye into all the world and preach the gospel to every creature." This commission prescribes the present duty of the Church, one that is not to be deferred or languidly performed until a new and more effective dispensation be inaugurated. The promise of Christ to be with His Church, as then commissioned, to the end of the world implies that its obligation to teach the nations is to continue until the final consummation. (CH-STA)

The first great event which is to precede the second coming of Christ is the universal proclamation of the gospel. Christ repeatedly taught that the gospel is to be preached to all nations before His second coming. Thus, in Matthew 24: 14, He says, "his gospel of the kingdom shall be preached in all the world for witness unto all nations; and then shall the end come"; and in Mark 13:10. "'the gospel must first be published among all nations." (CH-STA)

Remember the great commission! Was this great commission the great mistake of history? If such be our view, we will never go upon this great mission in which consists, nevertheless, the very reason for the existence of the Church on earth. Only if we catch the apostles' viewpoint and can say to our souls with the clearness of conviction which felt, that there is salvation in Jesus alone, will we be inspired with the zeal that filled them, to evangelize the world. (BBW, TSW)

The salvation of the world hangs, in our human mode of speaking, on the clearness and the strength of our conviction that there is salvation in none other than Jesus, that there is none other name under heaven, given among men, wherein they must be saved. Oh, the cruelty of that indifference, miscalled broadness of mind, that would withhold from a perishing world the only healing draught, on the pretense, forsooth, that it is not needed. bo remember that the whole world lies in iniquity—ill to death with the dreadful disease of sin, —and that you have in your hands the one curative potion, the only water of life which can purge away sin and restore to spiritual health and beauty. Remember the great commission! (BBW-TSW)

GROWTH IN GRACE

When there is no growth, there is no life. (AA-TRE)

In plants and animals, growth is natural and involuntary process. It goes on without effort, and by a law of natural development. This is true also of the growth of the body of a man. In the divine life, the case is different. It does not owe its existence or its continuance, and much less its increase, to any law of nature. It will not grow of itself, as does the plant or the animal. Therefore, the exhortation, grow in grace. We cannot exhort a young animal to grow. This, therefore, is a preliminary truth, the conviction of which should be engraved on our hearts, that our religion will perish, if left alone. It will wither and die, unless using the appointed means, is caused to grow. (CH-CP)

One circumstance attends the growth in grace of a real Christian and that is, the clearer and deeper insight which he obtains into the evils of his own heart. Now this is one of the best evidences of growth; but the first conclusion is apt to be, "I am growing worse every day; I see innumerable evils springing within me which I never saw before." This person may be compared to one shut up in a dark room where he is surrounded by many loathsome objects. If a single ray of light be let into the room, he sees the more prominent objects; but if the light gradually increases, he sees more and more of the light by which he has been surrounded. It was there before, but he did not perceive it. His increased knowledge of the fact is a sure evidence of increasing light. (AA-TRE)

GUILT

Sin, of necessity, involves guilt; and guilt is a fearful looking for of judgment. (CH-CP)

It is impossible for us to exaggerate our guilt in the sight of God. We are more guilty than we ever have conceived, or ever can conceive ourselves to be and depend upon it, the more honestly and truly we feel this, the more forbearing will we be towards those who neglect or injure us. (CH-CP)

HAPPINESS

The soul of man, formed for God, can only be holy or happy in communion with God. (CH-CP)

(Happiness) is healthful. It tends to holiness. It is to the graces of the Spirit what the light of the sun is to nature. It renders them more healthful, vigorous, and beautiful. Happiness belongs to heaven, misery, to hell. (CH-CP)

-And Youth

Think not, dear young people, that true religion will detract from your happiness. It is a reproach cast upon your Maker, to indulge such a thought. It cannot be. A God of goodness never required anything of his creatures which did not tend to their true felicity. (AA-TRE)

HARSHNESS

(Christ is dishonored) by the censorious, not only in making nonessentials of too much importance, but also in misrepresenting the spirit of their Master His religion does not justify their harsh judgments. (CH-CP)

HEART

-Necessary in Worship

No outward service, however enjoined, is acceptable to God when the heart is not right. The principle that God requires to be worshipped in spirit and in truth, is peculiar to the Bible. It does not belong to paganism, nor to corrupt forms of Christianity. (CH-CP)

-Deceitful

The deceitful heart of man will turn itself into every conceivable form and shape but that of true holiness; of this it may assume the shadow, but never the reality. (AA-PT)

-Hardened by God

In what sense is God said to harden men? See Rom. 9: 18, and John 12:40. This is doubtless a judicial act wherein God withdraws from sinful men, whom he has not elected to life, for the just punishment of their sins, all gracious influences, and leaves them to the unrestrained tendencies of their own hearts, and to the uncounteracted influences of the world and the devil. (AAH-OT)

HEAVEN

-Its Blessedness

Christ is the center of attraction in heaven. From him radiate the rays of divine glory which enliven, attract, and beautify all the innumerable host of worshippers. (AA-PT)

The incomprehensible blessedness of heaven shall arise from the vision of God. This vision beatifies and transforms the soul into the divine image, transfusing into it the divine life, so that it is filled with the fulness of God. This vision of God is in the face of Jesus Christ, in whom dwells the plenitude of the divine glory bodily. God is seen in fashion as a man, and this manifestation of God in the person of Christ is inconceivably ravishing. (CH-STA)

And I am reminded also, that as the twinkling stars are lost in the blaze of the rising sun, so there is one Person in the highest heavens, visible to all who enter that place, whose glory irradiates all the celestial mansions; whose love and smiles diffuse ineffable joy through all the heavenly hosts, and in whom every believer has an absorbing interest with which no other can be compared. On His head He wears many crowns, and in His hand He holds a scepter by which He governs the universe; but He exhibits, visibly, the marks of the violent death which, for us, He once endured. (AA-TRE)

Heaven is full of light; all darkness and doubt are absent. (AA-PT)

-Its Difference from Hell

Heaven is a place and state in which the Spirit reigns with absolute control. Hell is a place and state in which the Spirit no longer restrains and controls. The presence or absence of the Spirit makes all the difference between heaven and hell. (CH-STA)

HELL (See Future Punishment)

HERESY

It is against this rock—the substitution of Christ in the place of sinners and his making full satisfaction to the justice and law of God, thus working out for us a perfect righteousness by which we may be justified—that the assaults of philosophy, falsely so called, and of heresy in all its forms have been directed from the beginning. But it remains what it has ever been—the foundation of the faith, hope, and life of the Church. (CH-STA)

HISTORY

-And God's Purpose

History in all its details, even the most minute, is but the evolution of the eternal purposes of God. (CH-STA)

The sequence of the events which constitute what we call the world's history, and in which we are enmeshed, dark and inscrutable as may be their nexus and meaning and issue to us, is after all not the result of accident or chance, nor yet of necessity or fate, nor of human caprice or Satanic malice—but the orderly working out of the purpose of our Father in heaven, the infinitely wise and holy One, the infinitely righteous and loving One. (BBW-SSW)

The whole course of history is represented as the development of the plan and purposes of God, and yet human history is little else than the history of sin. No one can read the simple narrative concerning Joseph, as given in the book of Genesis, without seeing that everything in his history occurred in execution of a preconceived purpose of God. This is but an illustration. What is true of the history of Joseph is true of all history. It is the development of the plan of God. God is in history, and although we cannot trace His path step by step, yet it is plain in the general survey of events, through long periods, that they are ordered by God to the accomplishment of His divine purposes. (CH-STA)

God uses the nations with the absolute control that a man uses a rod or a staff. They are in His hands, and He employs them to accomplish His purposes. He breaks them in pieces like a potter's vessel, or e exalts them to greatness, according to His good pleasure. (CH-STA)

-And Christianity

Christianity is a "historical religion," and a "Christianity" wholly unrelated to historical occurrences is just no Christianity at all. Jesus is a historical. What He was, no less than what He did, is a matter of historical testimony. When we turn our backs on historical facts as of no significance of our "Christianity," we must turn our backs as well on Jesus He who would have a really "unhistorical Christianity" must know no Jesus whether on earth or in heaven. And surely a Christianity without Jesus is just no Christianity at all. (BBW, TSW)

-And the History of Redemption

The history of redemption through all its dispensations, Patriarchal, Abrahamic, Mosaic, and Christian, is the key to the philosophy of human history in general. The race is preserved, continents and islands are settled with inhabitants, nations are elevated to empire, philosophy and the practical arts, civilization and liberty are advanced, that the Church, the Lamb's bride, may be perfected in all her members and adorned for her Husband. (AAH-CF)

HOLINESS

By holiness is meant, 1. Purity. 2. Opposition to all evil. 3. All positive moral excellence. This exists imperfectly in man, perfectly though limited in angels, perfectly and without limit in God. There is a beauty in holiness When it is said that holiness is beautiful, it is meant not merely that it is an object of approbation, or of respect, or of fear or veneration, but of complacent delight; that it gives a peculiar pleasure, and that of the highest kind, which from analogy is called beauty. This beauty is revealed most clearly in the Lord Jesus Christ. He is represented as most beautiful. The Scriptures are filled with descriptions of the beauty of holiness as manifested in Jesus Christ. The Church is represented as ravished with his beauty. The beauty of holiness in us is the manifestation of God in us. (CH-CP)

The great thing is to be holy; to be illuminated by the Spirit; to shine as lights in the world, so that our spirit, opinions, and conduct shall be a continual rebuke to evil. This requires that we should keep ourselves unspotted from the world and in fellowship with God, his truth, and his people. (CH-CP)

HOLY SPIRIT

-A Divine Person

This Spirit is not an agency, but an agent who teaches and selects, who can be sinned against and grieved, and who, in the New Testament, is unmistakably revealed as a distinct person. (CH-STA)

-His Name

The Third Person of the Trinity is called "the Spirit," first, to indicate that He is the power or efficiency of God, i.e., the person through whom the efficiency of God is directly exercised; and secondly, to express His relation to the other persons of the Trinity. (CH-STA)

-His Importance

We might as well strike from the Bible the name and doctrine of God as the name and office of the Holy Spirit. In the New Testament alone He is mentioned not far from three hundred times. It is not only, however, merely the frequency with which the Spirit is mentioned, and the prominence given to His person and work, but the multiplied and interesting relations in which He is represented as standing to the people of God, the importance and number of His gifts, and the absolute dependence of the believer and of the Church upon Him for spiritual and eternal life, which render the doctrine of the Holy Ghost fundamental to the gospel. The work of the Spirit in applying the redemption of Christ is represented to be as essential as that redemption itself. It is therefore indispensable that we know what the Bible teaches concerning the Holy Ghost as to both His nature and office. (CH-STA)

Wherever men are busying themselves with holy and happy meditations on the Holy Ghost and his work, it is safe to say the foundations of a true spiritual life are laid, and the structure of a rich spiritual life is rising. (BBW, SSW)

-Source of Life

Whatever God does, He does by the Spirit. He is the immediate source of all life. Even in the external world the Spirit is everywhere present and everywhere active. Matter is not intelligent. It has its peculiar properties which act according to established laws. The intelligence, therefore, manifested in vegetable and animal structures is not to be referred to matter, but to the omnipresent Spirit of God. It is He who causes the grass to grow and gives breath to all living creatures (Ps.104:29-30) (CH-STA)

-His Work

The Holy Ghost is the immediate author of all truth, of all holiness, of all consolation, of all authority, and of all efficiency in the children of God individually and in the Church collectively. (CH-STA)

We cannot prescribe limits to the Holy Spirit in His ways of leading benighted souls into the path of life. The Holy Spirit, who operates where and when He will, is often at work on the minds of those whom we would least suspect to be thus visited. (AA-TRE)

The Holy Spirit does not work independently of the Word, but through the Word; nor does he work irrespectively of our constitutional faculties of reason, conscience, and free will, but through them. (AAH-CF)

-And Christ

The Spirit, we are taught, especially opens the eyes to see the glory of Christ, to see that He is God manifested in the flesh, to discern not only His divine perfections, but his love to us, and His suitableness in all respects as our Saviour, so that those who have not seen Him can yet believe on Him and rejoice in Him. This apprehension of Christ is transforming; the soul is thereby changed into His image from glory to glory by the Spirit of the Lord. (CH-STA)

-The Seal of God

Those whom God seals, on whom he impresses his seal, he authenticates as his people, he secures from destruction, and he makes them as his own. They are known by that seal to be his. Any man therefore who has the seal of God impressed upon him is thereby proved to be one of his children; he is secure from destruction and is marked as belonging to God, claimed by him as his own. What is the seal of God? It is the Holy Spirit. His presence in the soul authenticates it as born of God, secures it from apostacy, and marks it as the property of God, the purchase of the Redeemer s blood. (CH-CP)

-Can Be Grieved

The greatest calamity that can befall an individual, a church, or a people is that God should take His Holy Spirit from them. And as this is a judgment which, according to the Scriptures, does often come upon individuals, churches, and people, we should above all things avoid grieving the Spirit or quenching His influences. We grieve the Spirit by resistance, by indulgence in sin, and especially by denying His agency and speaking evil of His work. (CH-STA)

As the Holy Ghost in his relation to us is set forth as the Spirit of truth, of holiness, of love, of consolation, and of glory, it follows, 1. That what is contrary to truth grieves the Spirit of truth. 2. Everything impure or unholy; cherishing impure or unholy feelings in our hearts; exciting them in the hearts of others. 3. All irreverence, ingratitude, or disobedience toward God, and all malignant or unamiable feeling or conduct toward our fellowmen, all disposition or conduct which tends to disturb the peace of the family, of the community, of the Church, or of the world, is opposed to the Spirit of love, who is thereby also the Spirit of peace. 4. So all that tends to produce misery or distress is opposed to him who is the Comforter. (CH-CP)

-Needed by Preachers

To be the organ of the Holy Ghost as the efficient and successful agent in communicating this truth, we must be full of faith and of the Holy Ghost. No false fire or fictitious zeal can supply the place of the Spirit. The holiness which flows from the presence of the Spirit gives peculiar power over the heart and consciences of men. (CH-CP)

HOPE

Hope. is the desire and expectation of future good. Christian hope is the desire and expectation of the blessings promised in the gospel of Christ. They are summed up in the expression, "the glory of God," i.e., the glory of which God is the author. For feeble and sinful worms of the dust to cherish such expectations would be the height of presumption and madness were it not for the foundation which we have for such hope. That foundation is, 1. The promise of God. 2. The infinite merit of the Son of God. 3. The love of God is infinitely great and entirely gratuitous. 4. The witness of God s Spirit with our spirit that we are the children of God. (CH-CP)

A good hope is a hope which is founded on the truth, on the promise of God, and the work of Christ. This hope, 1. Is a helmet. 2. Is an anchor. 3. Is the soul what wings are to the eagle. It elevates it above the world. It raises us toward heaven and fills us with its spirit. (CH-CP)

HUMILITY

Humility is that state of mind which arises from a proper appreciation of the truth regarding us. 1. A due appreciation of our insignificance as creatures. In this sense it is opposed to self-importance, to self-reliance, to pride of intellect. 2. A due appreciation of ourselves as sinners, including a sense of guilt and of pollution. It is opposed, therefore, to self-righteousness and to self-complacency. 3. A due appreciation of our weakness. Hence, a sense of inability for self-conversion, for sanctification, for usefulness. (CH-CP)

Humility is not only the consciousness of this insignificance, but the recognition and acknowledgment of it, and the acquiescence in it. Pride is the denial or forgetfulness of this fact, an unwillingness to be thus of no account, the assertion of our own importance, and the claim to have it acknowledged by others. (CH-CP)

God's plan of salvation is intended to humble man. We cannot acquiesce in that plan or enjoy its benefits unless we are humble. Men must stoop to enter heaven. (CH-CP)

As nothing is so offensive as pride, so nothing is so conciliating as humility. It disarms hostility, conciliates favor, gives facility of access and influence. (CH-CP)

I have thought that the reason why a covenant-keeping God sometimes permits His children to fall into shameful acts of transgression, is because nothing else but such a sight of themselves as these falls exhibit would sufficiently humble their proud hearts. (AA-TRE)

HYPOCRISY

The Scriptures teach, 1. That we owe special duties to God, as reverence, love, devotion, worship, constant obedience, etc. 2. That we owe duties to our fellowmen, as parents, children, citizens, neighbors, fellow-creatures. 3. That these duties are not only consistent, the one class with the other, but that they are alike indispensable. That he who claims to fulfill the one while he neglects the other is a self-deceiver or a hypocrite. (CH-CP)

IDOLATRY

The making any other end than God's glory our object, is the sum and essence of idolatry. (CH-CP)

The relation between the soul and God is far more intimate than that between the soul and any creature. Our life, spiritual and eternal, depends on our relation to our Maker. Hence our highest duty is to Him. The greatest sin a man can commit is to refuse to render to God the admiration and obedience which are his due, or to transfer to the creature the allegiance and service which belong to Him. Hence no sin is so frequently or so severely denounced in the Scriptures (as is idolatry) (CH-STA)

IGNORANCE

Error never can under any circumstances produce the effects of truth. There is reason to believe, therefore, that all ignorance of revealed truth, or error respecting it must be attended with a corresponding defect in the religious exercises of the person. (AA-TRE)

IMAGE OF GOD

God is a Spirit; the human soul is a spirit. The essential attributes of a spirit are reason, conscience and will. A spirit is a rational, moral, and a free agent. In making man after His own image, therefore, God endowed him with those attributes which belong to His own nature as a Spirit. Man is thereby distinguished from all other inhabitants of this world and raised immeasurably above them. He belongs to the same order of being as God Himself and is therefore capable of communion with his maker. If we were not like God, we could not know Him. We should (then) be like the beasts which perish. (CH-STA)

We are the children of God, and therefore, we are like Him. We are, therefore, authorized to ascribe to Him, without limitation and to an infinite degree, all the attributes of our own nature as rational creatures. If we are like God, God is like us. This is the fundamental principle of all true religion. (CH-STA)

IMMORALITY

-In Professing Christians

It is universally admitted that an immoral life is inconsistent with a state of grace, that those who willfully continue in the practice of sin shall not inherit the kingdom of God. For sanctification is inseparable from justification, and the one is just as essential as the other. (CH-STA)

IMPUTATION

In what sense is Christ's righteousness imputed to believers? Imputation is an act of God as sovereign judge, at once judicial and sovereign, whereby (1) he makes the guilt and legal responsibilities of our sins really Christ and punishes him for them. "He was wounded for our transgression; the punishment of our peace was upon him" (Isa. 53: 5 and 11). (2) He makes the righteousness of Christ ours and then treats us as persons legally invested with those rights. (Rom. 4: 6; 10:4). (AAH-OT)

As Christ is not made a sinner by the imputation to him of our sins, so we are not made holy by the imputation to us of his righteousness. The transfer is only of guilt from us to him, and of merit from him to us. He justly suffered the punishment due to our sins, and we justly receive the rewards due to his righteousness. (AAH-OT)

INCARNATION

The glory of the Incarnation is that it presents to our adoring gaze, not a humanized God or a deified man, but a true God-man—one who is all that God is and at the same time all that man is; on whose almighty arm we can rest, and to whose human sympathy we can appeal. We cannot afford to lose either the God in the man or the man in the God; our hearts cry out for the complete Godman whom the Scriptures offer us. (BBW-SSW)

INDECISION

When the truth is heard from the pulpit, the sinner is often brought to a stand. He is convinced that the course of his life is wrong, and that if persisted in, it must end in ruin. For a moment he hesitates--halts between two opinions--between truth and error, between duty and transgression: between the choice of life or death.

The prophet addressed the idolatrous Israelites with the question, "How long halt ye between two opinions? If the Lord be God, follow him; but if Baal, then follow him. The object of Elijah was to bring them to a decision, one way or the other. Nothing is more unreasonable than hesitation in a matter so important. God hates this perpetual vacillation. "I would thou wert cold or hot," says Christ. "So then, because thou art lukewarm, and neither cold nor hot, I will spue thee out of my mouth." (BBW-SSW)

INFANTS

-Death of

All the members of the human race dying in infancy are believed to be saved through the mer its of Christ. (AAH-CF)

-Members of Church

Infants were members of the Church under the Old Testament economy. This is conclusively proved by the fact that infants, by the command of God, were circumcised on the eighth day after their birth. This is really the turning point in the controversy concerning the Church membership of infants. Since the Church is one under both dispensations, and infants were members of the Church under the theocracy, they are members of the Church now, unless the contrary can be proved. (AAH-CF)

INFIDELITY (Skepticism)

Guard solicitously against all approaches towards infidelity. Reject unbelieving thoughts and sceptical doubts from the beginning. The best security will be to study diligently the evidence of religion and be ready to meet the cavils of infidelity at all points. Make yourselves well acquainted with the best authors on this subject and let your faith rest on the firm ground of evidence. (AA-TRE)

INHERITANCE

-Of God's Children

Heirs to titles and estates, to kingdoms and empires, are frequently born, and such events are blazoned with imposing pomp, and celebrated by poets and orators; but what are all these honors and possessions but the gewgaws of children, when compared with the inheritance and glory to which every child of God is born an heir! But this being a birth from above, and all the blessings and privileges of the young heir, of a hidden and spiritual nature, the world around cannot be expected to take a lively interest in the event. (AA-TRE)

INSIGNIFICANCE

-Of Human Beings

We are finite, limited on every hand as to the place we occupy, as to the powers we possess, as to the excellence we can attain, and as to the blessedness we can enjoy. God is infinite. There is no limit to his presence, to his intelligence and knowledge, to his divine goodness or to his power. The sum of all finites is as nothing to the infinite. The whole universe, therefore, is as nothing to God. What then are we? We are so insignificant a part of this universe that were we blotted out of existence, none but an omniscient eye would miss us. (CH-CP)

INSPIRATION

-Its Definition

On this subject the common doctrine of the Church is, and ever has been, that inspiration was an influence of the Holy Spirit on the minds of certain select men which rendered them the organs of God for the infallible communication of His mind and will. They were in such a sense the organs of God that what they said God said. (CH-STA)

These books are, one and all, in thought and verbal expression, in substance and form, wholly the Word of God, conveying with absolute accuracy and divine authority all that God meant them to convey, without human additions or admixtures. This was accomplished by a supernatural influence the Spirit of God acting upon the spirits of the sacred writers, called 'inspiration;' which accompanied them uniformly in what they wrote, and which, without violating the free operation of their faculties yet directed them in all they wrote, and secured the infallible expression of it in words. (AAH-CF)

-Plenary (Not Partial)

All the books of Scripture are equally inspired. Alike are infallible in what they teach. Inspiration extends to all the contents of these several books. It is not confined to moral and religious truths, but extends to the statements of facts, whether scientific, historical, or geographical. It is not confined to those facts the importance of which is obvious, or which are involved in matters of doctrine. It extends to everything which any sacred writer asserts to be true. (CH-STA)

The view presented above is known as the doctrine of plenary inspiration. Plenary is opposed to partial. The Church denies that inspiration is confined to parts of the Bible and affirms that it applies to all the books of the sacred canon. It denies that the sacred writers were merely partially inspired; it asserts that they were fully inspired as to all they teach, whether of doctrine or fact. This of course does not imply that the sacred writers were infallible in areas other than the special purpose for which they were employed. They were not imbued with plenary knowledge. As to all matters of science, philosophy, and history, they stood on the same level with their contemporaries. They were infallible only as teachers and when acting as the spokesmen of God. Nor does the Scriptural doctrine on this subject imply that the sacred writers were free from errors in conduct. (CH-STA)

If our Lord and His apostles declare that the Old Testament is the Word of God; that its authors spake as they were moved by the Holy Ghost; that what they said, the Spirit said; if they refer to the facts and to the very words of Scripture as of divine authority; and if the same infallible guidance was promised to the writers of the New Testament and claimed by themselves; and if their claim was authenticated by God Himself—then there is no room for, as there is no need of, these theories of partial inspiration. The whole Bible was written under such an -influence as preserved its human authors from all errors and makes it for the Church the infallible rule of faith and practice. (CH-STA)

-Not Mechanical

The Church has never held what has been stigmatized as the mechanical theory of inspiration. The sacred writers were not machines. Their self-consciousness was not suspended, nor were their intellectual powers superseded. Holy men spake as they were moved by the Holy Ghost. Moreover, as inspiration did not involve the suspension or suppression of the human faculties, so neither did it interfere with the free exercise of the distinctive mental characteristics of the individual. If a Hebrew was inspired, he spake Hebrew; if a Greek, he spake Greek; if an educated man, he spoke as a man of culture; if uneducated, he spoke as such a man was wont to speak. The inspired penmen wrote out of the fulness of their own thoughts and feelings and employed the language and modes of expression which to them were the most natural and appropriate. Nevertheless, and none the less, they spoke as they were moved by the Holy Ghost, and their words were His words. (CH-STA)

-Different From Revelation

Revelation is the Spirit's act of communicating divine knowledge to the mind. Inspiration is the same Spirit's act of controlling those who make the truth known to others. (CH-STA)

INTERCESSION

To intercede, in the Scriptures, is to approach a person for another. In this sense Christ intercedes for his people, and we intercede for each other. Our intercession is simply approaching God in prayer on behalf of others. This is a commanded duty. "I exhort therefore, that, first, supplications, prayers, intercessions, and giving of thanks be made for all men." (1 Tim. 2:1.) James says, "Pray one for another." Our Lord commands us to pray for our enemies, to bless those who curse us. This then is a great duty, a great privilege, and a great source of consolation; one too often neglected and undervalued. (CH-CP)

INTERPRETATION OF SCRIPTURE
-General Rules

There are two principles which must control the interpretation of the Scriptures. That is, when a passage admits of two interpretations, the choice between them is to be determined, first, by the analogy of Scripture. If one interpretation contradicts what the Bible elsewhere teaches and other accords with it, then we are bound to accept the latter. Or, secondly, the interpretation must be decided by established facts. That is, if one interpretation agrees with such facts and another contradicts them, then he former must be true. (CH-CP)

The fundamental principle of interpretation of all writings, sacred or profane, is that the words are to be understood in their historical sense, that is in the sense in which they were used by their authors and intended to be understood by those to whom they were addressed. (CH-STA)

We must take the Scriptures in their plain historical sense—in that sense in which they were designed to be understood by those to whom they were addressed-or we do thereby reject them as a rule of faith. (CH-STA)

The Scriptures are to be interpreted under the guidance of the Holy Spirit, which guidance is to be humbly and earnestly sought. As only those who have a moral nature can discern moral truth, so only those who are spiritually minded can truly receive the things of the Spirit. (CH-STA)

-Of Figurative Sections

The figurative representations of Scripture are intended not to impress the imagination but instruct the understanding. They must therefore be interpreted to convey definite truth. They are not to be understood literally; nor is the analogy which they suggest being pressed too far. Nevertheless, they are never to be explained away as mere figures of speech. (CH-CP)

-If Opposed by Facts

There is also a distinction to be made between the Bible and our interpretation. The latter may come into competition with settled facts, and then it must yield. Science has in many things taught the Church how to understand the Scriptures. The Bible was for ages understood and explained according to the Ptolemaic system of the universe; it is now explained, without doing the least violence to its language, according to the Copernican system. It may cost the Church a severe struggle to give up one interpretation and adopt another, as it did in the seventeenth century, but no real evil need be entailed. The Bible has stood and still stands in the presence of the scientific world with its claims unshaken. (CH-STA)

INTOLERANCE

-Of Christianity

But Christianity is so intolerant, that it will bear no other religion; it seeks to overthrow every other system. If it would have admitted the claims of other religions, it would have escaped persecution. But no; it denounced every other system and mode of worship as hateful to God, and destructive to the soul. And it made every disciple a proselyter. And everyone now, whether male or female, bond or free, Jew or Greek, who professes Christianity, takes upon himself or herself the obligation to convert others to Christianity. (AA-PT)

JEHOVAH

Jehovah, from the Hebrew verb to be expresses self-existence and unchangeableness; it is the incommunicable name of God, which the Jews superstitiously refused to pronounce, always substituting in their reading the word Adonai, Lord. Hence it is represented in our English version by the word LORD, printed in capital letters. (AAH-OT)

The Jehovah of the Old Testament is our Lord; our Saviour was the Saviour of the saints who lived before His advent in the flesh. The divine person who delivered the Israelites out of Egypt, who led them through the wilderness, who appeared in His glory to Isaiah in the temple, and towards who is coming the eyes of the people of God were turned in faith and hope from the beginning, is He whom we recognize as God manifest in the flesh, our Lord and Savior Jesus Christ. He, therefore, who was the head of the theocracy is the head of the Church. (CH-STA)

JESUS CHRIST

-His Person

The facts which the Bible teaches concerning the person of Christ are, first, He was truly man, i.e., He had a perfect or complete human nature. Hence everything that can be predicated of man (that is, of man as man, and not of man as fallen) can be predicated of Christ. Secondly, He was truly God, i.e., He had a perfect divine nature. Hence everything that can be predicated of God can be predicated of Christ. Thirdly, He was one person. The same person, self, or ego who said, "I thirst," said, "Before Abraham was, I am." This is the whole doctrine of the incarnation. (CH-STA)

-Truly God

The Scriptures declare that Christ is truly God. All divine names and titles are applied to Him. He is called God, the Mighty God, the great God, God over all, Jehovah, Lord, the Lord of lords and the King of kings. All divine attributes are ascribed to Him. He is declared to be omnipresent, omniscient, almighty, and immutable, the same yesterday, today, and forever. He requires that men should honour Him as they honour the Father, that they should exercise the same faith in Him that they do in God. He declares that He and the Father are one, that those who have seen Him have seen the Father also. He calls all men unto Him and promises to forgive their sins, to send them the Holy Spirit, to give them rest and peace, to raise them up at the last day, and to give them eternal life. God is not more, and cannot promise more, or do more than Christ is said to be, to promise, and to do. (CH-STA)

-The Logos

As the eternal Word, the Logos, the manifested and manifesting Jehovah, He is the source of all knowledge to the intelligent universe and especially to the children of men. He was and is the light of the world. He is the truth. In Him dwell all the treasures of wisdom and knowledge, and from Him radiates all the light that men receive or attain. (CH-STA)

-Truly Man

The Scriptures teach that Christ had a complete human nature. That is, He had a true body and a rational soul. This is plain from His being born of a woman. He was conceived in the womb of the Virgin Mary and was nourished of her substance to be consubstantial with her. His body increased in stature, passing through the or dinar y process of development from infancy to manhood. It was subject to all the affections of a human body. It was subject to pain, pleasure, hunger, thirst, fatigue, suffering, and death.

It is no less plain that Christ had a rational soul. He thought, reasoned, and felt; He was joyful and sorrowful; He increased in wisdom; He was ignorant of the time when the day of judgment would come. He must, therefore, have had a finite human intelligence. These two elements, a true body and a rational soul, rove that Christ had a complete human nature. (CH-STA)

There are no human traits lacking to the picture that is drawn of him: he was open to temptation; he was conscious of dependence on God; he was a man of prayer; he knew a "will" within him that might conceivably be opposed to the will of God; he exercised faith; he learned obedience by the things that he suffered. It was not merely the mind of a man that was in him, but the heart of a man as well, and the spirit of a man. In a word, he was all that a man—a man without sin and error is. (BBW- SSW)

-Gracious and Truthful

"We beheld his glory," says the Apostle, "full" "complete, perfect" of grace and truth. And perfection of love and truth avails for all their manifestations. This man, the man Christ Jesus, could not act in any relation otherwise than lovingly, could not speak on any subject otherwise than truly. He is the pure fountain of love and truth. (BBW-TSW)

-His Joy

Jesus does not rejoice in sinners: it is not sin He loves or sinners as sinners. What He rejoices in is the rescue of sinners from their sin. And the deeper the sin the greater the rescue and the greater the joy, say unto you, "there is joy before the angels of God over one sinner that repenteth." (BBW-TSW)

-The Redeemer

The doctrine of the redemption is the distinguishing doctrine of the Bible. The person and work of the Redeemer is therefore the great theme of the sacred writers. (CH-STA)

-His Sufferings

All that Christ did and suffered would have been necessary had only one human soul been the object of redemption, and nothing different and nothing more would have been required had every child of Adam been saved through His blood. (CH-STA)

Vicarious suffering is suffering endured by one person of another, i.e., in his place. It necessarily supposes the exemption of the party in whose place the sufferings of Christ were vicarious, the meaning is that He suffered in the place of sinners. He was their substitute. He assumed their obligation to satisfy justice. What He did and suffered precluded the necessity of their fulfilling the demands of the law in their own persons. (CH-STA)

He did not suffer in either kind or degree what sinners would have suffered. In value, His sufferings infinitely transcended theirs. The death of an eminently good man would outweigh the annihilation of a universe of insects. So, the humiliation, sufferings, and death of the eternal Son of God immeasurably transcended in worth and power the penalty which a world of sinners would have endured. (CH-STA)

Christ, although in Himself perfectly holy, bore our sins. He was "made sin" (2 Cor. 5:21), i.e., treated as a sinner. The words uttered by our Lord upon the cross, "My God, my God, why hast thou forsaken me?" show that He was suffering the hiding of His Father's face. What that experience was it is impossible for us to understand. (CH-STA)

-His Death

Christ did not die simply to make the salvation of those for whom he died possible, to remove the legal obstructions to their salvation—but that he died with the design and effect of securing their salvation and of endowing them gratuitously with an inalienable title to heaven. (AAH-CF)

-His Active & Passive Obedience

The work of Christ was therefore of the nature of a satisfaction to the demands of the law. His obedience and sufferings, by His whole righteousness, active and passive, He, as our representative and substitute, did and endured all that the law demands. (CH-STA)

-Destroyer of Satan

He came to destroy the works of the devil; and that He did thus triumph over him, and his angels proved that He was what He claimed to be, the promised almighty King and conqueror who was to found that kingdom of God of which there is to be no end. (CH-STA)

-His Lordship

The great end of life, the only thing worth living for is, to secure the reign of Christ in our own souls, and to bring others to call him Lord. (CH-STA)

Christ is the King of every believing soul. He translates it from the kingdom of darkness. He brings it into subjection to Himself. He rules in and reigns over it. Every believer recognizes Christ as his absolute sovereign, as Lord of his inward as well as of his outward life. Every believer completely yields to Him reason, conscience, and heart, making Him the object of reverence, love, and obedience. (CH-STA)

Christ is called Lord in the New Testament with as much constancy and preeminence as Jehovah is called Lord in the Old Testament. This was the word which all the readers, whether of the Hebrew or Greek Scriptures, under the old economy were accustomed to use to express their relation to God. They recognized Him as their owner, as their supreme sovereign, and as their protector. The same feelings of reverence, adoration, and love, the same sense of dependence and desire of protection are expressed throughout the New Testament in calling Jesus Lord. (CH-STA)

As He is our Lord, in the sense of being our absolute proprietor, our maker, preserver, Redeemer, and sovereign, having the right to do with us as seems good in His sight, love His will the highest rule of duty and His for the great end of our being. (CH-STA)

We belong to Him not only because we are His creatures, but also because we have been purchased by His blood (1. Cor. 6:19-20). His will, and not our own, must govern our conduct and determine the use we make of our powers. All we, whether of knowledge, wealth, or influence, is His. He is the object or end of our living. His glory and the advancement of His kingdom are the only legitimate objects to which believers can devote their powers or resources. (CH-STA)

-His Miracles

Every miracle of Christ, therefore, was a visible manifestation of His divinity. By a mere word, an effortless exercise of His will, He healed the sick, opened the eyes of the blind, restored the lame, raised the dead, fed thousands with a few loaves of bread, and calmed the raging of the sea. He thus manifested forth His glory, giving visible demonstration that He was God in fashion as a man. (CH-STA)

When Moses, the prophets, or the apostles wrought miracles, they expressly disclaimed the idea that it was by their own efficiency. Christ, however, wrought miracles by His own inherent power; and it was to His efficiency the apostles attributed the miracles wrought through them. Christ never referred this miraculous power to any source outside Himself. He claimed it as His own prerogative, and He conferred the power upon others. (CH-STA)

-Head of the Church

As Christ is the only head of the Church, it follows that its allegiance is to Him, and that whenever those outside the Church undertake to regulate its affairs or to curtail its liberties, its members are bound to obey Him rather than men. They are bound to resist by all legitimate means such usurpations and to stand fast in the liberty wherewith Christ has made them free. They are under equal obligation to resist all undue assumption of authority by those within the Church, whether it be by the brotherhood, or by individual officers, or by Church councils or courts. The allegiance of the people terminates on Christ. They are bound to obey others only so far as obedience to them is obedience to Him. (CH-STA)

-The Advocate

We have an advocate, Jesus Christ the righteous. He is qualified for this office 1. Because he is the Son of God; a divine person; entitled to appear before God, whose intercession must be right and sure to be heard. His divinity gives infinite dignity and worth to his work, and efficacy to all he does in our behalf. 2. He is the Son of Man; clothed in our nature, and therefore able to obey and suffer in our stead, and to sympathize in our infirmities. 3. He is righteous and a propitiation for our sins. He has done all that justice and holiness require to our pardon and acceptance. (CH-CP)

The intercession of Christ involves several activities: (1) He appears before God as the sacrifice for our sins and as our High Priest, on the ground of whose work we receive the remission of our sins, the gift of the Holy Spirit, and all needed good. (2) He defends us against the sentence of the law and the charges of Satan, who is the great accuser. (3) He offers Himself as our surety, not only that the demands of justice shall be shown to be satisfied, but that His people shall be obedient and faithful. (4) He sanctifies the prayers and all the services of the redeemed, rendering them acceptable to God through the savor of His own merits. (CH-STA)

-Our Life

(Christ) is the end of our life. It is Christ for us to live. While others live for themselves; some for their country, some for mankind, the believer lives for Christ. It is the great end and design of his life to promote his glory and to advance his kingdom. (This is a true) test of character. The difference between the true and nominal Christian lies here. The one seeks and regards Christ as his life, only as he delivers from death. The other, as the end and object of life. (CH-CP)

-Our Knowledge of

There can be no true knowledge of God, but through Christ. This the Bible teaches because whosoever denieth the Son, the same hath not the Father, etc. He is the way, and no man cometh unto the Father but by him. Because the glory of God is revealed in the person of Christ. Not to see it, recognize, and acknowledge it, is to refuse to acknowledge God as God. God as revealed in nature, in the Old Testament and in Christ, is the same God. It is absurd to pretend to believe in and admire the sun under a cloud and refuse to do so when it is clear. And so, it is to acknowledge our Father at a distance, and not when at hand. There can be, therefore, no true knowledge of God without the knowledge of Christ. (CH-CP)

-Our Love of

Love to the Lord Jesus is the indispensable condition of salvation (Eph. 6: 24; 1 Cor. 16:22). The conditions of salvation are unalterable. They are always the same, and for all men. We can alter them neither for ourselves nor others. What say you? Do you love the Lord Jesus Christ? On this question depends on eternity. Here, those who love and those who do not love to form a distinct class, though intermingled. Hereafter they will be separated. Do you desire to love? That is love, if it only leads to a constant endeavor to do his will, and to associate with his people. (CH-CP)

What is it to love Christ, and how can we tell whether we love him or not? Love to Christ includes reverence for his person. He is an object of adoration to all who love him. Adoration is the expression of love. He is also the object of (delight). We delight in his excellence, and in his love, and are grateful for his benefits. And therefore, intercourse with him is a pleasure, and not a burden; and in looking forward to heaven, our desire is to be with Christ, and to behold his glory. If we love Christ, we shall be zealous for his glory. Any neglect or irreverence shown the Saviour will wound our hearts. Any honor rendered him will give us delight. We will love those who love and honor him and avoid those who neglect and abuse him. Those who love Christ keep his commandments. This is the test of love, not emotion, not excited feeling, but obedience. (CH-CP)

JEWS

To prevent the universal spread of idolatry, to preserve the knowledge of the truth, to gather in His elect, and to prepare the way for the coming of the promised Redeemer, God entered covenant with the father of the faithful (Abraham) and with his descendants through Isaac, constituting them his visible kingdom and making them the depositaries and guardians of His supernatural revelations. (CH-STA)

The two fundamental errors of Judaism were, 1. That natural descent from Abraham, or at least external union with the chosen people was essential to salvation, and 2. That works -- what a man does and what he is -- his inward state, was the ground of his acceptance with God. (CH-CP)

JOY

Joy is either a transient emotion, or a permanent, cheerful, and happy frame of mind. It enters the nature of hope, insomuch as hope is always attended with joy; but it differs from hope since the object of the one is future, and of the other present. Worldly joy is that which arises from the possession and expectation or possession of worldly good. Religious joy is that which comes from the expectation or possession of spiritual good. Religious joy is that which comes from the expectation or possession of spiritual good. (CH-CP)

The three great Christian graces are, Peter says, faith, love, and joy. As to these graces the Scriptures teach us, 1. That they are inseparable. They never appear one without the others. 2. They stand in a certain relation to each other as cause and effect; faith is the cause of love and love the cause of joy. (CH-CP)

Joy is healthful in all its natural influence and tendencies. Pain and sorrow are the reverse. The one is the inseparable companion of holiness; the others are inseparable from sin. The one tends, therefore, to produce holiness, and the others, sin. Pain and sorrow may be useful as medicine, not as food. Joy, however, is the natural atmosphere of the soul, out of which it cannot live. Or it is as oxygen in the air; it is its vital principle. Take joy out of heaven, and what would it be? It would be as though the oxygen of our air were removed; all that lives would do for our own good, therefore, we should rejoice. (CH-CP)

(Joy) beautifies, adorns, and renders attractive the Christian character. A gloomy Christian is not only a burden to himself, but also a source of unhappiness and of evil to those around him. We are bound, therefore, to be joyful as a means of honoring God and being useful to our fellowmen. (CH-CP)

JUDGING OTHERS

We have the right and duty to declare what God's judgment is, so far as it is revealed, e.g., that no one who denies Christ, or says that Jesus is accursed, is of God; that no unclean person, or unjust, or murderer, or drunkard hath any part in the kingdom of God. But beyond this we have no right to go. 1st. We have no right to pronounce that sin which God has not so declared—meats, days, etc. 2d. We have no right to judge the heart, or to pass sentence upon motives. Paul refused to be thus judged by the Corinthians. (CH-CP)

JUDGMENT OF GOD

Men are to be judged according to their works; the secrets of the heart are to be brought to light. God's judgment will not be founded on the professions or the relations of men, nor on the appearance or reputation which they sustain among their fellows, but on their real character and on their acts, however secret and covered from the sight of men those acts may have been. God will not be mocked and cannot be deceived; the character of every man will be clearly revealed not only in the sight of God, but also in the sight the man himself. All self-deceptions will be banished. Every man will see himself as he appears in the sight of God. (CH-STA)

Will all sinners fare alike on that day? All impenitent sinners will be condemned to everlasting misery; but there will be a wide difference between the punishment of those who sinned in ignorance, and those who sinned during light and against light. It will be more tolerable for Sodom and Gomorrah than for Bethsaida and Capernaum. Every man shall receive according to his work. (AA-PT)

The Judge of all the earth will do right. No human being will suffer more than he deserves, or more than his own conscience shall recognize as just. (CH-STA)

JUSTIFICATION

-Its Definition

(Justification) is a judicial declaration that the law is satisfied—not a sovereign waiving of the penalty. (AAH-CF)

Justification is a judicial of God proceeding upon that sovereign imputation, declaring the law to be perfectly satisfied in respect to us. This involves, 1st, pardon; 2d, restoration to divine favor. (AAH-OT)

-Its Foundation

The imperative question remains, how shall a man be just with God? If our moral excellence be not the ground on which God pronounces us just, what is that ground? The Bible and the people of God with one voice answer, "The righteousness of Christ Every believer relies for his acceptance with God, not on himself but on Christ, not on what he is or has done, but on what Christ is and has done for him. (CH-STA)

-Its Effects

The effects of this justification declared to be, 1. Peace with God and peace of conscience. 2. Freedom of access to God. 3. The enjoyment of his favor and gift of the Spirit. This secures sanctification. 4. Security from the accusation of the law, from the power of Satan, from apostasy, from any cause of evil. 5. Participation with Christ in all the benefits of his redemption. We become the. sons of God, and if sons, then heirs. (CH-CP)

-And Forgiveness of Sins

The sins which are pardoned in justification include all sins, past, present, and future. The righteousness of Christ is a perpetual donation. It is a robe which hides or, as the Bible expresses it, covers from the eye of justice the sins of the believer. Although they are sins deserving the wrath and curse of God, the necessity for the infliction of that curse no longer exists. For in justification the believer receives the promise that God will not deal with him according to his transgressions. (CH-STA)

-And Sanctification

Justification and sanctification are. inseparably connected. We are justified by his righteousness only because we are united to him, but united to him, we are partakers of his life; and if partakers of his life, we live as he lives. It is impossible, therefore, that any unholy person, i.e., anyone who determines to live in sin, or who does not strive to die unto sin and to live unto God, can have any actual hope of justification. God justifies only Christ's body. Their sanctification is not the ground, but it is the evidence and effect of it. This doctrine has been the cornerstone of the Church in all ages. (CH-CP)

KINDNESS

The Author of our being has ordained laws, according to which the most exquisite pleasure is connected, not with the direct pursuit of our own happiness, but with the exercise of benevolence. On this principle it is, he who labors wholly for the benefit of others, and as it were forgets himself, is far happier than the man who makes himself the centre of all his affections, the sole object of all his exertions. On this principle it was, that our Saviour said, "It is more blessed to give than to receive." (AA-TRE)

KINGDOM OF GOD

-Defined

The kingdom of God or of Christ in the New Testament, means in general that kingdom of the Messiah which the prophets in the Old Testament predicted should be established. (CH-CP)

The kingdom of God has existed in our world ever since the fall of Adam. Consisting of those who acknowledge, worship, love, and obey Jehovah as the only living and true God, it has ever been the light and life of the world. It is the salt by which it is preserved. It is the leaven by which it is ultimately to be pervaded. To gather His people into this kingdom, and to carry it on to its consummation, is the end of all God's dispensations and the purpose for which His eternal Son assumed our nature. He was born to be a king. To this end He lived and died and rose again, that He might be Lord of all those given to Him by the father. (CH-STA)

-Its Various Names

The kingdom of God on earth is called the kingdom of Christ, or of the Son of God, because it is administered by Him. The royal authority is vested in Him. It is called the kingdom of God because Christ is God, and because it is the kingdom which God was to establish on earth in distinction from the kingdoms of men. It is called the kingdom of heaven because it is spiritual and heavenly, and because it is to be consummated in heaven. (CH-STA)

- "Thy Kingdom Come"

According to the common Church doctrine, what you for when we say, Thy kingdom come, is that the authority of Jesus Christ as king shall be universally recognized, and his control over all hearts shall be absolute, and all evil be banished, and that consummation be reached which is called the kingdom of glory. That is, they pray for the state described by Paul when he says that all enemies shall be put under his feet. (CH-CP)

-And Satan's Kingdom

There are two great kingdoms in the world: that of God and that of Satan, of truth and of error, of light and of darkness, of holiness and of sin. All men are the subjects of the one or the other. There can be no neutrality. Not to submit to the one, is submission to the other. (CH-CP)

When a man is condemned and confined to a dungeon, he is in darkness and misery. When pardoned and brought out into the light, he is brought under all the influences which are essential to his physical well-being. So, it is with those who are translated from the kingdom of darkness into the kingdom of God's dear Son. (CH-CP)

KNOWLEDGE

-Essential for Salvation

Everywhere in the Scriptures it is asserted or assumed that the feelings follow the understanding. We must know God to love Him. In accordance with this principle that knowledge is essential to holiness, true religion and life everlasting are said to consist in the knowledge of God (John 17:3), and men are said to be saved and sanctified by the truth. (CH-STA)

In the Scriptures, knowledge and holiness, ignorance, and sin, are always associated. Those who have the knowledge of God and divine things are holy, and they only; and those who know not the things of the Spirit are the unregenerated. This is not an arbitrary usage. Knowledge produces holiness, and ignorance produces sin. (CH-CP)

-Not merely Intellectual

The knowledge of Christ is not the apprehension of what he is, simply by the intellect, but also a due apprehension of his glory as a divine person arrayed in our nature, and involves not as its consequence merely, but as one of its elements, the corresponding feeling of adoration, delight, desire, and complacency. (CH-CP)

-Is Power

Let us not deceive ourselves: in religion as in everything else knowledge is power. That is a platitude. But platitudes have this to be said for them—they are true. Nothing - not fervor, not devotion, not zeal - can supersede the necessity of knowledge. If knowledge without zeal is useless; zeal without knowledge is worse than useless—it is positively destructive. (BBW, SSW)

-Of God is Universal

The Bible asserts that the knowledge of God is universal. This it does both directly and by necessary implication. The apostle directly asserts that the heathen have the knowledge of God, and such knowledge as to render their impiety and immorality inexcusable (Rom. 1:19-21).

The Scripture everywhere addresses men as sinners; it calls upon them to repent; it threatens them with punishment in case of disobedience or promises pardon to those who turn from their sins. All this is done without any preliminary demonstration of the being of God. It assumes that men know that there is a God and that they are subject to His moral government. In teaching the universal sinfulness and condemnation of men, their inexcusableness for idolatry and immorality, and in asserting that even the most degraded are conscious of guilt and just exposure to the divine judgment, the Bible takes for gr anted that the knowledge of God is universal, that it is written on the heart of every man. (CH-STA)

LABOR

The farmer must labor; so, must the student, and so also the Christian. Good fruit will not grow of itself; neither will the mind, nor will piety (spirituality). We go back unless we go forward. We go forward only by labor. We cannot float up stream. (CH-CP)

THE LAMB OF GOD

In the Revelation he is called the Lamb twenty times, and in different relations. 1.As a sacrifice. The Lamb that was slain. As he in whose blood the saints had washed their robes. 2. As the ruler of the Church and of the world, he is set forth as the Lamb. This teaches that the (God-man) has the attributes of a lamb; and hence, a. That opposition to him is unprovoked and malignant. b. That his people may confide in his gentleness and tenderness. He is not like a ferocious, or even an austere ruler, but one whose scepter is love, who rules by and in love. 3.As judge he is called the Lamb. This teaches that even in the administration of justice, Christ acts with the greatest tenderness and forbearance. (CH-CP)

LANGUAGE

Language has its rights. The meaning of words cannot be changed at the pleasure of individuals. The word of God, and its equivalents in other languages, have a definite meaning, from which no man is at liberty to depart. (CH-STA)

The language of the Bible is the language of common life, and the language of common life is founded upon apparent and not upon scientific truth. It would be ridiculous to refuse to speak of the sun rising and setting, because we know it is not a satellite of our planet. (CH-STA)

THE LAW OF GOD

-Ceremonial and Civil

Both the ceremonial and judicial laws of the Jews have ceased to have any binding force under the Christian economy. (AAH-CF)

-Its Demands

The law demands perfect obedience and satisfaction of justice. This Christ has rendered. Those who renounce their own righteousness and believe that Christ has made a full satisfaction in their stead, and put their trust in what he has done, are immediately absolved from all guilt, and accepted as righteous in the sight of God. Thus, are cleansed from guilt by faith in Christ. (CH-CP)

-Moral

The Scriptures being the ONLY and COMPLETE rule of faith and practice, whatever is revealed therein as the will of God is a part of the moral law for Christian men; and whatever is not revealed therein as his will either directly or by necessary implication, is not part of our moral obligation at all. (AAH-CF)

This moral law has been summarily comprehended in the two tables of the law, called the Ten Commandments, is a fact not disputed. By this it is not meant that every duty which God now requires of Christian men may be directly derived from the Decalogue, but that the general principles of the infinite law of moral perfection, as adjusted to the general relations sustained by men to God, and to one another, may be found there. (AAH-CF)

-And Sin

Multitudes live in sin, without knowing it. What they really do is sin, though not so in their consciousness. so, Paul persecuted Christians. Such is generally the case with the heathen, such with the men of the world. The first necessity therefore is that the mind should be enlightened by the law. The gospel being a provision for the relief of the guilty, it cannot be embraced by those who do not feel their guilt. (CH-CP)

The Spirit convinces of sin through the law. Therefore, we must bring ourselves to that standard and not judge ourselves among ourselves or compare ourselves with ourselves. (CH-CP)

Sin derives its power from the law. It is the law which gives sin its power to condemn. What, therefore, satisfies the law, destroys the power of sin, and thus deprives death of its sting. Christ having by his righteousness and death satisfied the demands of the law, gives us victory over death. (CH-CP)

-And Conscience

This moral law, at least in its essential principles, and as far as was necessary for the guidance of men in a state of innocence, was revealed in the very constitution of man's nature; and although it has been greatly obscured by sin, it remains sufficiently clear to render even the heathen without excuse. (AAH-CF)

-And the Christian

While Christ fulfilled the law FOR us, the Holy Spirit fulfills the law IN us, by sanctifying us into complete conformity to it. And in obedience to this law the believer brings forth those good works which are the fruits though not the ground of our salvation. (AAH-CF)

LIBERTY

Liberty is not freedom from restraint or authority. This cannot be predicated of any creature. All rational beings are under the authority of reason and right. And as these are in infinite perfection in God, all creatures are under absolute subjection to him. And this subjection is the highest liberty. In renouncing subjection to God, man lost his liberty. He became the slave of sin. (CH-CP)

There is no real liberty but where the gospel reigns. The reign of the gospel secures civil and religious liberty, not only by restraining the power of ruler s within legitimate bounds, but also by making the people act on the principle that they must obey God rather than man. (CH-CP)

-Of the Christian

The liberty wherewith Christ has made us free consists of freedom from all illegitimate authority, and of subjection to truth, reason, and God, and final deliverance of his people and of it the "whole creation" from the bondage of corruption. (CH-CP)

-And Ability

Liberty and ability are distinct and should not be confounded. Free agency is the power to decide according to our character; ability is the power to change our char acter by a volition. The former, the Bible and consciousness affirm belongs to man in every condition of his being; the latter, the Bible and consciousness teach with equal explicitness does not belong to fallen man. The two things, therefore, ought not to be confounded. (CH-STA)

By LIBERTY we mean the inalienable prerogative of the human soul of exercising volition as it pleases. In this sense man is as free now as before the fall. By ABILITY we mean the capacity either to will in opposition to the desires and affections of the soul at the time, or by a bare exercise of volition to make oneself desire and love that which one does not spontaneously desire or love. We affirm that liberty is, and that ability in this sense is not, an element of the soul. (AAH-CF)

LIFE

-Spiritual

We are in a far higher sense dependent upon God for spiritual life than for corporal or intellectual life. For the latter we are indeed dependent; but they are communicated and continued according to fixed laws, while our spiritual life is not. It cannot in any way be produced in ourselves or communicated to others without a direct intervention of God. It is in this point analogous to a miracle. And we should feel our impotency to change our own heart, or to convert others. (CH-CP)

The life secured by Christ for His people was the life forfeited by sin, and that life which the believer derives from Christ is spiritual and eternal life, the exaltation and complete blessedness of his whole nature, both soul and body. (CH-STA)

LIGHT

Light is pure. It cannot be defiled. So, it is the fit emblem of holiness. God is absolute holiness. There is nothing in him of an opposite character. He stands opposed to evil as light does to darkness by an opposition of nature, necessary, immutable, eternal. Darkness cannot exist in light. The one excludes or is the negative of the other. God and sin are opposed and cannot exist in fellowship. (CH-CP)

THE LORD'S SUPPER

-Its Design

As the death of the incarnate Son of God for us men and for our salvation is of all events the most important, it should be held in perpetual remembrance. It was to this end that our blessed Lord instituted this sacrament and accompanied the institution with the command, "This do in remembrance of me." (CH-STA)

The Lord's Supper is presented under various aspects in the Scriptures. 1. It is presented primarily as a commemoration of the death of Christ. 2. It is presented as the seal of the covenant of grace, and as the acknowledgment of our acceptance of that covenant and our appropriation of its benefits. 3. It is presented as an act of communion with Christ. 4. It is presented as an act of communion with our fellow Christians. (CH-CP)

-Its Participants

Any man who sincerely desires to thank the Lord Jesus for his redemption, and who purposes to live in obedience to his commands, is authorized and bound to come to the table of the Lord, and aid in proclaiming and perpetuating the knowledge of his death. (CH-CP)

-Its Blessing

As our natural food imparts life and strength to our bodies, so this sacrament is one of the divinely appointed means to strengthen the principle of life in the soul of the believer and to confirm his faith in the promises of the gospel. (CH-STA)

The reason why believers receive so little by their attendance on this ordinance is that they expect so little. They expect to have their affections stirred and their faith somewhat strengthened, but they only rarely expect so to receive Christ as to be filled with all the fulness of God. Yet Christ in offering Himself to us in this ordinance offers us all of God we can receive. For in Christ, we are complete, that is filled with the fulness of God (Col. 2:10). (CH-STA)

THE LOST

No man is lost for the (lack) of an atonement, or because there is any other barrier in the way of his salvation than his own most free and wicked will. (AAH-OT)

LOVE

-Its Pre-eminence

Without this (love) all other passions are worthless, all professions, all hopes, are empty and vain. No amount of knowledge, or orthodoxy, or of power, natural or supernatural, no almsgiving or devotion to the poor no church member ship, no assiduity in all religious duties, is of any avail. (CH-CP)

-To God

The love of God comprehends in it the love of all that is good and the hatred of all that is evil. (CH-CP)

Love to Christ is not (simply) an emotion, or a feeling. It is that in the soul which makes it delight in Christ; which leads it to prefer the honor and interests of Christ to all other objects; and which leads us to live, labor, suffer and die for him gladly. (CH-CP)

-To Brethren

The special law of Christ's kingdom is that its members should love one another with brotherly love—a love which leads to the recognition of all Christians as brethren belonging to the same family and entitled to the same privileges and blessings, and a love which ministers to their necessities so that there be no lack. (CH-STA)

MAN

-Universal Belief in God

All men, in every age and in every part of the world, under all forms of religion and of every degree of culture, have felt and acknowledged that they are subject to a personal Being higher than themselves. No forms of speculative philosophy, however plausible or however widely diffused or confidently held in the schools or in the closet, have ever availed to invalidate this instinctive or intuitive judgment of the mind. (CH-STA)

-His Universal Need

Wherever we meet a man, no matter of what name or nation, we not only find that he has the same nature with ourselves; that he has the same organs, the same senses, the same instincts, the same feelings, the same faculties, the same understanding, will, and conscience, and the same capacity for religious culture, but that he has the same guilty and polluted nature, and needs the same redemption. Christ died for all men, and we are commanded to preach the gospel to every creature under heaven. Accordingly, nowhere on the face of the earth are men to be found who do not need the gospel or who are not capable of becoming partakers of the blessings which it offers. (CH-STA)

-State of his Nature in Glory

It is altogether probable that our nature, in virtue of its union with the divine nature in the person of Christ, and in virtue of the union of the redeemed with their exalted Redeemer, shall hereafter be elevated to a dignity and glory far greater than that in which Adam was created or to which he ever could have attained. (CH-STA)

MARRIAGE

. Marriage was ordained of God, and is therefore a divine institution, involving a religious as well as a civil contract. (AAH-CF)

MATERIALISM

Materialism is that system which ignores the distinction between matter and mind, and refers all the phenomena of the world, whether physical, vital, or mental, to the functions of matter. (If) it can be shown that unintelligent force cannot account for all the phenomena of the universe, and that there is such an objective entity or substance as mind, the theory is refuted. (CH-STA)

MEANS OF GRACE

What are the means of grace? The word, sacraments, and prayer. There are no others. (CH-CP)

It is through the Word, sacraments, and prayer that God communicates constant supplies of grace. They are the means of calling the activity of spiritual life into exercise. But these means of grace are inoperative unless they are received and used by faith. Faith does not, indeed, give them their power, but it is the condition on which the Spirit of God renders them efficacious. (CH-STA)

You may do what you please to a dead tree; you may spread around it the richest soil, plant it by rivers of water, and let in upon it the brightest light, and spread about it the purest atmosphere, yet it remains as dead as ever. It is so in the divine life. The most abundant supplies of light, the freest access to all that is adapted to its nourishment may be supplied, and there can be no growth without the inward principle. Now this is communicated, and maintained, and increased in power only by the word, sacraments, and prayer. (CH-CP)

MEDIATOR

A mediator is one who intervenes between contesting parties for the sake of making reconciliation. (AAH-CF)

The saints and angels are not mediators between us and God or us and Christ Because it is explicitly asserted that Christ is the only Mediator between God and man. 1 Tim. 2:5. The very suggestion of supplementing the work of Jesus Christ with that of other mediators is infinitely derogatory to him. (AAH-CF)

The mediatorial office involves all the three great functions of prophet, priest, and king; and Christ discharged them all, both in his estate of humiliation and exaltation. (AAH-CF)

MEDITATION

What is meditation? It is the serious, prolonged, devout contemplation of divine things. (CH-CP)

The mind should be stored with the truth and with the words of Scripture. We should cultivate the habit of casual meditation, or of recurring to the word of God continually a. as a matter or subject of thought, b. for direction, c. for support, and d. for consolation. (CH-CP)

Sir Isaac Newton said that if he differed from other men, it was in the power of attention. Whether this is correct of Newton or not, the point of difference between one Christian and another, so far as second or proximate causes are concerned, is mainly in the power or habit of contemplating divine truth long enough to allow it to produce its proper effect. (CH-CP)

To mind the things of the flesh is to make them the object of thought, desire, and pursuit. The things of the Spirit are those things which the Spirit reveals as the proper objects of thought, desire, and pursuit. And to mind them is thus to make them the object of our meditation, desire, and pursuit. The things of the Spirit are God, Christ, truth, holiness, the interests of Christ's kingdom and heaven. (CH-CP)

MERCY

Hosea says, "I will have mercy and not sacrifice;" that is, moral duties are of higher obligation than positive commands. God had commanded sacrifices, but he had also commanded the exercise of mercy. When the two came into conflict, so that one must yield to the other it was the positive that was to give way. (CH-CP)

MESSIAH

How can it be proved that the promised Messiah of the Jewish Scriptures has already come, and that Jesus Christ is that person? We prove that he must have already come by showing that the conditions of time and circumstances, which the prophets declare should mark his advent, are no longer possible. We prove, secondly, that Jesus of Nazareth was that person by showing that every one of those conditions was fulfilled in him. (AAH-OT)

MINISTERS

-Their Duty

The duty of candidates for the ministry—To feel that they are bound to go wherever God may call them; that it is not for them to choose. (CH-CP)

-And God's Will

How does God reveal his will to his ministers, as to where they should labor? He does it first, by his inward dealings with them, and secondly, by his outward dispensations. First, as to his inward dealings. 1st. He furnishes them with the gifts requisite to some special field of labor. 2d. He addresses their understandings. He presents to them the (needs) of the different parts of the great field; the faculties for usefulness; the demand for laborers. 3d. He addresses their conscience. 4th. He addresses their hearts, awakens an interest in particular portions of the field, and infuses into them an earnest desire for the work. Secondly, as to his outward dispensations. 1st. He removes obstacles out of the way, such as (lack) of health, obligations to dependent parents, and other hindrances of a like nature. 2d. He sends messages to them by friends. 3d. He sometimes stirs up the church to call them here or there. (CH-CP)

-Must Count the Cost

Men who enter the ministry should count the cost. They should understand what are the responsibilities which they assume, and the vows which they make. Let this then be graven on the palms of your hands. You must preach. You cannot turn back; you cannot turn aside to any other work; you cannot rightly engage in anything which does not subserve the preaching of the gospel. (CH-CP)

-Are Not Priests

(Scriptures) bid us simply to confess our faults one to another. There is not a word said about confession to a priest in the Bible. The believer, on the contrary, has immediate access to Christ, and to God through Christ (1 Tim. 2: 5; John 14: 6; 5:40; Matt. 11:28), and is commanded to confess his sins immediately to God. 1 John 1: 9. No priestly function is ever ascribed to the Christian ministry in the New Testament. (AAH-CF)

-The Mouthpiece of God

If the minister is the mouthpiece of the Most High, charged with a message to deliver, to expound and enforce; standing in the name of God before men, to make known to them who and what this God is, and what his purposes of grace are, and what his will for his people—then, the whole aspect of things is changed. Then, it is the primary duty of the minister to know his message; to know the instructions which have been committed to him for the people, and to know them thoroughly; to be prepared to declare them with confidence and with exactness, to commend them with wisdom, and to urge them with force and defend them with skill, and to build men up by means of them into a true knowledge of God and of his will, which will be unassailable in the face of the fiercest assault. (BBW-SSW)

CHRISTIAN MINISTRY

-Preparation for

A low view of the functions of the ministry will naturally carry with it a low conception of the training necessary for it. (BBW-SSW)

A comprehensive and thorough theological training is the condition of a qualified ministry. When we satisfy ourselves with a less comprehensive and thorough theological training, we are only condemning ourselves to a less qualified ministry. (BBW-SSW)

No second-hand knowledge of the revelation of God for the salvation of a ruined world can suffice the needs of a ministry whose function it is to convey this revelation to men. For such a ministry as this the most complete knowledge of the wisdom of the world supplies no equipment; the most fervid enthusiasm of service leaves without furnishing. Nothing will suffice for it but to know; to know the Book; to know it at first hand; and to know it through and through. And what is required first for training men for such a ministry is that the Book should be given them in its very words as it has come from God' s hand and in the fulness of its meaning, as has been ascertained by the labors of generations of men of God who have brought to bear upon it all the resources of sanctified scholarship and consecrated thought. (BBW-SSW)

MIRACLES

-Their Definition

A miracle, therefore, may be defined to be an event brought about in the external world by the immediate efficiency or simple volition of God. (CH-STA)

-Their Historicity

The truth of Christianity depends on the historical truth of the account of the miracles recorded in the New Testament. (CH-STA)

To say that these (miracles) never occurred, simply because, according to the ephemeral theory of the hour, they could not occur, is the infinite of folly. It is a thousand-fold more certain that they occurred than that the best authenticated facts of history are true. For such facts we have only ordinary historical evidence; for the truth of Christ's miracles, and especially of his resurrection, we have the evidence of all the facts of history from his day to the present. The actual state of the world, and the existence of the Church, necessitate the admission of those facts, to which God himself bore witness of old in signs, and wonders, and divers (various) miracles, as He does still in a manner irresistible, in the gift of the Holy Ghost. (CH-STA)

-Their Continuance

There is nothing in the New Testament inconsistent with the occurrence of miracles in the post-apostolic age of the Church. The Apostles were indeed chosen to be the witnesses of Christ, to bear testimony to the facts of his history and to the doctrines which He taught. And among the signs of an Apostle, or necessary credentials of his commission, was the power to work miracles. (Rom. 15:18; 2 Cor. 12:12.) When the Apostles had finished their work, the necessity of miracles, so far as the great end they were intended to accomplish was concerned, ceased. This, however, does not preclude the possibility of their occurrence, on suitable occasions, in after ages. It is a mere question of fact to be decided on historical evidence. In some few cases the nature of the event, its consequences, and the testimony in its support, have constrained many Protestants to admit the probability, if not the certainty of these miraculous interventions. (CH-STA)

-False or Counterfeit

The difficulty of discriminating between miracles and these lying wonders. i.e., between the works of God and the works of Satan, has been anticipated and provided for by the sacred writers themselves (see Deut. 13:1-3; Matt. 7:22-23; 24:24, Thess. 2:9). (CH-STA)

These passages teach that supernatural events, i.e., events transcending the power of material causes and the ability of man, may be brought about by the agency of higher intelligences, and that no such supernatural events are to be regarded as of any authority if produced for a wicked purpose. (CH-STA)

Satan will not cooperate to confirm the truth or to promote good. God cannot cooper ate to confirm what is false or to promote evil. Thus, the character of the agent and the design for which a supernatural event is brought about determine whether it is truly a miracle or one of the lying wonders of the devil. (CH-STA)

The Kingdom of Satan can easily be recognized by its character. No isolated event is ever to be recognized as a miracle. The man, and the doctrine and their relation to the whole system of past revelations and miraculous interventions, will in every case be sufficient to discriminate the identity of the supernatural cause. (AAH-OT)

MISSIONARIES

-Not Unique Servants

The work of foreign missions is not a distinct part of the general work of the church. The commission under which the Church acts has equal reference to all parts of the field. The work of the missionary is therefore not different from the work of a minister. A man who enlists as a soldier, does not enlist for any one field. He is to go wherever he is sent. (CH-CP)

-Rewarded according to Faithfulness not Numbers of converts

The gospel is as glorious and excellent when men reject it to their own condemnation, as when they believe. And ministers, if faithful, are as well pleasing to God when unsuccessful, as when successful. This should comfort and sustain them under all their trials. The missionary who labors for years without a convert is still as incense in the estimation of God. Men do not so view the matter. Ministers through unbelief often regard themselves as rejected and disowned when no visible effects follow their labors. But God views the matter in a different light. Successful or unsuccessful, the faithful minister is equally acceptable to God. (CH-CP)

-Their Motivation

Motives which should induce us to give ourselves up to this work, to go where God may send us. 1. The command of Christ, which is explicit and obligatory, and is addressed to us as truly as though we were specially named in the commission. Disobedience as to going at all, or as to going where we ought to go, is certain to entail the greatest evils on our own soul. 2. Love to Christ and gratitude for the benefits of redemption. 3. The absolute necessity of the gospel to the salvation of the heathen. This is clearly the doctrine of the Bible and of the Church. If they do not hear, they cannot believe; and if they do not believe, they cannot be saved. (CH-CP)

MONEY

-Purpose of Investments

Ought not (business) enterprises now to be entered on for the very purpose of making gain to be applied to the promotion of the Redeemer's kingdom? And should not those whose efforts to increase their property God signally blessed, make a free-will offer ing of a portion of their profits to his service? (AA-PT)

MONOTHEISM

There is only one living and true God or divine Being. The religion of the Bible stands opposed not only to atheism, but to all forms of polytheism. (CH-STA)

MORALITY

-Bound to True Religion

The attempt to dissociate morality from religion leads to the destruction of morality. The latter cannot continue without the former. The great and efficient motives to moral duties are derived from religion. And as God is the source of all good, nothing good can continue in those who live in alienation from him. And because God judicially abandons the irreligious to immorality. (CH-CP)

-In Saved Sinner's Compared with Unfallen Man

The morality of the redeemed man is equally fuller and richer than the morality of unfallen man could ever have become. There are obligations of gratitude, for example, which fall on him—obligations on the one hand to a humility of quite distinctive character, and on the other hand to love of a peculiar which unfallen man must have remained a stranger. (BBW-SSW)

MORTIFICATION (Dying to Sin)

The same remarks are applicable to the mortification of sin. We are prone to view our depravity too much in the general, and under this to repent of it, and humble ourselves on account of it; whereas, to make any considerable progress in this part of sanctification, we must deal with our sins in detail. (AA-TRE)

No plant can live unless it is allowed to grow. If what reveals itself above ground be cut down as often as it appears, the root itself will die. This with noxious weeds is often a tedious process, but if per severed in, it must finally succeed. So, with the old man, or the principle of sin. If its acts, or actings are prevented or destroyed, the principle itself will grow weaker and weaker, until it finally dies. (CH-CP)

But as the "old man", though crucified, never becomes extinct in this life, this warfare between the flesh and the spirit never ceases until death. As these opposite moral principles operate through the same natural faculties and affections, it is a matter of course, that as the one gains strength the other must be proportionately weakened; and experience teaches that the most effectual way to subdue the power of sin is to cherish and exercise the principle of holiness. Every victory over any lust weakens its power; and by a steady growth in grace, such advantage is obtained over inbred sin, that the advanced Christian maintains the mastery over it, and is not subject to lose violent struggles which were undergone when this warfare commenced. (AA-TRE)

MYSTICISM

-Its Definition

Any system, whether in philosophy or religion, which assigns more importance to the feelings than to the intellect is called mysticism. The mystic assumes that the senses and reason are alike untrustworthy and inadequate sources of knowledge, that nothing can be received with confidence as truth, at least in the higher departments of knowledge, in all that relates to our own nature, to God, and our relation to Him, except what is revealed either naturally or supernaturally in the feelings. (CH-STA)

-And the Apostles

In no case do we find the apostles calling upon the people, whether Jews or Gentiles, to look within themselves, to listen to the inner Word. They were to listen to the outward Word, to believe what they heard, and to pray for the Holy Spirit to enable them to understand, receive, and obey what was thus externally made known to them. (CH-STA)

-An Objection against

(An) objection to the mystical doctrine is that there is no criterion by which a man can test these inward impulses or revelations and determine which are from the Spirit of God and which are from his own heart or from Satan, who often appears and acts as an angel of light. Many men who are under the influence of some evil spirit honestly believe themselves to be inspired. (CH-STA)

NATIONS

God uses the nations with the absolute control that a man uses a rod or a staff. They are in His hands, and He employs them to accomplish His purposes. He breaks them in pieces like a potter s vessel, or He exalts them to greatness, according to His good pleasure. (CH-STA)

NATURAL MAN

There are two classes of men in the world, the natural and the spiritual; those who are controlled by their own nature, and those who are controlled by the Spirit of God. The former is governed as to their thoughts, opinions, feelings, and outward life, by the principles of human nature in its present state. Such men never rise above the sphere of the natural. They look at the things which are temporal. They live for the present. The spiritual are those in whom the Spirit of God dwells and reigns. (CH-CP)

NATURAL THEOLOGY

-Affirmed

Those who live under the light of nature, (Paul) says, are justly chargeable with impiety and immorality, because the perfections of the Divine Being, his eternal power and Godhead, have, from the creation, been manifested by the things which are made. Yet men have not acknowledged their Creator. They neither worshipped him as God, nor were thankful for his mercies, but served the creature more than the Creator. In thus departing from the Fountain of all excellence, they departed from excellence itself. Their foolish hearts were darkened, and their corruption manifests itself not only by degrading idolatry, but by the various forms of moral evil both in heart and life. These sins are committed against the law which is written on every man's heart; so that they know that those who do such things are worthy of death and are therefore without excuse even in their own consciousness. (CH-WL)

-All men, in every age and in every part of the world, under all forms of religion and of every degree of culture, have felt and acknowledged that they are subject to a personal Being higher than themselves. Men ignorant of the true God have fashioned for themselves imaginary gods (Rom. 1:23) whose wrath they have endeavored to appease and whose favour they have endeavored to win. (CH-STA)

-Inadequate for Salvation

Here it is that natural theology utterly fails. It cannot answer the question, how can man be just with God? or, how can God be just and yet justifying the ungodly? Mankind have anxiously pondered this question for ages and have gained no satisfaction. The ear has been placed on the bosom of humanity, to catch the still, small voice of conscience, and got no answer. It has been directed heavenward and received no response. Reason, conscience, tradition, history, unite in saying that sin is death; and, therefore, that so far as human wisdom and resources are concerned, the salvation of sinners is as impossible as raising the dead. Every conceivable method of expiation and purification has been tried without success. (CH-STA)

-Cosmological Argument

Every effect must have an adequate cause. The world is an effect. Therefore, the world must have had a cause outside of itself and adequate to account for its existence. (CH-STA)

It may be stated in the form of a syllogism, thus-Major Premise: - Every new existence or change in anything previously existing must have had a cause pre-existing and adequate. Minor Premise: - The universe as a whole and in all its parts is a system of changes. Conclusion: - Hence the universe must have a cause exterior to itself, and the ultimate or absolute cause must be eternal, uncaused, and unchangeable. The judgment is unavoidable; the opposite is unthinkable. Something exists now, therefore something must have existed from eternity, and that which has existed from eternity is the cause of that which exists now. (AAH- OT)

-Moral Argument

As the image of the sun reflected from a mirror or from a smooth surface of a lake reveals to us that the sun is and what it is, so the soul of man, just as clearly and just as certainly, reveals that God is and what He is. The reflection of the sun does not teach us everything that is true concerning that luminary; it does not reveal its internal constitution nor tell us how its light and heat are maintained from age to age. In like manner the soul, as the image of God, does not reveal all that God is. Yet in both cases, and equally in both cases, what is revealed is true, that is, trustworthy. (CH-STA)

Man is essentially and universally a religious being. The sense of absolute dependence and moral accountability is inherent in his nature, universal and necessary. Conscience always implies responsibility to a superior, in moral authority, and therefore in moral character. is especially implied in the sense of guilt which accompanies every violation of conscience. God is manifested and recognized in conscience as a holy, righteous, just, and intelligent will, i.e., a holy personal spirit. (AAH-OT)

-Teleological Argument

Design supposes a designer. The world everywhere exhibits marks of design. Therefore, the world owes its existence to an intelligent author. (CH-STA)

The argument is, such is the nature of design that it of necessity implies an intelligent agent; and, therefore, wherever or whenever we see evidence of design, we are convinced that it is to be referred to the operation of mind. On this ground we are not only authorized but compelled to apply the argument from design far beyond the limits of experience and to say that it is just as evident that the world had an intelligent creator as that a book had an author. If man can believe that a book was written by a chance or blind, unconscious force, then, and not otherwise, can he rationally deny the validity of the argument from design in proof of the existence of a personal God. (CH-STA)

If a father by providing a home for his children gives indisputable evidence of intelligence and love, then are those attributes to be ascribed to Him who fitted up this world to be the home of His creatures. (CH-STA)

OATHS

The proper occasions upon which an oath may be taken are all those in which seriously and perfectly lawful interests are involved, and in which an appeal to the witness of God is necessary to secure confidence and end strife (Heb. 6:16); and, whenever the oath is imposed by competent authority upon those subject to it. (AAH-CF)

An oath cannot bind to that which is unlawful, because the obligation of the law is imposed upon us by the will of God, and therefore takes precedence of all obligations imposed upon us by the will of men or by ourselves; and the lesser obligation cannot relieve from the greater. The sin is in taking the oath to do the unlawful thing, not in breaking it. Therefore, Luther was right in breaking his monastic vows. (AAH-CF)

OBITUARIES

"Now about that time, Herod the king, stretched forth his hands to vex certain of the church. And he killed James, the brother of John, with the sword." From this we may learn that, to go safely to heaven, it is not necessary that we should have a laudatory obituary on earth. I have often been shocked with the thought, that while a man's eulogy is pronounced upon earth, the poor soul may be writhing and blaspheming in the torments of hell! (AA-TRE)

OBEDIENCE

Obedience to God, obeying his commands from a pious (sincere) spirit, is the most acceptable worship we can render to him. (CH-CP)

Be active in the service of God. Obeying produces believing. (CH-CP)

OBLIGATION

No tongue can tell our obligations to Christ, as our Redeemer, from the awful bondage into which we were by our apostacy from God. (CH-CP)

OLD AGE

Your work is never ended while you are in the body. It is a sad mistake for aged persons to relinquish their usual pursuits and resign everything into the hands of their children. Many have dated their distressing melancholy from such a false step. The mind long accustomed to activity is miserable in a state of stagnation; or rather, having lost its usual nutriment, it turns and preys upon itself. (AA-TRE)

Let not the infirm and aged say that they can now do nothing for God. They can do much; and for ought they can tell, more than they ever did in the days of their vigor. It is a beautiful sight to see men laden with fruit, even in their old age. (AA-TRE)

It is not desirable for a Christian to live to be incredibly old; especially when all active service in the cause of Christ is precluded. Old age is a peculiarly unfavorable season for growth in grace. Many of the natural auxiliaries to piety (spirituality) are then removed; and at the same time, many infirmities cluster ar ound us; so that a declension in religion is not uncommon in the protracted years of the aged. (AA-TRE)

A man is never too old nor decrepit to be covetous. Covetousness is peculiarly the vice of the aged, and when indulged, strikes its roots deeper, the older we grow. (AA-TRE)

ORIGINAL RIGHTEOUSNESS

In the moral image of God, or original righteousness, are included the perfect harmony and due subordination of all that constituted man. His reason was subject to God, his will was subject to his reason, his affections and appetites to his will, and the body was the obedient organ of the soul. (CH-STA)

ORIGINAL SIN

Inasmuch as Adam acted as the head of the whole race, all men were on probation and fell with him in his first transgression. The Scriptures therefore teach that we come into the world under condemnation. We are by nature, i.e., we were born, the children of wrath. This fact is assumed in all the provisions of the gospel and in all the institutions of our religion. (CH-STA)

It is an undeniable fact that the penalty which Adam incurred has fallen upon his whole race. The earth is cur sed for them as it was for him. They must earn their bread by the sweat of their brows. The pains of childbirth are the common heritage of all the daughters of Eve. All men are subject to disease and death. All are born in sin, destitute of the moral image of God. There is not an evil consequent on the sin of Adam which does not affect his race as much as it affected him. (CH-STA)

ORTHODOXY

Orthodoxy will not last without piety (spirituality). An unconverted ministry forsakes the truth. This all history proves. (CH-CP)

PANTHEISM

Pantheism merges everything into God. The universe is His existence. All reason is His reason; all activity is His activity; the consciousness of creatures is all the consciousness of God Himself; good and evil, pain and pleasure, are phenomena of God-modes in which God reveals Himself. He is not, therefore, a person whom we can worship and in whom we can trust. He is only the substance of which the universe and all that it contains are the ever-changing manifestation. Pantheism admits of no freedom, no responsibility, no conscious life after death. (CH-STA)

Pantheism not only destroys the foundation of morals but renders all rational religion impossible. (CH-STA)

It is no extravagance to say that pantheism is the worst form of atheism. For mere atheism is negative. It deifies neither man nor evil. But pantheism teaches that man, the human soul, is the highest form in which God exists, and that evil is as much a manifestation of God as is good; Satan is the ever-blessed and adorable Redeemer. Beyond this it is impossible for the insanity of wickedness to go. (CH-STA)

PARADISE

We read in the parable of the rich man and Lazarus, that "'the beggar died, and was carried by the angels into Abraham's bosom" (Luke 16:22). It is undeniable that in his case the transition from earth to heaven was immediate. Still more explicit is the declaration of our Lord to the penitent thief, "Today shalt thou be with me in paradise" (Luke 23:4). There can be no doubt that in "paradise" here is heaven (cf. 2 Cor. 12:2-4; Rev. 2:7); consequently, when Christ promised the dying thief that he would that day be in paradise, He promised that he would be in heaven. (CH-STA)

PAUL & ISAIAH

To pronounce Homer and Newton idiots would be no more irrational than to set down Isaiah and Paul as either imposters or fanatics. It is as certain as any self-evident truth that they were wise, good, sober-minded men. That such men would falsely claim to be the authoritative messengers of God and to be endowed with supernatural powers in confirmation of their mission is a contradiction. (CH-STA)

PEACE

Next to the blessing of peace with God and in our own conscience, is that of peace with our fellow men. "As much as lieth in you, live peaceably with all men. And again, "Follow peace with all men." The true source of all the wars, contentions, and disturbances which are in the world, is the pride, the envy, the covetousness, and other evil passions of our nature. Eradicate these, and in their place introduce pure and kind affections, and you will experience a double peace—peace within and peace without. (AA-TRE)

No system was ever so admirably adapted to produce universal peace as Christianity, and the only reason why this effect has not followed its reception everywhere, is that its true spirit has not been imbibed. Just so far as this blessed system is cordially embraced, it cuts up by the roots all causes of contention, except that which has for its subjects, sin and error. It teaches us not only to love our friends and brethren, but also our bitterest enemies, to return blessing for cursing, and kindness for ill treatment. (AA-TRE)

PELAGIANISM

The Pelagian, believing human nature to be uncontaminated, and needing nothing but a correct knowledge of the truth, rejects all supernatural aid, and maintains that every man has full ability to perform all good actions, and to reform what is amiss, by simply attending to the instructions of the Word, and exercising his own free will, by which he is able to choose and pursue what course he pleases. (AA-TRE)

The opposition between Pelagianism and the gospel is so open and so radical that the former has never been regarded as a form of Christianity at all. It has, in other words, never been the faith of any organized Christian Church is little more than a form of rationalism. (CH-STA)

Another consequence of his principles which Pelagius unavoidably drew was that men could be saved without the gospel. As free will in the sense of plenary ability, belongs essentially to man as much as reason, men whether Heathen, Jews, or Christians, may fully obey the law of God and attain eternal life. The only difference is that under the light of the Gospel, this perfect obedience is rendered easier. (CH-STA)

PERFECTION

The more holy a man is the more humble, self-renouncing, self-abhorring, and the more sensitive to every sin he becomes, and the more closely he clings to Christ. The moral imperfections which cling to him he feels to be sins, laments and strives to overcome them. Believers find that their life is a constant warfare, and they need to take the kingdom of heaven by storm and watch while they pray. They are always subject to the constant chastisement of their Father's loving hand, which can only be designed to correct their imperfections, and to confirm their graces. And it has been notoriously the fact that the best Christians have been those who have been the least prone to claim the attainment of perfection for themselves. (AAH-OT)

The word "perfect" is applied to some men in Scripture either to mark comparative excellence, or to assert genuine sincerity in profession and service. But the inspired biographies of the men themselves — such as David, Acts 13:22; Noah, Gen. 6: 9; and Job1:1, prove very clearly that the perfection intended was not a sinless one. (AAH-CF)

PERSEVERANCE

Although it is certain, on the part of God, that if we are elected and called, we shall be saved; yet it requires constant watchfulness, and diligence, and prayer to make that calling and election sure to us. - 2 Pet. 1:10. The orthodox doctrine does not affirm certainty of SALVATION because we have ONCE believed, but certainty of PERSEVERANCE IN HOLINESS, therefore, in opposition to all weaknesses and temptations, is the only sure evidence of the genuineness of experience, or of the validity of our confidence as to our future salvation, and surely such an assurance of certainty cannot encourage either carelessness or immorality. (AAH-OT)

This is a great work, and one absolutely necessary. If a man thinks it enough to believe in Christ and then live as he pleases, he turns the grace of God into licentiousness, and lays up wrath against the day of wrath. We must subdue the flesh, i.e., our corrupt nature, the world, and the devil. (CH-CP)

PHARISEEISM

(Humility) stands opposed to self-righteousness. It is the effect of conviction of sin, which produces the consciousness that we are destitute of all merit in the sight of God. How essential this is, the Scriptures everywhere teach. The Pharisee and the Publican are presented in contrast, the one offensive and the other acceptable in the sight of God. A moral man puffed up with a sense of his good desert, is more offensive than an immoral man bowed down with a sense of guilt. When we consider the number and aggravations of our sins, we are lost in wonder that we can be so infatuated as to arrogate merit to ourselves. (CH-CP)

PHILOSOPHY

No man has the right to hang the millstone of his philosophy around the neck of the truth of God. (CH-STA)

Jesus Christ is the true God. The revelation which He made of Himself was the manifestation of God. He and the Father are one. Philosophy must veil her face in the presence of Jesus Christ as God manifest in the flesh. She may not presume in that presence to say that God is not, and is not known to be, what Christ Himself most clearly was. (CH-STA)

The false teachers in Colosse were Jews, but not Judaizer s. They were philosophers. They designed to substitute philosophy for Christianity, not by denying the latter, but by explaining it. They distinguished between faith and knowledge. Faith was for the people, knowledge for the educated few. The objects of faith were the historical and doctrinal statements of the Bible. The objects of knowledge were the speculative truths underlying those statements, and into which they were to be sublimated. All that philosophy vainly pretends to do is accomplished in Christ. In Christ are all the treasures of wisdom and knowledge, and he is the only source of knowledge. The knowledge which he gives is sure, satisfying, sanctifying. (CH-CP)

PHYSICIANS

There is danger, as Richard Greenham, 1535-1594, says, "that the bodily physician will look no further than the body, while the spiritual physician will totally disregard the body, and look only at the mind". (AA-TRE)

Christ is not only the only physician, and one able to heal with certainty all our maladies, but he is always accessible to everyone and at all times. It is not any one form of spiritual disease, or any one degree of it, but all forms and all degrees. Anyone in the last stage of spiritual death may come to him with the certainty of being received and cured. He demands no conditions. He asks no terms. He requires no preparation and will receive no recompense. (CH-CP)

POLYGAMY

Experience shows that physically, economically, and morally, polygamy defeats all the ends for which marriage was designed and is inconsistent with human nature and the relations of the sexes, while monogamy proves in the highest degree adapted to effect those ends. (AAH-CF)

THE POOR

In our public system of religious instruction in cities and villages, the poor are too much overlooked. There must be some more effective measures for conveying the gospel to the destitute poor than our splendid churches furnish. (AA-PT)

In every Christian church there are men and women who wish to do good, but they know not how to go about it. Let each of these go out into the lanes and dark alleys of the city and persuade at least one to go with them to the house of prayer: all such exertions are useful to the person himself, whatever may be the effect on others. Let the meetinghouse be seated with benches, and every seat be in common; so that the first person who comes shall have the right to occupy it. And let the missionary to these people speak kindly to them, and inquire into their wants and afflictions, and make known cases of extreme suffering to those whose office it is to relieve distress. (AA-PT)

-In Spirit

The poor in spirit are those who are conscious of their spiritual poverty. They stand opposed to those who falsely assume and assert that they are rich and know not that they are wretched and miserable, and poor and blinded and naked. Poorness of spirit includes, therefore, 1. A sense of ignorance and a willingness to be taught. 2. A sense of unworthiness, as opposed to a spirit of self-righteousness. 3. A sense of pollution, as opposed to a disposition to admire our own excellence and to regard ourselves as attractive in the sight of others. 4. A sense of helplessness. 5. Poverty of spirit is a sense of wretchedness, i.e., of the utter incompetency of the world to fill the desires of the soul. (CH-CP)

POVERTY

Poverty and suffering are by infinite wisdom judged best for the traveler to Zion. Let the Lord's people be contented with their condition, and thankful that they are preserved from snares and temptations which they would have found it difficult to withstand. (AA-TRE)

POWER

-Of God's Creatures

The power of the creature is not self-sustained. It is not an ability to exist, act and accomplish its purposes (apart from) God, and independently of him; but it is ability which he constantly sustains. It is in him we live and move and have our being. (CH-CP)

-The Power of Man

We get the idea of power from our own consciousness. That is, we are conscious of the ability of producing effects. Power in man is confined within very narrow limits. We can change the current of our thoughts, or fix our attention on a particular object, and we can move the voluntary muscles of our body. Beyond this our direct power does not extend. It is from this small measure of efficiency that all the stores of human knowledge and all the wonders of human art are derived. (CH-STA)

-The Power of the Gospel

No series of miracles could give stronger evidence of the divine origin and power of the gospel than the actual and permanent reformation of wicked men; and the sceptic may be challenged to account for such effects on any natural principles. (AA-TRE)

PRAISE

In Scripture men and all rational creatures are called upon and required to praise God. 1. For all his divine perfections, natural and moral, his infinite greatness; for his wisdom, power, holiness, justice, goodness, and truth. 2. For his wonderful works, of creation, of providence, of redemption. 3. For all his blessings, of creation, providence, and redemption. These are inexhaustible topics of praise, for all creatures and for all eternity. (CH-CP)

The happiest, holiest, and most useful Christians, those most heavenly in their disposition and state, are those who praise God most and best. (CH-CP)

PRAYER

Prayer is the expression, uttered or unuttered, of all the feelings and desires which (a spiritual) state of mind produces or excites. (CH-STA)

As prayer is converse with God, it includes those spiritual exercises, those goings forth of the soul towards God in thought and feeling, which reveal themselves in the forms of reverence, gratitude, sorrow for sin, an awareness of dependence, and obligation. In this sense, the man who lives and walks with God prays always. He fulfills to the letter the injunction, "Pray without ceasing. "It is our duty and high privilege to have this constant converse with God. The heart should be like the altar of incense on which the fire never went out. (CH-STA)

Faith and prayer are our chief resource under all the various and heavy afflictions of this life. (AA-TRE)

-Requisites of Acceptable Prayer

(1) Sincerity. The first and most obviously necessary requisite of acceptable prayer is sincerity. God is a Spirit. He searches the heart. He is not satisfied with words or with external homage. He cannot be deceived and will not be mocked. It is a great offence, therefore, to utter words before Him in which our hearts do not join. (CH-STA)

(2) Reverence. God is an infinitely exalted Being - infinite in His holiness as well as in knowledge and power. He is to be held in reverence by all who are round about Him. This holy fear is declared to be -the first element of true religion. We offend God, therefore, when we address Him as we would a fellow creature or use forms of expression of undue familiarity. Nothing is more characteristic of the prayers recorded in the Bible than the spirit of reverence by which they are pervaded. (CH-STA)

(3) Humility. We must have both a due sense of our insignificance as creatures and a proper apprehension of our ill-desert and uncleanness in the sight of God as sinners. This is the opposite of self-righteousness, of self-complacency, and self-confidence. (CH-STA)

(4) Importunity. Persistence in prayer is so important that on three different occasions our Lord impressed its necessity upon His disciples. (CH-STA)

(5) Submission. Every man who duly appreciates his relation to God will, no matter what his request, be disposed to say, "Lord, not my will, but thine, be done." God deals with us as a wise benefactor. He requires that we appreciate the value of the blessings for which we ask, and that we manifest a proper earnestness of desire. (CH-STA)

(6) Faith. We must believe (a) that God exists, (b) that He is able to hear and answer our prayers, (c) that He is disposed to answer them, and (d) that He certainly will answer them, if consistent with His own wise purposes and with our best good. (Lack) of confidence in these precious promises of God, (lack) of faith in His disposition and readiness to hear us, is one of the greatest and most common defects in the prayers of Christians. Every father desires the confidence of his children and is grieved by any evidence of distrust; God as our father demands from us the feelings which children ought to have towards their earthly parents. (CH-STA)

(7) Reliance on the name of Christ. The prayers of Christians must be offered in His name. When we are told to pray in the name of Christ, we are required to urge that we be heard based on who Christ is and what He has done. We are not to trust to our own merits, or our own character, nor even simply to God's mercy; we are to plead the merits and worth of Christ. It is only in Him, in virtue of His mediation and worth, that, according to the gospel, any blessing is conferred on the apostate children of men. (CH-STA)

-Importance of Frequent Prayer

The believer needs, to maintain his spiritual health and vigor, regular and stated seasons of prayer, as the body needs its daily meals. (CH-STA)

We read that Christ often retired for the purpose of prayer and not unfrequently spent whole nights in that exercise. If the spotless soul of Jesus needed these seasons of converse with God, none of His followers should venture to neglect this important means of grace. Let each day at least begin and end with God. (CH-STA)

Prayer is essential to the existence and growth of the spiritual life. It is the breath of the new man. By this means he obtains quick relief from unnumerable evils and draws down from heaven blessings of the richest and sweetest kind. (AA-TRE)

-A Powerful Instrument

Possess your minds fully of the persuasion that prayer is efficacious, when offered in faith and with importunity, to obtain the blessings which we need. God has made Himself known as the Hearer of prayer: yea, He has promised that we shall have, as far as may be for His glory and our good, whatever we ask. The most important events may be brought about by prayer. (AA-TRE)

Prayer will, moreover, be your most effectual guard against sin and the power of temptation: FOR SATAN TREMBLES WHEN HE SEES THE WEAKEST SAINT UPON HIS KNEES. (AA-TRE)

Moses by his prayer saved the Israelites from destruction; at the prayer of Samuel the army of the Philistines was dispersed. These facts (in James 5:17) are referred to by the Apostle James, for the purpose of proving that the prayer of a righteous man availeth much. Prayer is a power. Queen Mary of Scotland was not beside herself, when she said she feared the prayers of John Knox, more than an army. (CH-STA)

-United

Not only pray for them yourself but engage other Christian friends also to pray for them. When many good people join their requests together, their cry is more acceptable and prevalent. When the church united in prayer for Peter in chains, he was soon delivered, and in the very time of their prayers. All believers have, through Christ, a great interest in heaven, and the Father is willing to grant what they unitedly and importunately ask in the name of His dear Son.

PRAYERLESSNESS

A prayerless man is thoroughly irreligious and spiritually dead. (CH-STA)

A prayerless Christian and a pulseless man are alike impossible. The pulse is the great criterion or index of the health of the body; so, prayer is of the health of the soul. (CH-CP)

PREACHING

-The One Great Object

It is the great object of the ministry to preach the unsearchable riches of Christ, i.e., to proclaim him as possessing all divine perfections in an infinite degree. If men are brought to see and acknowledge this, then are they converted and saved. (CH-CP)

The only way to save men is not by preaching the doctrines of natural religion, nor by holding up law, nor by expounding the anthropological doctrines of the Bible. These things are important in their place, but they ae subordinate to preaching Christ, that is, holding him up in his person, his work, and his relation to us as the great object of knowledge, and as such, the great object of love, the only ground of confidence and our only all-sufficient portion.

It is by being brought to the knowledge of Christ that men are to be converted and the world saved. (CH-CP)

Therefore, brethren, as ye go hence, go to preach Christ. Let that be your theme and that your object. If faithful, you will receive a crown of righteousness. If unfaithful, it would have been better had you never been born. (CH-CP)

PREDESTINATION

If only we were all willing to sit simply at the feet of the inspired writers and take them at their word, we should have no difficulties with Predestination. The difficulties we feel about Predestination are not derived from the Word. The Word is full of it, because it is full of God, and when we say God and mean God—God in all that God is—we have said Predestination. Our difficulties with Predestination arise in an unwillingness to acknowledge ourselves to be wholly at the disposal of another. We wish to be at our own disposal. (BBW-SSW)

The high mystery of predestination is to be handled with special prudence and care. This necessity arises from the fact that it is often abused, and that its proper use is in the highest degree important. (AAH-CF)

PRESERVATION

By preservation is meant that all things external to God owe the continuance of their existence, with all their properties and powers, to the will of God. (CH-STA)

PRIDE

-Its Offensiveness

The reasons why pride is thus offensive are, 1. Because it is an utter falsehood. It is a false estimate. It supposes that to be true which is not true. It supposes that we are what we are not. 2. Because it is founded on ignorance of God, of his law and of its requirements. 3. Because it is the opposite of the state of mind which becomes our true character and our true relation to God. 4. Because it is in its own nature offensive and disgusting for the loathsome to assume that it is attractive, the impotent that it is strong, the evil that it is good, the revolting that it is beautiful. 5. Because it is the source of malignity, contempt, cruelty, and injustice. (CH-CP)

-Its Cure

Its cure is a. A due sense of our insignificance and dependence. b. A due sense of our unworthiness. c. Being filled with due apprehensions of the glory of God. (CH-CP)

1. Always humble yourselves, i.e., never seek exaltation or honor or praise. 2. Do not dwell on your own superiority, real or imaginary. 3. Condescend to men of low estate. 4. Seek not your own but the things of Jesus Christ, and how you may do good to others. (CH-CP)

PRIESTHOOD OF BELIEVERS

The sense in which all believers are priests is, 1. That they all have liberty of access to God. This is the main idea. This is the great distinction and blessedness intended to be expressed by the term. 2. They offer to God the sacrifice of a broken Heart, the incense of prayer, the thank-offering of praise. They minister before God and are in this sense priests. 3. They make intercession for others. (CH-CP)

The Old Testament priests were a distinct class, separated from the people. They could not engage in ordinary avocations, nor seek support in the ordinary way. Those who ministered at the altar were partakers of the altar. In like manner, Christians are a people separated world, and consecrated to God. They cannot belong to the world, seek its objects, or enjoy its pleasures. (CH-CP)

PROCRASTINATION

Beware of devolving the duty of today on tomorrow. This is called procrastination, which is said, justly, to be "the thief of time." Remember that every day and every hour has its own appropriate work; but if that which should be done this day is deferred until a future time, to say the least, there must be an inconvenient accumulation of duties in the future. But as tomorrow is to everybody uncertain, to suspend the acquisition of an important object may be the occasion of losing forever the opportunity of receiving it. The rule of sound discretion is, never put off till tomorrow what ought to be done today. (AA-TRE)

PROFESSION OF FAITH

By a credible profession is meant a profession of the true religion sufficiently intelligent and sufficiently corroborated by the daily life of the professor to be credited as genuine. Every such profession is ground for the presumption that the person is a member of the true Church, and consequently constitutes him a member of the visible Church and lays an obligation upon all other Christians to regard and treat him accordingly. (AAH-CF)

PROGRESSIVE REVELATION

The progressive character of divine revelation is recognized in relation to all the great doctrines of the Bible. What at first is only obscurely intimated is gradually unfolded in subsequent parts of the sacred volume until the truth is revealed in its fulness. This is true of the doctrines of redemption, the person and work of the Messiah, the nature and office of the Holy Spirit, and a future state beyond the grave. And this is especially true of the doctrine of the Trinity. (CH-STA)

PROMISES OF GOD

The attributes of the divine promises are, 1. That they are exceeding great and precious. The blessings promised are exceeding great and are such as give them value to us. 2. They are sure, a. Because spoken by God, and therefore his veracity is pledged, and his power and infinite wisdom are secured for their fulfillment. b. Because they are all yea and amen in Christ; that is, he has rendered them by his work certain, having performed the condition on which they were suspended, and having received power to carry them into effect. 3. They are immutable. (CH-CP)

PROPERTY

Every person who loves the Lord Jesus should strive, by all lawful means, to acquire something to expend in this holy cause (of missions); and no Christian ought, in this day, to think of accumulating property for any other purpose, than for the promotion of Christ's kingdom. The Master NEEDS now all that his disciples have it in their power to give. The hundreds of millions of the heathen who are perishing for lack of knowledge, call for our exertions and our liberal charities. (AA-PT)

-Believers belong to Christ

Redemption is deliverance by purchase. The redeemed become the property of the Redeemer. "Ye are not your own: for ye are bought with a price." (Believers) have no right to use their bodies, their time, or talents for themselves, at their own discretion, and for their own advantage. They belong to Christ, in the sense in which a slave belongs to his master. This right of property and the consequent right of control extends not merely to the body, but to the soul. It is the soul that has been bought. Therefore, our souls are not our own. Our reason, our conscience, our hearts, our whole rational and immortal nature, belong to Christ. He determines what we are to think, what to believe what to approve, what to condemn, what to love, and what to hate. (CH-CP)

PROPHECY

The leading events recorded in the New Testament were predicted in the Old. Of this any man can satisfy himself by a comparison of the two. The coincidence between the prophecies and the fulfillment admits of no rational solution except that the Bible is the work of God, or that holy men of old spake as they were moved by the Holy Ghost. (CH-STA)

PROPHETS

According to Scriptural usage a prophet is one who speaks for another. Any man receiving a revelation from God, or inspired in the communication of it is, in the Scriptures, called a prophet. (CH-STA)

A prophet of God is one qualified and authorized to speak for God to men. Foretelling future events is only incidental. (AAH-OT)

The fundamental note of the Old Testament is Revelation. Its seers and prophets are not men of philosophic minds who have risen from the seen to the unseen, and, by dint of much reflection, have gradually attained to elevated conceptions of him who is the author of all that is. They are men of God whom God has chosen, that he might speak to them and through them to his people. Israel has not in and by them created for itself a God. God has through them created for himself a people. (BBW-SSW)

PROTESTANTISM

Against all undue assumptions of authority, Protestants hold fast to two great principles: (1) the right of private judgment and (2) the exclusivity of the Scriptures as the infallible rule of faith and practice. (CH-STA)

PROVIDENCE OF GOD

-Its Definition

Providence literally means foresight, and then a careful arrangement prepared beforehand for the accomplishment of predetermined ends. Providence includes the two great departments (a) of the continued PRESERVATION of all things as created, and (b) of the continued GOVERNMENT of all things thus preserved, so that ALL the ends for which they were created, are infallibly accomplished. (AAH-OT)

-Its Nature

Of this providential government the Scriptures teach (1) that it is universal, including all the creatures of God and all their actions. The external world, rational and irrational creatures, things great and small, ordinary, and extraordinary, are equally and always under the control of God. (2) The Scriptures also teach that this government of God is powerful. It is the universal sway of omnipotence which renders certain the accomplishment of His designs. (3) It is wise; (4) God's providence is holy. That is, there is nothing in the ends proposed, the means adopted, or the agency employed, which is inconsistent with His infinite holiness. (CH-STA)

-Its Importance

This doctrine of providence is the foundation of all practical religion, and the denial of it is practically atheism, for we are then without God in the world. (CH-STA)

A firm faith in the universal providence of God is the solution of all earthly troubles. It is almost equally true that a clear and full apprehension of the universal providence of God is the solution of most theological problems. (BBW-SSW)

QUALIFICATIONS FOR THE CHRISTIAN MINISTRY

The only evidence of a call to any office is the possession of the qualifications. But these qualifications are various. 1st. Regeneration, which is presupposed. 2d. Intellectual qualifications, including ability, knowledge, and orthodoxy. 3d. The spiritual qualifications, including, (a) High appreciation of the importance of the office. (b) A strong desire for it from proper motive. (c) A willingness to go anywhere and to submit to everything in the discharge of its duties. (d) A sense of responsibility or obligation, so that we can say, "Woe is me if I preach not the gospel!" 4th. Bodily qualifications; good health and the necessary gifts of utterance. (CH-CP)

RATIONALISM

By rationalism is meant the system or theory which assigns undue authority to reason in matters of religion. (CH-STA)

Rationalism assumes that human intelligence is the measure of all truth. This is an insane presumption on the part of such a creature as man. (CH-STA)

The protest which our religious nature makes against the narrow, cold, and barren system of rationalism is a sufficient proof that it cannot be true, because it cannot meet our most urgent necessities. (CH-STA)

(Rationalism) proceeds on an essentially false principle. It assumes the competency of reason to judge of things entirely beyond its sphere. God has so constituted our nature that we are authorized and necessitated to confide in the well-authenticated testimony of our senses within their appropriate sphere. And in like manner, we are constrained to confide in the operation of our minds and in the conclusions to which they lead within the sphere which God has assigned to human reason. But the senses cannot sit in judgment on rational truths. We cannot study logic with the microscope or scalpel. It is no less irrational to depend upon reason or demand rational or philosophical demonstration for truths which become the objects of knowledge only as they are revealed. From the nature of the case the truths concerning creation, the probation and apostasy of man, the purpose and plan of redemption, the person of Christ, the state of the soul in the future world, the relation of God to His creatures, etc., since they depend not on general principles of reason, but in great measure on the purposes of an intelligent, personal Being can be known only so far as He chooses to reveal them and must be received simply on His authority. (CH-STA)

REASON

Let us rely on our senses within the sphere of our sense perceptions, on our reason within the sphere of rational truths, and on God, and God alone, in all that relates to the things of God. Only he who consents with the docility of a child to be taught of God truly knows. (CH-STA)

Christians, therefore, concede to reason all the prerogatives it can rightfully claim. God requires nothing irrational of His rational creatures. He does not require faith without knowledge, or faith in the impossible, or faith without evidence. Christianity is equally opposed to superstition and rationalism. (CH-STA)

This knowledge of God is the foundation of all religion; therefore, to deny that God can be known is really to deny that rational religion is possible. In other words, it makes religion a mere sentiment or blind feeling instead of its being what the apostle declares it to be. A RATIONAL SERVICE (Rom. 12:1) homage of the reason as well as of the heart and life. (CH-STA)

Paul does not depreciate reason. The senses have their sphere. Reason has its sphere. But there is a supernatural or spiritual sphere into which reason cannot enter. This conclusion is sustained by consciousness. What do you know? There lies the grave! Where does it lead to? What lies beyond it? (CH-CP)

RECONCILIATION

The core of Paul's Gospel is indeed expressed in this one word, Reconciliation; and it behooves us to consider carefully what he means by it. It is perfectly easy to see what Paul means by this reconciliation, the ministry of which he declares to be his only function. It is, shortly, not the reconciliation of man to God. but the reconciliation of God to man—a reconciliation which God has Himself undertaken and which He has accomplished at the tremendous cost of the death of His Son, on the ground of which He is able to release men from their trespasses. (BBW-TSW)

REDEMPTION

-Its Definition

In its application to the work of Christ the word redemption means deliverance by purchase. This is plain because it is a deliverance not by authority, or power, or teaching, or moral influence, but by blood, by the payment of a ransom. (CH-STA)

Redemption, in the Christian sense of the term, is deliverance through the blood of Christ from the power and consequences of sin. Christ came to save sinners. He saves none but sinners. The Bible clearly teaches that the death of Christ is necessary; had there been any other way in which men could be saved, Christ is dead in vain (Gal. 2:21; 3:21).

-Its Objects

The two great objects to be accomplished by the work of Christ are, the removal of the curse under which mankind labored on account of sin: and their restoration to the image and fellowship of God. Both these are essential to salvation. We have guilt to be removed, and souls dead in sin to be quickened with a new principle of divine life. Both these objects are provided for in the doctrine of redemption as presented in the Scriptures and held in the Church. In the opposing theories devised by theologians, either one of these objects is ignored or one is unduly subordinated to the other. (CH-STA)

-Its Two Parts

There are two distinct parts of redemption. One is referred to Christ, the other to the Spirit. Christ acts as our prophet, priest and king. The Spirit applies the redemption purchased by Christ. He convinces of sin. He renews, enlightens, sanctifies, leads, and comforts. He dwells in us and constantly works in us to will and to do. He is in us the source or principle of spiritual life. (CH-CP)

-Its Design

The end or design of the whole scheme of redemption is the praise of the glory of the grace of God, i.e., its purpose is to exhibit to the admiration of intelligent creatures the glorious attribute of divine grace, or the love of an infinitely holy and just God towards guilty and polluted sinners. (CH-STA)

-Its Evidences

Are we then redeemed? Not if we regard ourselves as our own. Not if we use our bodies, our time and talents as belonging to ourselves. Not if we seek our own glory. Not if we act in obedience to our own will. We are redeemed from the devil and hell, only if we recognize Christ as our owner; only if love to him constrains us to live to his glory and makes his will the rule of our conduct. (CH-CP)

-The Greatest Work

So far as we know, the redemption of man, i.e., delivering him from the guilt and power of sin - is the greatest work in the history of the universe - the greatest as a manifestation of the glory of God. (CH-CP)

The redemption of the world by Jesus Christ is the middle point in the history, not of our race only, but of the universe. (CH-CP)

THE REFORMATION

-And Missions

When the Reformation came, the Protestants had as much as they could do to live. They had arrayed against them everywhere the tremendous power of the Romish Church, and in most cases all the power of the State. They had to defend their doctrines against the prejudices and learning of the age; to organize their Churches, and alas! they were distracted among themselves. Under these circumstances it is not to be wondered at that the command, "Go ye into all the world, and preach the gospel to every creature" was almost forgotten. It is only within the last fifty years that the Church has been brought to feel that its great duty is the conversion of the nations. More, probably, has been done in this direction during the last half century than during the preceding five hundred years. It is to be hoped that a new effusion of the Spirit like that of the day of Pentecost may be granted to the Church whose fruits shall as far exceed those of the first effusion as the millions of Christians now alive exceed in number the one hundred and twenty souls then gathered in Jerusalem. (CH-STA)

REGENERATION

-Its Definition

The subjective change wrought in the soul by the grace of God is variously designated in Scripture. It is called a new birth, a resurrection, a new life, a renewing of the mind, a dying to sin and living to righteousness, translation from darkness to light. In theological language it is called regeneration. (CH-STA)

-Its Nature

In regeneration the Spirit does everything. In sanctification, he excites and aids and gives efficacy to the means. (CH-CP)

The soul is passive in regeneration. It is the subject and not the agent of the change. The soul cooperates or is active in what precedes and in what follows the change, but the change itself is something experienced and not something done. (CH-STA)

I have all along admitted that the mode of the Spirit's operation in regeneration is altogether inscrutable: and an attempt to explain it is worse than folly. We may, however, without intruding into things unseen, or attempting to dive into the unsearchable nature of the divine operations, say that God operates on the human mind in a way perfectly consistent with its nature, as a spirit, and a creature of understanding and will. (AA-TRE)

No believer ever ascribes his regeneration to himself. He does not regard himself as the author of the work, or his own relative goodness, his greater susceptibility to good impression, or his greater readiness of persuasion, as the reason why he rather than others is the subject of this change. He knows that it is a work of God, and that it is a work of God's free grace. (CH-STA)

RELIGION

True religion never has existed and never can exist where the truths revealed in the Bible are unknown. (CH-STA)

These principles - immutability of the divine law, the necessity of its demands being satisfied, the impossibility of sinners making that satisfaction for themselves, the possibility of its being rendered by substitution, and the accomplishment of this work in our behalf by a wonder fully constituted person—are the great constituent principles of the religion of the Bible. (CH-STA)

The religion of redeemed man is a deeper and richer religion than that of unfallen man could ever have been. The sad experiences through which he has passed; the glorious experiences into which by redemptive grace he has been brought; have not only deepened and enriched his religious nature but have also deepened and enriched the content of his religious understanding and his religious. there are aspects of the divine nature, there are whole regions of religious experience, to the apprehension and enjoyment of which only the redeemed soul has access. (BBW-SSW)

REPENTANCE

-In Salvation

What is saving repentance? It includes— 1st. A sense of personal guilt, pollution, and helplessness. 2d. An apprehension of the mercy of God in Christ. 3d. Grief and hatred of sin, a resolute turning from it unto God, and a persistent endeavor after a new life of holy obedience. (AAH-OT)

(Repentance) in a religious sense is the turning from sin unto God. When genuine it is a fruit of regeneration, and a gift of the Spirit. In the wide sense in which it is used it includes the whole process of conversion. (CH-CP)

-Distinguished from Conversion

Conversion is generally used to designate only the first actings of the new nature at the commencement of a religious life, or the first steps of a return to God after a notable backsliding (Luke 22: 32); while repentance is a daily experience of the Christian as long as the struggle with sin continues in his heart and life. Ps.9:12,13; Luke 9:23; Gal. 6:14; 5:24. (AAH-CF)

REPROOF

-Giving it

All members of the church have a duty to perform towards erring brethren. When they see them going astray, they should not act towards them as if they hated them but should rebuke them in the spirit of meekness. Christian reproof from one Christian to another seems to be almost banished from our churches. There is a quick eye to discern a brother's faults, and a ready tongue to speak of them to others; but where do we now find the faithful reprover of sin, who goes to the man himself, without saying a word to anyone, and between themselves, faithfully warns, exhorts, and entreats a straying brother to return. (AA-TRE)

This duty (reproving works of darkness-Eph. 5:11), 1. Is a difficult one. It should be performed with humility, with wisdom, with gentleness, and with a benevolent spirit, as well as with a zeal for the law and honor of God. 3. It should be done officially, by ministers in the pulpit and out of it; by private Christians, whenever the occasion calls for it; not when it is obvious that it would be useless or worse, for we are not to cast our pearls before swine. 4. It is often better done privately than publicly. (CH-CP)

-Receiving It

As concerns those who receive rebuke, (a.) That they should recognize the right and duty of their brethren to administer it. (b.) That they should receive it as coming from the Lord. (c.) That as neither the Church nor the believer, whether the rebuker or the rebuked, is perfect, imperfection in the character of the reprover, in his manner or spirit, would not justify us in resenting or resisting it. The Church is one. We should bear each other's burdens, sympathize in each other's sorrows, and endeavor to correct each other's faults. (CH-CP)

REPUTATION

Endeavor to acquire and maintain a good reputation. A good name is rather to be chosen than great riches. A ruined fortune may be recovered, a lost reputation never. (AA-TRE)

He who sacrifices reputation for present comfort buys it at too dear a rate. The merchant who, when he fails, loses his reputation for truth and integrity, will meet with but little favour from the world, and will have little chance of rising again. But he who has been unfortunate, and yet maintains his integrity and preserves his character unsullied, is often able to enter again into business under favorable auspices; and is encouraged and aided in his attempts to gain a living, by men of wealth and standing. Such a man is often successful to such a degree, that he has it in his power to compensate those from whom benefit was derived in the day of his calamity. (AA-TRE)

RESPONSIBILITY

-Moral

What are the essential conditions of moral responsibility? To be morally responsible a man must be a free, rational, moral agent. 1st. He must be in present possession of his reason to distinguish truth from falsehood. 2d. He must also have in exercise a moral sense to distinguish right from wrong. 3d. His will, in its volitions or executive acts, must be self-decided, i.e., determined buy its own spontaneous affections and desires. If any of these are wanting, the man is insane, and neither free nor responsible. (AAH-OT)

RESTITUTION

When a Christian has personally injured a brother or scandalized by his unChristian conduct the Church of Christ, he ought to be willing, by a public or a private confession to declare his repentance to those that are offended. If we have done wrong, we stand in the position of one maintaining a wrong until, by an expressed repentance and, where possible, redress of the wrong, we place ourselves on the side of the right. (AAH-CF)

RESTORATION

It is the duty of the brethren, or of the Church, when offended, to forgive the offending party and restore him fully to favour upon his repentance. As to public scandals, the Church is bound to forgive them when the Lord has done so. (AAH-CF)

RESURRECTION

-Of Christ

Not only is the resurrection of Christ asserted in the Scriptures but is also declared to be the fundamental truth of the gospel. "If Christ be not risen," says the apostle, "'Then is our preaching vain, and your faith is also vain ye are yet in your sins." (1 Cor. 15:14). Indeed, it may be safely asserted that the resurrection of Christ is the most important fact in the history of the world. CCH-STA)

It has been customary in the past to look upon the resurrection of Jesus as the very citadel of the Christian position. Friend and foe have been one in so regarding it. Upon it, as his Gibraltar, the Christian man has entrenched himself. It has seemed to him to the rock on which he could securely build the house of his faith, and upon which the rain may descend, and the floods come, and the winds blow without effect. Similarly, it has seemed to the assailants of Christianity, that so long as this rock stood unconquered all their energy was in vain. (BBW-SSW)

There are only three theories which can be possibly stated to account for these facts. Either the original disciples of Christ were deceivers and deliberately concocted the story of the Resurrection; or they were woefully deluded; or the Resurrection was a fact. (BBW-SSW)

In addition to being the most important, the resurrection of Christ is the best-authenticated fact in the history of the world: (1) It was predicted in the Old Testament. (2) It was foretold by Christ Himself. (3) It was a fact admitting of easy verification. (4) Abundant, suitable, frequently repeated evidence was afforded of its actual occurrence. (5) The witnesses to the fact that Christ was seen alive after His death upon the cross were numerous competent, and on every account worthy of confidence. (6) Their sincerity of conviction was proved by the sacrifices, even that of life, which their testimony entailed upon them. (7) Their testimony was confirmed by God bearing witness together with them in signs and wonders, and divers (various) miracles, and gifts of the Holy Ghost (Heb. 2:4). (8) The effects which His gospel has produced in the state of the world admit of no other rational solution than the truth of His death and subsequent resurrection. The Christian Church is His monument. All believers are His witnesses. (CH-STA)

-Of Believers

We should not think that the redemption and resuscitation of the body is a small matter. The body is an essential part of human nature, and the glorified body will add to the felicity of the redeemed in a degree which we have no means of calculating. The inspired writers, therefore, when speak of the blessedness of heaven, speak sparingly of the state of the separate soul; but when they describe the resurrection, they seem to be enraptured. (AA-TRE)

REVELATION

It is of utmost importance that we should not misconceive the relation between "general" and "special" revelation. This relation is not one of contrast and opposition, but rather one of supplement and completion. They do not stand as two systems, each complete, over against one another; but together they form one organic whole. (BBW-SSW)

REVIVAL OF RELIGION

-Its Definition

(Revival) is confined to a sudden change from general inattention to a general attention to religion, to those seasons in which the zeal of Christians is manifestly increased, and in which large numbers of persons are converted to God. (CH-CP)

-True or False?

The criteria for the decision between true and false revivals are the same as those for deciding between true and false religion. These are, First, their origin. Are they due to the preaching of the truth? Secondly, their character. Is the excitement humble, reverential, peaceful, benevolent, holy; or is the feeling manifested proud, censorious, malicious, denunciatory, schematical, irreverent? Thirdly, their permanent fruits. This is the only certain test. (CH-CP)

-Its Design

If God revives his people, it is that he may communicate life through them to others. It is of vast importance, therefore, to ourselves and others, that we should really draw rear to God in an effectual manner. (CH-CP)

REWARD

Men will be rewarded according to fidelity. Not according to their success, but according to their desirous effort to serve Christ. (CH-CP)

RULERS

The proximate end for which God has ordained magistrates is the promotion of the public good, and the ultimate end is the promotion of his own glory. The specific way in which the civil magistrate is to endeavor to advance the glory of God is through the promotion of the good of the community (Rom. 13:4) in temporal concerns, including education, morals, physical property, the protection of life and property, and the preservation of order. (AAH-CF)

SABBATH

-A Universal & Permanent Observance

That the Sabbath belongs to the class of universal laws, binding all men and all ages, is evident, 1. Because it was instituted before the giving of the Law. 2. Because the ground of its observance was a general ground, in which all nations were concerned. 3. Because it was predicted that it would be observed under the reign of the Messiah. 4. Because its observance has been in fact continued, by divine injunction, by the whole Christian Church. 5. It is incorporated in the decalogue. (CH-CP)

-Its Change to the Lord's Day

The reason why the seventh day was originally appointed was that it was to commemorate the work of creation. This is the foundation of all religion, and it is therefore of fundamental importance that it should be remembered. 2. The special reason for the observance of the first day was the commemoration of the resurrection of Christ, on which rested the truth of the gospel. If Christ rose, then the gospel is true. If the world was created, then there is a personal God, the maker, preserver, and ruler of the universe

No one, therefore, can overestimate the importance of the observance of the Sabbath. (CH-CP)

-Importance of Sabbath Worship

Surely, if ever there was one who might justly plead that the common worship of the community had nothing to offer him it was the Lord Jesus Christ. But every Sabbath found him seated in his place among the worshipping people, and there was no act of stated worship which he felt himself entitled to discard. Even in his most exalted moods, and after his most elevating experiences, he quietly took his place with the rest of God's people, sharing with them in the common worship of the community. "He entered, as his custom was, into the synagogue, on the Sabbath day." "As his custom was!" Jesus Christ made it his habitual practice to be found in his place on the Sabbath day as the stated place of worship to which he belonged. As Sir William Robertson Nicoll well insists, "we cannot afford to be wiser than our Lord in this matter. If anyone could have pled that his spiritual experience was so lofty that it did not require public worship, if anyone might have felt that the consecration and communion of his personal life exempted him from what ordinary mortals needed, it was Jesus. But he made no such plea. Is it reasonable, then, that any of us should think we can safely afford to dispense with the pious custom of regular participation with the common worship of our locality?" (BBW-SSW)

SACRAMENTS

-Their Design

What is the design of the sacraments? 1st. That they should signify, seal, and exhibit to those within the covenant of grace the benefits of Christs redemption and thus as a principal means of grace edify the church. Matt. 3:11; Gen. 17:11; 1 Cor. 10:2-21; 11:23-26; 12:13; Rom. 2:28; 4:11; 3:27; 1 Pet. 3:21. 2d. That they should be visible badges of membership in the church, to put a visible difference between the professed followers of Christ and the world, Gen. 34:14; Ex. 12:48; Eph. 2:19. (AAH-OT)

-And Sanctification

What efficacy do the Scriptures ascribe in this work (of sanctification) to the Sacraments? The true view is, "that the sacraments are efficacious means of gr ace, not merely exhibiting but actually conferring upon those who worthily receive them the benefits which they represent; " yet this efficacy does not reside properly in them, but accompanies their proper use in virtue of the divine institution and promise, through the accompanying agency of the Holy Ghost, and as suspended upon the exercise of faith upon the part of the recipient, which faith is at once the condition and the instrument of the reception of the benefit. —Matt. 3:11; Acts 2:41; 10:47; Rom. 6:3; 1 Cor. 12:13; Titus 3:5; 1 Pet. 3: 21. (AAH-OT)

-Source of their Power

The power or efficiency of the sacraments does not reside in the elements, in the water used in baptism or in the bread and wine used in the Lord's Supper. It is not in the sacramental actions, either in giving or in receiving the consecrated elements. Neither does the virtue or efficiency reside in or flow from the person by whom the sacraments are administered. It does not reside in his office. There is no supernatural power in the man, by virtue of his office, to render the sacraments effectual. Nor does their efficiency depend upon the character of the administrator in the sight of God, nor upon his intention, that is, his purpose to render them effectual. The efficacy of the sacraments is due solely to the blessing of Christ and the working of His Spirit. (CH-STA)

SALVATION

-And Knowledge

It is the common faith of the Christian world that, so far as adults are concerned, there is no salvation without the knowledge of Christ and faith in Him. This has ever been regarded as the ground of the obligation which rests upon the Church to preach the gospel to every creature. (CH-STA)

-And Satan's Kingdom

Man by his apostasy fell under the dominion of Satan, and his salvation consists in his being translated from Satan's kingdom into the kingdom of God's creation. (CH-STA)

-Its Condition

The knowledge of Christ and faith in Him are declared (in Scripture) to be essential to salvation. (CH-STA)

From the Scriptures, as a whole - from the New Testament and from the Old as interpreted by infallible authority in the New - we learn that the plan of salvation has always been one and the same; it has always had the same promise, the same Saviour, and the same condition. (CH-STA)

-Its Design

We certainly shall never do justice indeed to the Biblical conception of salvation taken as a whole, save by giving to that term its widest conceivable connotation. In the Biblical conception of it, we shall not be able to say it too emphatically, salvation broadens ifs beneficent reach to cover every evil that afflicts the afflicted race of man. (BBW-TSW)

SANCTIFICATION

-Its Nature

Sanctification consists in two things: first, gradual removal and destruction of the power of the principles of evil still infecting our nature; and secondly, the growth of the principle of spiritual life until it controls the thoughts, feelings, and acts and brings the soul into conformity to the image of Christ (Eph. 4:22-24). (CH-STA)

-Its Source

Sanctification does not exclude all cooperation on the part of its subjects, but, on the contrary, calls for their unremitting and strenuous exertion, it is nevertheless the work of God. It is not carried on as a mere process of moral culture by moral means; it is as truly supernatural in its method as in its nature. (CH-STA)

It must be remembered that while the subject is passive with respect to that divine act of grace whereby he is regenerated, after he is regenerated he co-operates with the Holy Ghost in the work of sanctification. The Holy Ghost gives the grace, and prompts and directs in its exercise, and the soul exercises it. Thus, while sanctification is a grace, it is also a duty. (AAH-CF)

-Not Perfection

The doctrine of Lutherans and Reformed, the two great branches of the Protestant Church, is that sanctification is never perfected in this life; sin is not in any case entirely subdued. Even the most advanced believer has need, if he continues in the flesh, to pray daily for the forgiveness of sins. (CH-STA)

-Different from Justification

There are several ways, then, in which justification differs from sanctification: (1) The former is a transient act, the latter a progressive work. (2) Justification is a forensic act, God acting as judge, declaring justice satisfied so far as the believing sinner is concerned, whereas sanctification is an effect due to divine operation. (3) Justification changes, or declares to be changed, the relation of the sinner to the justice of God; sanctification involves a change of character. (4) The former, therefore, is objective, the latter subjective. (5) The former is founded on what Christ has done for us; the latter is the effect of what He does in us. (6) Justification is complete and the same in all, while sanctification is progressive and is more complete in some than in others. (CH-STA)

SATAN

That there is one fallen angel exalted in rank and power above all his associates is clearly taught in the Bible. He is called Satan (the adversary), the traducer, the evil one, the prince of the power of the air, the prince of darkness, the god of this world, Beelzebub, Belial, the tempter, the old serpent, and the dragon. These and similar titles set him forth as the great enemy of God and man, the opposer of all that is good and the promoter of all that is evil. (CH-STA)

-His Power

1. (The Scriptures) ascribe to him great power and authority over other fallen spirits. 2. They ascribe to him power in the world and over the world. He is the god of the world. This means, a. that he controls the men of the world. b. That the aims, ends and agency of the world tend to the promotion of his kingdom. c. That this service and subjection, although unintentional and ignorantly rendered, are of the nature of homage. Paul thus teaches that idolaters are worshippers of demons. The things which they sacrifice they sacrifice to devils. 3. They ascribe to him a power over the souls of men, controlling in the children of disobedience, harassing, and impeding in the children of God. 4. That the whole power of Satan over spirits, over the world and over the souls of men, is exerted against God and his kingdom. It is exerted in promoting evil and counteracting good. In individual men, in promoting error, in blinding the mind to the truth, in fostering unbelief, in exciting evil passions, in tempting to sin, as in the cases of Judas and Ananias; and in leading to despair. (CH-CP)

With respect to the souls of men, Satan and his angels are utterly destitute of any power either to change the heart or to coerce the will, their influence being simply moral, and exercised in the way of deception, suggestion, and persuasion. (AAH-OT)

-His Temptations

About the temptations of Satan, it is certain, first, that he does tempt the children of men; all men; us as well as others. Secondly, how he does this we do not know. Thirdly, we cannot distinguish between his temptations and the suggestions of our own evil hearts, any more than we can between the leading of the Spirit and our own exercises. Fourthly, the temptations of Satan are subtle, powerful, and greatly to be dreaded; not to be despised or made light of. Most men are led captive by him at his will. (CH-CP)

If you wish to know where he will be likely to meet you, I will say, in your own room, in the church, on your bed, and in your daily intercourse with men. A single thought, which suddenly starts up in your mind will show that the enemy is near and is suggesting such thoughts as without his agency never can be accounted for. "Watch, therefore," "resist the devil, and he will flee from you. (AA-TRE)

I am much inclined to think that Satan is far less dangerous when he comes as "a roaring lion" and frightens the soul with his horrid blasphemies, than when "he transforms himself into an angel of light" and seduces our affections gradually and secretly away from God and attaches them sinfully to the world. (AA-TRE)

-His "Fiery Darts"

These (conflicts) arise from horribly wicked thoughts, blasphemous, atheistically, or abominably impure, which are injected with a power which the soul cannot resist, and sometimes continue to rise in such thick succession that the mind can scarcely be said to be ever entirely free from them. I have known persons of consistent piety (spirituality) and sound intellect who have been infested with the continual incursion of such thoughts for weeks and months together: so that they had no rest during their waking hours; and even their sleep was disturbed with frightful dreams. These may emphatically be called to "the fiery darts of the wicked one" They may be compared to balls or brands of fire cast into a house full of combustibles. The object of the enemy by such assaults is to perplex and harass the child of God, and to drive him to despair; and as many who are thus tempted are ignorant of Satan's devices, and of the "depths" of his subtlety, and charge upon themselves the fault of all these wicked thoughts, the effect aimed at does actually take place. (AA-TRE)

But it is not upon ignorant, weak, and diseased persons only that these furious assaults are made. Such a man as Luther was in frequent conflicts of this kind; and he was so persuaded that these were the temptations of the devil, that he speaks of his presence with as much confidence as if he had seen him by his side. (AA-TRE)

Sometimes, indeed, Satan injects his fiery darts, enkindled in hell, to frighten the timid soul and drive it to despair; but in this he often overshoots his mark, and drives the poor trembling soul nearer to his Captain, whose broad shield affords ample protection. (AA-TRE)

THE SAVIOR

-To be Remembered Constantly

We are to remember the hand which holds us up from Hell every moment. A man floating on the ocean might as well forget the plank which sustains him; or the man suspended over an abyss, forget the rope which holds him up, as we, to forget Christ. (CH-CP)

We cannot look back without seeing Christ. We cannot look beneath, above, or around us in the present, but he fills the whole horizon. We cannot look forward, but he is the effulgence which sheds its glory on our eternal career. To remember Christ, therefore, is all our duty, for it is to live on him, to live for him, and to live with him. (CH-CP)

SCRIPTURE

-Its Inspiration (see INSPIRATION)

-Its Unity

The several books of which the Scriptures are composed were written by many different authors living during fifteen hundred years, and yet they are found to be an organic whole, the product of one mind. They are as clearly a development as the oak from the acorn. (CH-STA)

-Its Completeness

By the completeness of the Scriptures is meant that they contain all the extant revelations of God designed to be a rule of faith and practice for the Church. It is not denied that God reveals Himself, even His eternal power and Godhead, by His works, and has done so from the beginning of the world. But all the truths thus revealed are clearly made known in His written Word. (CH-STA)

-Its Perspicuity

The Bible is a plain book. It is intelligible by the people. And they have the right and are bound to read and interpret it for themselves, so that their faith may rest on the testimony of the Scriptures and not on that of the Church. Such is the doctrine of Protestants on this subject.

It is not denied that the Scriptures contain many things hard to understand, that they require diligent study, that all men need the guidance of the Holy Spirit to come to right knowledge and true faith. But it is maintained that in all things necessary to salvation they are sufficiently plain to be understood even by the unlearned. (CH-STA)

-Its Old Testament Canon

When Christ or His apostles quote the "Scriptures," or the "law and the prophets" and speak of the volume then so called, they give their sanction to the divine authority of all the books which that volume contained. All, therefore, that is necessary to determine for Christians the canon of the Old Testament is to ascertain what books were included in the "Scriptures" recognized by the Jews of that period. This is a point about which there is no reasonable doubt. The Jewish canon of the Old Testament included all the books, and no others, which Protestants now recognize as constituting the Old Testament Scriptures. On this ground Protestants eject the so-called apocryphal books. They were not. included in the canon of the Jews. They were, therefore, not recognized by Christ as the Word of God. (CH-STA)

-Its New Testament Canon

The principle on which the canon of the New Testament is determined is equally simple. Those books, and those only, which can be proved to have been written by the apostles, or to have received their sanction, are to be recognized as of divine authority. The reason of this rule is obvious. The apostles were the duly authenticated messengers of Christ, of whom He said, "He that hear eth you heareth me. (CH-STA)

-Its Historic Nature

The books of the Old Testament were written to meet the wants of God's people before Moses, under Moses, and in the successive periods from Moses to the advent. The books of the New Testament, especially the epistles, were not written as essays or discourses but as letters to congregations to meet their historical wants. But all, both under the old and new economy, was so ordered that all truth necessary or desirable has been made known. (CH-CP)

-How It Reveals God

In what ways do the Scriptures reveal God? They reveal God 1st, by his names. 2d. By the works which they ascribe to him. 3d. By the attributes which they predicate of him. 4th. By the worship they direct to be paid to him. 5th. By the manifestation of God in Christ. (AAH-OT)

-How It is to be Studied

How are we to search the Scriptures? 1. Reverently and submissively, with the fixed determination to believe every truth which they affirm. Everything is right which they command, and everything is wrong which they condemn. We are not to sit in judgment on the Scriptures. 2. With diligence, 3. With dependence; convinced that without divine guidance we shall obtain neither right speculative knowledge, nor right spiritual views. 4. Therefore with prayer, previous and continued. 5. With self-application. (CH-CP)

-And Science

As the Bible is of God, it is certain that there can be no conflict between the teachings of the Scriptures and the facts of science. It is not with facts, but with theories, believers must contend. Many theories apparently or inconsistent with the Bible have, from time to time, been presented. But these theories have proved either to be false or to harmonize with the Word God, properly interpreted. The Church has been forced more than once to alter her interpretation of the Bible to accommodate the discoveries of science. But this has been done without doing any violence to the Scriptures or in any degree impairing their authority. (CCH-STA)

-And Reason

While (Scripture) makes known truths far above the reach of sense or reason, it reveals nothing which contradicts either. It harmonizes with our whole nature. It supplements all our other knowledge and authenticates itself by harmonizing the testimony of enlightened consciousness with the testimony of God in His Word. (CH-STA)

SECURITY OF BELIEVERS

The effect of this union to Christ, which pertains to the individual believer and to the Church as a whole, is security. No man can pluck them out of the hand of Christ. All given to him shall come to him, and he will raise them up at the last day. The gates of hell can never prevail against the Church. This security rests, 1. On the promise and covenant of God. 2. On the fact that Christ lives, and his life secures the life of the believer and of the Church. 3. On the fact that he has power in heaven and earth. 4. On the fact that he has a covenant right to the co-operation of the Holy Spirit, and because he has conquered sin and Satan. (CH-CP)

Our security is perseverance. This is often insisted on in the Scriptures. When a man is overboard, it is not the first grasp of the rope that saves him. That is essential; but it is equally essential that he hold on. So, a soldier in battle. So, the Christian. He may hold on through life but make shipwreck at the end. (CH-CP)

SEDUCTION

These Christians were exposed to the severest persecutions, and the most insidious seductions. The dire situation was analogous to that of the ancient Hebrews surrounded by their enemies, who often persecuted and allured them. The apostle strives to impress upon his readers, that their danger was the same, their crime if they forsook Christ would be greater, and their punishment far more severe. We need this caution and exhortation. A ship sailing rapidly in a smooth sea, among hidden reefs and shoals, is often in more danger than when tossed about by a hurricane in mid-ocean. In the one case all on board are secure and careless, in the other all are watchful and alert. Our danger is, 1. From within; an evil heart, not to be despised, not to be neglected, but seriously watched. 2. From the influence of the world, its avocations, its amusements, its spirit, its opinions leading to indifference, (tolerance) and infidelity. (CH-CP)

SELF CONTROL

-Mentally

Cultivate the habit of controlling your thoughts. Do not let them be governed by accident or fortuitous association. Keep the rudder always in your hand. (CH-CP)

Much of the service of Christ consists in bringing down every imagination, and every thought into subjection to his teaching, and in the inward life of the soul, as he is Lord, not of the body only, or of the outward life, but of the soul and all its states and exercises. (CH-CP)

-Physically

The body belongs to Christ, is the subject of redemption, and the temple of the Holy Spirit. It is a profanation, therefore, to make our members the instruments of unrighteousness. (CH-CP)

The service of Christ includes the regulation of our outward life in obedience to his will. It is avoiding everything in our conduct which is unholy, unjust, unkind, impure, or unbecoming our character as his servants and children. (CH-CP)

SELF DECEPTION

-In Salvation

I have often noticed how tenaciously the most profane and obstinate sinners will cleave to the hope of having been once converted if they have ever been the subjects of religious impressions. Miserable delusion! (AA-TRE)

SELF DEPENDENCE

It is by faith that the spiritual life is made to grow; and the doctrine free grace, without any mixture of human merit, is the only true object of faith. Christians are too much inclined to depend upon themselves, and not to derive their life entirely from Christ. (AA-TRE)

To be emptied of self-dependence, and to know that we need aid for every duty, and even for every good thought, is an important step in our progressing piety spirituality. (AA-TRE)

SELF DENIAL

Practice self-denial every day. Lay a wholesome restraint upon your appetites. Be not conformed to this world. Let your dress, your house, your furniture, be plain and simple, as becomes a Christian. (AA-TRE)

All acts of self-denial, the refusal to gratify the lusts of the flesh, even when natural and proper, is an assertion of the supremacy of the soul over the body and tends to strengthen its authority. (CH-CP)

SELF EXAMINATION

-Its Object

(An) object of self-examination is a knowledge of ourselves, as Christians, i.e., whether our conduct be consistent, our motives pure, and our progress in the divine life what it ought to be. This should be a daily exercise. We should call ourselves to account every day, to see we have failed. (CH-CP)

-Its Requirements

Self-examination requires, 1. A right standard of judgment. This is the word of God. 2. Self-examination requires an impartial, faithful, and attentive judge. No matter how accurate the rule, if we are partial, unfaithful, and indifferent in implying it, we shall err. 3. It requires time. There must be a day of judgment. There are set times which are especially appropriate; for example, the close of the day, sacramental occasions, any period of emergency. The great evil is, that the work is neglected because of the (lack) of a set time for it. (CH-CP)

Take more time for praying to "the Father which is in secret", and for looking into the state of your soul. Redeem an hour daily from sleep if you cannot obtain it otherwise; and as the soul's concern are apt to get out of order and more time is needed for thorough self-examination than an hour a day, set apart, not periodically but as your necessities require, days of fasting and humiliation before God. On these occasions, deal faithfully with yourself. Be in earnest to search out all your secret sins and repent of them. (AA-TRE)

SELFISHNESS

Live not merely for yourselves, but also for the good of others. Selfishness contracts the soul and hardens the heart. The man absorbed in selfish pursuits is incapable of the sweetest, noblest joys of which our nature is susceptible. (AA-TRE)

The Author of our being has ordained laws, according to which the most exquisite pleasure is connected, not with the direct pursuit of our own happiness, but with the exercise of benevolence. On this principle it is, that he who labours wholly for the benefit of others, and as it were for gets himself, is far happier than the man who makes himself the centre of 1 his affections, the sole object of all his exertions. this principle it was, that our Saviour said, "It is more blessed to give than to receive." (AA-TRE)

SELF SACRIFICE

A life of self-sacrificing unselfishness is the most divinely beautiful life that man can lead. (BBW-TSW)

-Christ's Example

(Christ) did not cultivate self, even His divine self: He took no account of self. He was led by His love for others into the world, to forget Himself in the needs of others, to sacrifice self once for all upon the altar of sympathy. Self-sacrifice brought Christ into the world. And self-sacrifice will lead us, His followers, not away from but into the midst of men. Wherever men suffer, there will we be to help. Wherever men fail, there will we be to uplift. Wherever men succeed, there will we be to rejoice. Self-sacrifice means not indifference to our times and our fellows: it means absorption in them. It means forgetfulness of self in others. It means not that we should live one life, but a thousand lives, - binding ourselves to a thousand souls by the filament of so loving a sympathy that their lives become our s. (BBW-TSW)

Our Lord took no account of Himself, only because the value of the souls of men pressed upon His heart. And following Him, we are not to consider our own things, but those of others, just because everything earthly that concerns us is as nothing compared with their eternal welfare. (BBW-TSW)

SEMI-PELAGIANISM

The two great points in dispute between the Augustinians and Semi-Pelagians were decided in favour of the former. Those points were (1.) That original sin, or the corruption of nature derived from Adam, was not simply a weakening of our power for good, but was spiritual death; really sin, incapacitating the soul for any spiritual good. And (2.) That in the work of conversion it is not man that begins, but the Spirit of God. The sinner has no power to turn himself unto God but is turned or renewed by divine grace before he can do anything spiritually good. (CH-STA)

SENSUALITY

Another danger against which you must be watchful is pleasure - sensual pleasure. Worldly amusements, however innocent they may appear, are replete with hidden dangers. These scenes exhilarate the spirits, and excite the imagination, until reason and conscience are hushed, and the real end of living is forgotten. For the sake of pleasure, everything important and sacred is neglected, and the most valuable part of human life is wasted in unprofitable engagements. (AA-TRE)

SEPARATION FROM THE WORLD

Those who identify themselves with the world, who are not distinguishable from it in their spirit, their pursuits, their principles of action, their mode of living, will undoubtedly perish with the world. If not separated from it here, they will not be separated from it hereafter. (CH-CP)

SERVANTS OF CHRIST

Remember that you serve a living, not a dead Christ. You are to trust in His blood. In it alone have you life. But you are to remember that He was not broken by death, but broke death; and having purchased you to Himself by His blood, now rules over your souls from His heavenly throne. He is your master whom you are to obey. He has given you commandment to bring all peoples to the knowledge of Him. And He has promised to be with you, even to the end of the world. Live with Him. Keep fast hold upon Him; be in complete touch with Him. Let your hearts dwell with Him in the heavenly places, that the arm of His strength may be with you in your earthly toil. Let this be that by which all men know you: that in good report and in bad, in life and in death, in the great and in the small affairs of life - in everything you do down to the minutest acts of your everyday affairs - you are the servants of the Lord Christ. So will you be truly His disciples, and so will He be your Savior - unto the uttermost. (BBW-TSW)

SERVICE

-Acceptable to God

It is only in loving Christ that we love God, in glorifying Christ that we can glorify God, and in serving Christ that we can serve God. (CH-CP)

All service render ed for a wrong object, from a bad motive, or in the abuse of a right frame of mind is an abomination to God. First, as a God of truth, because the service professes one thing, and the one who renders it professes another. Or what he does is of the nature of a lie, and of a lie to the God of truth. Second, as a God of holiness. Such hypocritical, insincere service is in its own nature offensive. (CH-CP)

SHEEP

-Humans better than

"How much better," our Savior exclaims, "is a man than a sheep!" But why, we may ask, is a man better than sheep? Precisely what is it in man which distinguishes him from all the other creatures which inhabit the world with him, and raises him above them all? There are two endowments of human nature which separate it fundamentally from all other earthly natures and form the foundations of its immeasurable superiority to them. Man is endowed as no other creature is, with an irresistible sense of dependence and an ineradicable sense of obligation. It is because man is conscious of his dependence that he is a religious being. And it is because he is conscious of his obligation that he is a moral being. And it is precisely in these two characteristics—that he is a religious and that he is a moral being—that the superior it to other earthly creatures consists of. (BBW-SSW)

SIN

-Its Description

Herein is sin: that we are not like God. As the opposite of reason is unreason, the opposite of wisdom is folly, and the opposite of good is evil, so the opposite of the divine holiness is sin. (CH-STA)

Anything less than loving God constantly with all the heart, all the soul, all the mind, and all the strength, and our neighbors as ourselves, is sin. (CH-STA)

The scriptural idea of sin is the (lack) of conformity of any act, state or feeling with the law of God. This assumes: That not merely the omission of required acts, but the absence of required states, any (lack) of conformity to the law of God is sin, the (lack) of zeal, of faith, of gratitude, of love. The standard is absolute perfection. Any and every thing short of it is sin. This is the testimony of God's Word, as also of reason and conscience. (CH-CP)

Sin is not (just) an act but a power, a principle, something innate, indwelling, permanent and active, an enemy of the most dangerous kind, not only because it is within and ever on the alert and powerful, and has so many allies, but also because it is so treacherous. (CH-CP)

-Its Elements

Sin includes guilt and pollution; the one expresses its relation to the justice, the other to the holiness of God. These two elements of sin are revealed in the conscience of every sinner. He knows himself to be liable to the justice of God and offensive in His holy eyes. (CH-STA)

-Its Representation

Sin is always represented in Scripture as a very great evil, - as degrading the soul, as producing all separating us from God, as justly deserving his very great misery, his wrath and curse. (CH-CP)

-And the Law

(Sin) has relation to law. As moral and rational beings we are of necessity subject to the law of right. This is included in the consciousness of obligation. The word ought would otherwise have no meaning. To say we ought to be to say that we are bound, that we are under author Is to that we are bound, that we are under authority of some kind. Sin is related to law, and law is not one of our own enacting. It is not mere idea or abstraction, it is not mere truth or reason, or the moral order of the universe, but the nature and will of God. (CH-STA)

-And God's Decrees

Sin according to the Scriptures, is permitted so that the justice of God may be known in its punishment, and His grace in its forgiveness. And the universe, without the knowledge of these attributes, would be like the earth without the light of the sun. (CH-STA)

-And God's Providence

About the sinful acts of men, the Scriptures teach (1) that they are so under the control of God that they can occur only by His permission and in execution of His purposes. (2) The Scriptures teach that the wickedness of men is restrained within certain bounds: "Surely the wrath of man shall praise thee: the remainder of wrath shalt thou restrain" (Ps. 76: 10). (3) Wicked actions are overruled for good. The wicked conduct of Joseph's brethren, the obstinacy and disobedience of Pharoah, and above all, the crucifixion of Christ, the persecutions of the Church, the revolutions, and wars among the nations, have been all so overruled by God as to fulfil His wise and merciful designs. (4) The Scriptures teach that God's providence in relation to the sins of men is such that the sinfulness thereof proceedeth only from the creature and not from God, who neither is nor can be the author or approver of sin. (CH-STA)

-And God's Holiness

We know that sin and misery exist in the world, and we know that God is infinite in power, holiness, and benevolence. But how to reconcile the prevalence of sin with the character of God we know not. (CH-STA)

-Its Consequences

Such is the nature of God, and such the relation which He sustains to His moral creatures, that sin, the transgression of the divine law, must involve the destruction of the fellowship between man and his creator, and the manifestation of the divine displeasure. The apostle therefore says that he who offends in one point, who breaks one precept of the law of God, is guilty of the whole. (CH-STA)

Sin is a burden and a torment; although it is loved and cherished as the cups of the drunkard are cherished, it would cease to reign in any rational creature if emancipation could be affected by an act of the will. There is no truth, then, of which men are more intimately convinced than that they are the slaves of sin, that they cannot alter their char acter at will. (CH-STA)

-Our Hatred of

No man has any right to presume that he hates sin in general unless he practically hates every sin in particular; and no man has any right to presume that he is sorry for and ready to renounce his own sins in general unless he is conscious of practically renouncing and grieving for each sin into which he falls. (AAH-CF)

-Or God to be Chosen

We must choose between sin and God. If we cherish or indulge sin, we renounce God. If we take God as our portion, we renounce sin. (CH-CP)

SINGING

The singing or music of the Church should be conducted on the following principles. 1st. On the principle that it is a means and not an end. Whenever the singing or music is so elaborate as to distract attention from God to itself, it is subversive of the end designed, and productive of evil. This is a common evil in the Greek, Latin, and often in Protestant churches. 2d. It should be as excellent, with the limitations specified, as possible, because it answers its end in proportion to its excellence and exalts and refines the people. 3d. It should be appropriate, i.e., not martial nor festive, but devotional music. 4th. It should be so conducted as to secure the co-operation of the people. This is their right, and it is a great good to them. (CH-CP)

SINGLEMINDEDNESS

Another thing which prevents growth in grace is that Christians do not make their obedience to Christ comprehend every other object of pursuit. Their religion is too much a separate thing, and they pursue their worldly business in another spirit. They try to unite the service of God and Mammon (money). Their minds are divided, and often distracted with earthly cares and desires which interfere with the service of God; whereas they should have but one object of pursuit, and all that they do and seek should be in subordination to this. Everything should be done for God and to God. (AA-TRE)

SINNERS

So, the sinner until reconciled to God is a sinner in all he does, whether his acts are in themselves indifferent, or in themselves right; whether they be acts of justice, benevolence, or religion. They are the acts of a sinner, and offensive to God. (CH-CP)

SOLDIERS OF CHRIST

The Christian is a soldier and must expect to encounter enemies, and to engage in many a severe conflict. The young convert may well be likened to a raw recruit just enlisted. He feels joyous and strong, full of hope and full of courage. When the veteran Christian warns him of coming dangers and formidable enemies, and endeavors to impress on his mind a sense of his weakness and helplessness without divine aid, he does not understand what he says. He apprehends no dangers or enemies which he is not ready to face and is ready to think that the aged disciples with whom he converses have been deficient in courage and skill or have met with obstacles which are now removed out of the way. (AA-TRE)

The Christian is called a soldier, and so is the minister. What does Paul mean to teach concerning the ministerial office, in calling ministers soldiers? 1. That the work in which they are engaged is an arduous one, calling for the exertion of all their powers. They have many enemies to overcome, within and without. Within, a. Sloth. b. Languor. c. (Lack) of faith. d. Despondency. e. Desire of ease. f. Desire of fame. g. Love of money, love of power. Without, a. Error. b. Infidelity. c. Disregard of the truth. d. Ignorance. e. Vice in all its forms. f. Malice and detraction. g. Satan and his emissaries. The work is not only arduous because of opponents to overcome, but also because of the work to be done. 2. Paul means to teach that his work demands a man's whole time and strength. 3. Paul teaches that the minister, in the discharge of his duties, is to exhibit all soldierly qualities. 4. Paul teaches that the minister, like the soldier, should be animated by a spirit of loyalty. The proper motive in a soldier is loyalty to his sovereign or to his country. So, in the case of the minister, loyalty to Christ, zeal for his glory, love for his person, the desire to establish and extend his kingdom, because it is his, is the distinctive and proper motive. (CH-CP)

SONSHIP

The general idea of sonship is participation of nature. In this sense Christ is, the Son of God. In this sense Adam and all mankind are God's children. And in this sense, the regenerated, who are brought to be partakers of God's nature, are specially his children. They are renewed after the image of God in knowledge, righteousness, and holiness. (CH-CP)

SORROW

The Christian has abundant cause to be habitually joyful; reasons which cannot be duly and believingly apprehended without producing joy. Sadness, therefore, is the fruit and evidence of unbelief, as spiritual joy is the fruit and evidence of faith. It is unnatural and wrong, unbelieving, and ungrateful for those who have all these sources of joy to be habitually sad and desponding. Nothing is more difficult to bear than for a father to see a child, surrounded by everything necessary to render him happy, habitually, and causelessly miserable. (CH-CP)

THE SOUL'S WORTH

If we compare the soul to anything else, the world and all it contains, we see the two do not admit of comparison. The one is infinitely less than the other. The relation of a grain of sand to the material universe, of an insect to all animated nature, of a new-born infant to the whole intelligent creation, or a single moment of pleasure, a draught of cold water to a long life of the highest blessedness, fail utterly to indicate the disparity between the value of our souls to us, and all other things. (CH-CP)

(The soul's) inherent value, as determined by its capacities, by what it can know, enjoy, or suffer, and by what it effects, is above all estimate. By this standard it is more valuable than all the irrational creatures combined. Less would be lost if a material globe, teeming with animal and vegetable life, should be blotted out, than if a single soul should perish. (CH-CP)

SPEECH

"Govern your tongue." More sin, it is probable, is committed, and more mischief done, by this small member, than in all other ways. The faculty of speech is one of our most useful endowments, but it is exceedingly liable to abuse. He who knows how to bridle his tongue is, therefore, in Scripture, denominated "a perfect man" (AA-TRE)

SPIRIT

By Spirit we mean the subject to which the attributes of intelligence, feeling, and will belong, as active properties. Where these unite there is distinct personality. (AAH-CF)

SPIRITUALITY

Constant effort to advance in piety (spirituality) is the only way to avoid declining, and declension leads to apostasy. (CH-CP)

STABILITY

Truth is permanent, error is changeable, and therefore in every department, unless a man's views are correct, there is no security for his stability. (CH-CP)

The only stable foundation is the Bible; the firm conviction that the Bible is the word of God, that what it teaches is true infallibly. The only ground of faith, which is stable, is the witness of the Spirit. True experimental religion is the only security against error, and the only security for stability. (CH-CP)

STRENGTH

In relation to the divine life, and to the duties therewith connected, is Christ our strength. He is the source from which that life is derived. It is sustained by him, and from him come the daily supplies needed for our daily duties. The strength to believe, the strength to understand. the strength to obey, the strength to resist temptation, the strength to bear afflictions, comes from Christ only. Paul said that of himself he could do nothing, but through Christ strengthening him, he could do all things. No limits can be assigned to this divine strength. History is filled with examples of men, weak in intellect, weak in character, feeble of purpose, who have been transformed into heroes by the power of Christ. They have subdued kingdoms, stopped the mouth of lions, put to fight the armies of the aliens. (CH-CP)

Paul bids Timothy during all besetting perplexities and dangers which encompassed him to strengthen his heart by bear ing constantly in remembrance. Jesus Christ conceived specifically as the Lord of the Universe, who has been dead, but now lives again and abides forever in the power of an endless life as the royal seed of David ascended in triumph to His eternal throne. (BBW-TSW)

STUDENTS OF THEOLOGY

Whatever you may have done in the past, for the future make all your theological studies "religious exercises." This is the great rule for a rich and wholesome religious life in a theological student. Put your heart into your studies; do not merely occupy your mind with them but put your heart into them. They bring you daily and hourly into the very presence of God; his ways, his dealing with men, the infinite majesty of his Being form their very subject matter. Put the shoes from off your feet in this holy presence! (BBW-SSW)

We are frequently told, indeed, that the great danger of the theological student lies precisely in his constant contact with divine things. They may come to seem common to him because they are customary. The words which tell you of God's terrible majesty or of his glorious goodness may come to be mere words to you—Hebrew and Greek words, with etymologies, and inflections, and connections in sentences. (BBW-SSW)

Are you, by this constant contact with divine things, growing in holiness, becoming every day more and more men of God? If not, you are hardening! And I am here today to warn you to take seriously ly your theological study, not merely as a duty, done for God's sake and therefore made divine, but as a religious exercise, itself charged with religious blessing to you as fitted by its very nature to fill all your mind and heart and soul and life with divine thoughts and feelings and aspirations and achievements. You will never prosper in your religious life in the Theological Seminary until your work in the Theological Seminary becomes itself to you a religious exercise out of which you draw everyday enlargement of heart, elevation of spirit, and adoring delight in your Maker and your Savior. (AA-TRE)

SUBMISSION TO GOD

Our whole happiness and well-being depend on our submitting ourselves to God. If we are in harmony with him, with his will and purposes, and allow him to execute his plan, and rejoice in the sovereignty of his will, then all things will work together for our good, and the end to which infinite wisdom and love conducts all things, will include our supreme and everlasting blessedness. If we submit our reason to his teaching we shall be preserved from all fatal and hurtful error and guided more and more into the knowledge of the truth. (CH-CP)

Submission is the practical recognition of the rightful authority of God over us as our sovereign. Our relation to God requires that our submission to him should be absolute, without reserve, without hesitation, and without limitation. (CH-CP)

God's word is the great storehouse of truth. To that and to all it contains we are to submit. (CH-CP)

SUFFERING

Learn from Christ how you ought to suffer. Let perfect submission to the will of God be aimed at. Never indulge a murmuring or discontented spirit. Repose with confidence on the promises. Commit all your cares to God. Become familiar with death and the grave. Wait patiently until your change comes; but desire not to live a day longer than may be for the glory of God. (AA-TRE)

TAKING OFFENSE

The quickness to resent an injury or insult is in proportion to the value we set upon ourselves. If, therefore, we are truly humble, if we are conscious of our vileness and unworthiness in the sight of God, we shall be little disposed to be offended when others manifest towards us a (lack) of respect or of kind feelings. We shall know in our hearts that we little deserve the respect or affection of any human being. (CH-CP)

The question is, what is our duty in reference to personal offenses? 1. We should not cherish any malignant or revengeful feelings towards those who injure us. 2. We should not retaliate, or avenge ourselves on our offenders. If the offense is of such a nature that the interests of society or of the Church require it to be punished, it is right in us to desire such punishment. 3. We should cherish towards those who offend us, the feelings of kindness, regarding them with that benevolence which forbids our wishing them any harm. 4. We should treat them in our outward conduct with kindness, returning good for evil, and acting towards them as though they had not injured us. (CH-CP)

TALENTS

What are talents? All our physical and mental gifts, all our attainments, all our influence, all our time, everything capable of being used in his service are talents. (CH-CP)

TEMPERAMENT

The fact is undeniable that there is a constitutional difference among men in this respect. Some dispositions are cheerful; others are sad or desponding. Some are inclined to be hopeful; others are always anticipating evil. So, some men are contemplative, others active. Some amiable; others morose. The natural temperament is not changed by regeneration. The same disposition, when natural, which characterized the man before conversion, or as a natural man, characterizes his religious exercises. This is the case unless the measure of divine grace be so great as to infuse, as it were, a new nature as well as a new heart into the soul of the convert. (CH-CP)

TEMPLE OF GOD

1. We should reverence ourselves. The temple of God was holy. It could not be profaned with impunity. If we are the temple of Christ, we should keep our hearts pure from all defilement of error, suspicion, or sin. 2. We should reverence our fellow Christians, from the highest to the lowest, as we reverence the temple of God. We should dread polluting their minds by error or evil. God will destroy those who defile his temple. (CH-CP)

TEMPTATION

-How to Resist

We should thus imitate him, in his manner of resisting temptation. 1. He never placed himself in danger. He refused to tempt God. 2. He resisted the first suggestions of evil. 3. He appealed to the authority of the Scriptures or used them as the sword of the Spirit. (CH-CP)

Watch and pray lest ye fall into temptation. Exercise the utmost care against the occasions and the beginnings of evil, and constantly look to God to protect you from being tempted, and to deliver you when temptation comes. He has taught us to say daily, Lead us not into temptation. (CH-CP)

-Uses of temptation

1. They teach us our weakness and reveal the depravity that is within us. 2. They teach us to depend on God. 3. They exercise and strengthen our graces. 4. They qualify us to sympathize with others and to aid them. (CH-CP)

TEN COMMANDMENTS

The Ten Commandments teach love to God and to man; and on these, the Saviour said, hang all the Law and Prophets. Matt. 22:37-40. These commandments were originally written by the finger of God himself on two tables of stone. The first four relate to the duties man owes to God, and the remaining six relate to the duties we owe to our fellowmen. (AAH-CF)

TESTIMONIES

-Not Adequate Ground for Faith

To make the testimony of others to the truth of Christianity the ground of faith, is inadmissible, for two obvious reasons. In the first place it is not sufficiently extensive. The obligation to believe rests on multitudes to whom that testimony is not addressed. In the second place, it is entirely inadequate. The great mass of men cannot be required to believe, on the testimony of the learned few, a religion which is to control their conduct in this world, and to decide their destiny in the next. Besides, learned men testify on behalf of the Koran as well as in favour of the Bible. That, therefore, cannot be an adequate ground of faith, which may be urged in support of error as well as of truth. (CH-WL)

-Effective Means of Helping Others

Religious conversation, in which Christians confidently tell of the dealings of God with their own souls, has been often a powerful means of quickening the sluggish soul, and communicating comfort. It is in many cases a great consolation to the desponding believer to know that his case is not entirely singular; and if a traveler can meet with one who has been over the difficult parts of the road before him, he may surely derive from his experience some salutary counsel and warning. (AA-TRE)

THEOLOGIANS

The office of the theologian is simply to ascertain, arrange and vindicate the truth as taught in the word of God. (CH-CP)

(The theologian) should remember that his business is not to set forth his system of truth (that is of no account), but to ascertain and exhibit what is God's system, which is a matter of the greatest moment. Complete havoc will be made of the whole system of revealed truth unless we consent to derive our philosophy from the Bible instead of explaining the Bible by our philosophy. (CH-STA)

It is important that the theologian know his place. He is not master of the situation. He can no more construct a system of theology to suit his fancy than the astronomer can adjust the mechanism of the heavens according to his own good pleasure. As the facts of astronomy arrange themselves in a certain order and will admit of no other, so it is with the facts of theology. Theology, therefore, is the exhibition of the facts of Scripture in their proper order and relation, with the principles or general truths which pervade and harmonize the facts themselves. (CH-STA)

If the office of the theologian, as is proper order truths which (CH-STA) as is so generally admitted, to take the facts of Scripture as the man of science does those of nature, and found upon them his doctrines, instead of deducing his doctrines from the principles or primary truths of his philosophy, it seems impossible to resist the conclusion that the doctrine of Augustine is the doctrine of the Bible. (CH-STA)

THEOLOGY

-Centered on Jesus Christ

All my theology is reduced to this narrow compass, JESUS CHRIST came into the world to save sinners. (AA-PT, Spoken on his death bed to his family).

-Its Proper Sphere

It must be remembered that theology is not philosophy. It does not assume to discover truth or to reconcile what it teaches as true with all other truths. Its province is simply to state what God has revealed in His Word and to vindicate those statements as far as possible from misconceptions and objections. (CH-STA)

The astronomer, the geologist, and the zoologist very soon discover that the facts of their several sciences stand in a certain relation to each other and admit of no other. If this relation is not recognized, the facts themselves will be denied or distorted. The only source of mistake is either an incomplete induction of the facts or a failure to allow them their due relative importance. One system of astronomy has given place to another only because the earlier astronomers were not acquainted with facts which their successors discovered. The same. to a greater or lesser extent, is true of all departments of natural science. It must be no less true in theology. What the facts of nature are to the (scientist), the facts of the Bible are to the theologian. It is true here, as in natural science, that it is only by an imperfect induction of facts, or by denying or perverting them, that their relative position in the scheme of salvation can be a matter of doubt or of diversity of opinion. (CH-STA)

THEORIES

-Different from Facts

There is a great distinction between theories and facts. Theories are of men. Facts are of God. The Bible often contradicts the former, never the latter. (CH-STA)

-Of Darwinian Evolution

(This theory) is a mere hypothesis incapable of proof. From the nature of the case, what concerns the origin of things cannot be known except by supernatural revelation. All else must be speculation and conjecture. (CH-STA)

The theory in question cannot be true because it is founded on the assumption of an impossibility. It assumes that matter does the work of mind. The doctrine of Darwin is that a primordial germ, with no "inherent intelligence, has developed, under purely natural influences, into all the infinite variety of vegetable and animal organisms with all their complicated relations to each other and to the world ar ound them. Not only does he assert that all this is due to natural causes and that the lower impulses of vegetable life pass by insensible gradations into the instinct of animals and the higher intelligence of man, but he also argues against the intervention of mind anywhere in the process. God, says Darwin, created the unintelligent living cell; after that first step, all else has followed by natural law, without purpose and without design. Whoever believes this can also believe that all the works of art, literature, and science in the world are the products of carbonic acid, water, and ammonia. (CH-STA)

Ordinary men reject this Darwinian theory with indignation as well as with decision not only because it calls upon them to accept the possible as demonstrably true, but because it ascribes to blind, unintelligent causes the wonders of purpose and design which the world everywhere exhibits, and because it effectually banishes God from His works. (CH-STA)

THINGS INDIFFERENT

About things indifferent, the rule laid down by the Scriptures is, that one man should not judge another, but determine for himself what is, and what is not injurious to his spiritual interests. Another rule is that we are bound to avoid things in themselves indifferent, even though harmless to ourselves, which are injurious to others. (CH-CP)

Nothing indifferent can be a proper ground of church discipline, or a condition of Church fellowship. (CH-CP)

TIME

The flow of time is ceaseless. It waits for no man. It is irrevocable. The past is gone forever. (CH-CP)

Take care of the minutes and the hours will take of themselves. Gather up the fragments. (CH-CP)

Think frequently and seriously on the inestimable value of time. Never forget that all that is dear and worthy of pursuit must be accomplished in that short span of time allotted to us here. (AA-TRE)

All the works of man must be performed in time, and whatever acquisition is made of any good, it must be obtained in time. Time, therefore, is not only short, but precious. (AA-TRE)

Life is short and uncertain. To act as though it were indefinitely long, or as though the possession of it was secure, is folly. This is a folly of which most men' are guilty, and to which all men are exposed. We are ourselves sensible how little we lay to heart the brevity and uncertainty of life. How much we live as though we should live always. At twenty or thirty we live and feel as to life's continuance as we did at ten or fifteen. At fifty or seventy, it is all the same. We live in the present, and the present is as real at one age as at another. It requires an effort, therefore, to bring this truth home to our minds, so that it shall really affect and control our lives. (CH-CP)

TONGUE

Permit me to suggest the following brief rules for the government of the tongue. Avoid loquacity (excessive speech) In the multitude of words there wanteth (lacks) not sin. If you have nothing to communicate which can be useful, be silent. Think before you speak. How many painful anxieties would be prevented by obeying this simple, common-sense precept. Especially, be cautious about uttering anything in the form of a promise, without consideration. Be conscientiously regardful of truth, even to a tittle, in all that you say. Never speak what will be likely to excite bad feelings of any kind in the minds of others. (AA-TRE)

TOTAL ABSTINENCE

Beware of the least approach towards the gulf of intemperance. On that slippery ground, many strong men have fallen, never to rise. The trophies of this insidious and destructive vice are widely spread on every side, and the wise and the good have conclude that there is no effectual security against the enemy, but in a resolute and persevering abstinence from inebriating drink. (AA-TRE)

TRANSLATION OF THE SCRIPTURES

The Bible was not so conceived as the Christians' book that they desired to keep it to themselves. Rather, reading it themselves thus diligently, they wished everyone else to read it, too. Finding it the source of life for themselves they ardently desired that others also should drink at its inexhaustible fountains. The missionary- value of the Bible was well understood. Its translation into other languages, Augustine, for example, looks upon as essentially a missionary act: God had given it originally in Greek only as an ad interim provision—the Greek Bible was merely the central reservoir whence it should flow out in translation to all the world. And nothing was closer to the hearts of Christians than that the beaten among whom they lived should be induced to read the Bible. (BBW-SSW)

TRIBULATION

It is a striking peculiarity in the religion of Christ, that in the conditions of discipleship, "taking up the cross" is the first thing. He never tempted any to follow Him with the promise of earthly prosperity, or exemption from suffering. On the contrary, He does indeed, promise to those who forsake father and mother, wife and children, brothers and sisters, houses and lands, a compensation of a hundredfold more than they had left, but He permits them not to fall into the delusion that this hundredfold was to consist in earthly good things, for He immediately adds, "WITH PERSECUTIONS". (AA-TRE)

All the tribulations which are suffered by the justified believer in this life are chastisements, designed for his benefit, and expressive of his heavenly Father's love—not penal evils, expressive of his wrath and unsatisfied justice. (AAH-CF)

TRINITY

-Its Elements

The unity of the divine Being; the true and equal divinity of the Father, Son, and Spirit; their distinct personality; and the relation in which they stand to one another, to the Church, and to the world, are not presented in a doctrinal formula in the Word of God; but the several constituent elements of the doctrine are asserted or assumed over and over from the beginning to the end of the Bible. (CH-STA)

-Its Importance

The doctrine of the Trinity is everywhere recognized as the foundation of religion. The Father elects, the Son redeems, the Spirit sanctifies. (CH-CP)

-A Practical Doctrine

It is a great mistake to regard that doctrine as a mere speculative or abstract truth which is of no practical concern to us or which we are required to believe simply because it is revealed. On the contrary, this doctrine concerning the constitution of the Godhead underlies the whole plan of salvation and determines the character of the religion of all true Christians. This judgment is only the expression of the deep conviction that anti-Trinitarians must adopt a radically different system of religion from that on which the Church builds her hopes. (CH-STA)

-Designed by God to be Constantly Remembered

In the formulas of baptism and of the apostolic benediction, provision was made to keep this doctrine constantly before the minds of the people. Every Christian is baptized in the name of the Father, of the Son, and of the Holy Ghost. The personality, the divinity, and consequently the equality of these three subjects are here taken for granted. (CH-STA)

-Distinct Personalities

The Scriptural facts are: (a) the Father says I; the Son says I; the Spirit says I; (b) the Father God says Thou to the Son, and the Son says Thou to the Father, and in like manner the Father and the Son use the pronouns He and Him in reference to the Spirit; (c) the Father loves the Son, the Son loves the Father, the Spirit testifies of the Son. The Father, Son, and Spirit are severally subject and object. They act and are acted upon or are the objects of action. Nothing is added to these facts when it is said the Father, Son, and Spirit are distinct persons; for a person is an intelligent subject who can say I, who can be addressed as Thou, and who can act and can be the object of action. (CH-STA)

When we say they are distinct persons we do not mean that one is as separate from the other as one human person is from every other. (AAH-CF)

-And Redemption

The Scriptures clearly teach that the several persons of the Trinity are engaged in the work of man's redemption. To the Father are referred the plan itself, the selection of its objects, and the mission of the Son to carry the gracious purpose into effect. To the Son, the accomplishment of all that is requisite to render the salvation of sinful men consistent with the perfections and law of God, and to secure the final redemption of those given to Him by the Father. The special work of the Spirit is the application of the redemption purchased by Christ. (CH-STA)

TROUBLE

Was not God's providence over all, could trouble come without his sending, were Christians the possible prey of this or the other fiendish enemy, when perchance God was musing, or gone aside, or on a journey, or sleeping, what certainty of hope could be ours? "Does God send trouble?" Surely, surely. He and he only. To the sinner in punishment, to his children in chastisement. To suggest that it does not always come from his hands is to take away all our comfort. (BBW-TSW)

TRUTH

-Defined

By truth is meant that which sustains, which answers expectation; which never disappoints; which is and is ever found to be consistent with reality. Falsehood and error, on the other hand, is that which is empty, vain; which does not sustain; which disappoints; which does not correspond with the real. (CH-CP)

-And God's Word

The proposition, "Thy word is truth" is equivalent to, the Scriptures are true; all they teach concerning God, man, his character, and his relation to God, concerning the person and work of Christ, the plan of salvation, the future life, and the future state of the Church, is true. Everything conforms to what is real. Everything may be confidently relied upon. Nothing will ever disappoint legitimate expectation. Those who assume the Scriptures to be true and act upon them will attain there they promise. Those who assume that what they teach is false and act, accordingly, will find their mistake. (CH-CP)

-All from God

God is then author o ur nature and the maker of heaven and ear th; therefore, nothing which the laws of our nature or the facts of the external world prove to be true can contradict the teaching of God's Word. Neither can the Scriptures contradict the truths of philosophy or science. (CH-STA)

We must not, then, as Christians assume an attitude of antagonism toward the truths of reason, or the truths of philosophy, or the truths of science, or the truths of history, or the truths of criticism. As children of light, we must be careful to keep ourselves open to every ray of light. If it is light, its source must be sought in him who is true Light; if it is truth, it belongs of right to him who is the plenitude of truth. (BBW-TSW)

Let us, then, cultivate an attitude of courage as over against the investigations of the day. None should be more zealous in them than we. None should be quicker to discern truth in every field, more hospitable to receive it, more loyal to follow it whithersoever it leads. It is not for Christians to be lukewarm regarding the investigations and discoveries of the time. Rather, the followers of the Truth indeed have no safety, in science or in philosophy, save in the arms of truth. It is for us, therefore, as Christians, to push investigation to the utmost; to be leaders in every science; to stand in the van of criticism; to be the first to catch in every field the voice of the Revealer of truth, who is also our Redeemer. The curse of the Church has been her apathy to truth, in which she has too often left to her enemies that Study of nature and of history and philosophy, and even that investigation of her own peculiar treasures, the Scriptures of God. (BBW-TSW)

-And Christ

. Since Jesus Christ our Lord, Founder of our religion, was the very incarnation of truth, no truth can be antagonistic to the religion which he founded. (BBW-TSW)

-And Salvation

Without holiness, no man can see God, and without truth there can be no believers. Our own salvation and that of others depends on the truth. Look at the heathen world and those once Christian countries which have lost the truth. (CH-CP)

-And Doctrine

In the Church Christianity has always been regarded as a system of doctrine. Those who believe these doctrines are Christians; those who reject them, are, in the judgment of the Church, infidels or heretics. If our faith be formal or speculative, so is our Christianity; if it be spiritual and living, so is our religion. But no mistake can be greater than to divorce religion from truth and make Christianity a spirit or life distinct from the doctrines which the Scriptures present as the objects of faith. (CH-STA)

-Importance of Retaining the Scriptural Forms of Expression

It is of great importance that the Scriptural form of presenting truth be retained. Rationalism was introduced into the Church under the guise of a philosophical statement of the truths of the Bible free from the outward form in which the sacred writers, trained in Judaism, had presented them. Thus, by the theory of accommodation, every distinctive doctrine of the Scriptures was set aside, and Christianity reduced to deism. It is, therefore, far more than a mere matter of method that is involved in adhering to the Scriptural form of presenting Scriptural truths. (CH-STA)

UNION WITH CHRIST

The relation both of the Church and of the believer to Christ is not an external one, but an internal and vital one. It is not by outward profession, nor be external rites that this relation is consummated or preserved, but by a living faith and the indwelling of the Spirit; and consequently, no individual man, and no body of men have a right to be regarded, treated, or obeyed as a part of the Church catholic, except so far as he or they give evidence of this real union with Christ. (CH-CP)

UNITY OF BELIEVERS

They love what God loves; they hate what God hates. They love those whom God loves, and so far as their character is concerned, they hate those whom God hates. The friends of God are their friends. This is the ground of the unity of communion between Christians, and why they love each other as brethren. (CH-CP)

In a word, the unity of the apostolic churches was grounded on the one thing they had in common—their common Christianity. Its bond was the common reception of the Holy Spirit, which exhibited itself in one calling, one faith, one baptism. And as the existence of no other foundation for unity is traceable in the history of the churches, so the duty of seeking no other mode of unity than would be built on this foundation is pressed on their consciences by either the Lord or his apostles. (BBW-SSW)

Nor is the unity, for which he prayed in his High Priestly prayer, one grounded on external organization, but one grounded in communion with him. (BBW-SSW)

UNITY OF MANKIND

Wherever we meet a man, no matter of what name or nation, we not only find that he has the same nature with ourselves; that he has the same organs, the same senses, the same instincts, the same feelings, the same faculties, the same understanding, will, and conscience, and the same capacity for religious culture, but that he has the same guilty and polluted nature, and needs the same redemption. Christ died for all men, and we are commanded to preach the gospel to every creature under heaven. Accordingly, nowhere on the face of the earth are men to be found who do not need the gospel or who are not capable of becoming partakers of the blessings which it offers. The spiritual relationship of men, their common apostasy, and their common interest in the redemption of Christ, demonstrate their common nature and their common origin beyond the possibility of reasonable or excusable doubt. (CH-STA)

VISIONS

What is here related is no doubt strictly true, but there is no propriety in calling it "a vision," since it can easily be accounted for by a vivid impression on the imagination. A vision is something supernatural seen with the bodily eyes; but this man was totally blind; the objects so clearly discerned must then have been from impressions on the imagination. But in saying this, it is not intended to deny that the cause was the Spirit of God. This divine Agent can and does produce vivid impressions on the imagination, which have so much the appearance of external realities, that many are persuaded that they do see and hear what takes place only in their own minds. (AA-TRE)

VOCATION

Religion does not take a man away from his work; it sends him to his work with an added quality of devotion. We sing, do we not?

"Teach me, my God and King
In all things Thee to see
And what I do in anything,
to do it as for Thee.

If done t'obey Thy laws,
E' en servile labors shine:
Hallowed is toil, if this the cause,
The meanest work divine."

The doctrine is the doctrine, the fundamental doctrine, of Protestant morality, from which the whole system of Christian ethics unfolds. It is the great doctrine of "vocation," the doctrine, to wit, that the best service we can offer to God is just to do our duty—our plain, homely duty, whatever that may chance to be. (BBW-SSW)

VOWS

The vow is a promise made to God. In the vow, God is the party to whom the promise is made. It is of like nature with an oath because we are bound to observe them on the same grounds—because of our obligation to truth, and because of our obligation to reverence God. Lightly to vow on a trifling occasion, or having vowed to fail to keep it, is an act of profanity to God. (AAH-CF)

WALKING WITH GOD

Walking with any one is a familiar Scripture phrase for fellowship or communion. Walking with God, therefore, is habitual communion with him. (CH-CP)

This walking with God is a rare and high attainment, as it implies more than casual or occasional intercourse. There is all the difference between the intercourse of ordinary Christians with God and habitual walking with him, that there is between an occasional inter course, however agreeable, with a man whom we meet occasionally, and our daily communion with an intimate friend, or members of our own family. Walking with God, therefore, means uniform, habitual communion with him. (CH-CP)

Communication cannot be one sided. There must be conversation, address, and answer. God does thus commune with us. He reveals himself to his people as he does not unto the world. He assures them of his love. He awakens in them confidence in his promises. He brings those promises to their minds and gives them the power of response. These promises become his answers to their requests. And they experience a renewal of faith, -love, zeal, etc., which is the manifestation of his presence with the soul. This is not imaginary. It is real. It is not enthusiasm (Fanaticism). It does not suppose anything miraculous, no responses by voice, no unintelligent impulses; but the consciousness of the presence of the Infinite Spirit with our spirits; the conviction that he hears and answers us. We have probably all seen examples of this walking with God, men. who lived in habitual communion with God through Christ. (CH-CP)

WAR

If possible, every nation should avoid war; but a state of warfare may be forced on a nation. Self-defence is the first law of our nature and is a duty. (AA-PT)

War is an incalculable evil, because of the lives it destroys, the misery it occasions, and the moral degradation it infallibly works on all sides—upon the vanquished and the victor, the party originally in the right and the party in the wrong. In every war one party at least must be in the wrong, involved in the tremendous guilt of unjustifiable war, and in most cases both parties are in the wrong. No plea of honor, glory or aggrandizement, policy, or profit, can excuse, much less justify, war; nothing short of necessity to the end of the preservation of national existence. (AAH-CF)

It is an evident truth, that every case in which human life is taken in war, is a case of murder; some persons must be accountable for the shedding of all the blood which is spilled. And if this be so, then that nation which, without sufficient reason, commences a war or provokes a war, has an awful responsibility resting on it; and so also, when a war is in progress, that nation which refuses to make peace, or insist on unreasonable conditions, is guilty of all the blood which may be shed, and all the misery produced. (AA-PT)

WARFARE, SPIRITUAL

-Our Adversary

If our adversary was a man, and possessed nothing beyond human strength, ingenuity, and cunning, we might defend ourselves by human means. But as we must contend with Satan, we need the armour of God. (CH-CE)

If it is not true that there is such a being as Satan, or that he possesses great power and intelligence, or that he has access to the minds of men and exerts his power for their destruction; if all this is obsolete, then there is no real necessity for supernatural power or for supernatural means of defence. If Satan and satanic influence are fables or figures, then all the rest of the representations concerning this spiritual conflict is empty metaphor. But if one part of this representation is literally true, the other has a corresponding depth and reality of meaning. If Satan is really the prince of the powers of darkness, ruler and god of this world; if he is the author of physical and moral evil; the great enemy of God, of Christ and of his people, full of cunning and malice; if he is constantly seeking whom he may destroy, seducing men into sin, blinding their minds and suggesting evil and sceptical thoughts; if all this be true, then to be ignorant of it, or to deny it, or to enter on this conflict as though it were merely a struggle between the good and bad principles in our own hearts, is to rush blindfold to destruction. (CH-CE)

-Inevitable

We are subjected to an inevitable conflict. It cannot be avoided by flight, by surrender, or by refusing to resist. It is a conflict, not for house and home, nor for liberty or security, but of life and death; not of the body, but of the soul; not temporal, but eternal. The enemy is sometimes designated as Satan and the powers of darkness, sometimes as the world, and sometimes as our own evil hearts, or ourselves. These all constitute one. They are different powers of the kingdom of darkness. Satan is the god of this world. The world is subject to him and constitutes one large corps of his army; and the flesh, i.e., our fallen nature, is his ally. (CH-CP)

-Not to be Taken Lightly

Some people make a mockery of Satan's temptations, as though they were the dreams of superstitious souls. Not so Paul, and Peter, and John - not so Luther and Calvin, and Zwingli. Not so any who understand the nature of the spiritual warfare. It is to the great injury of many professors, that they are not constantly on the watch against the wiles of the devil. (AA-TRE)

-Sometimes Subtle

Christians are more injured in this warfare by the insidious and secret influence of their enemies lulling them into the sleep of carnal security, than by all their open and violent assaults. No duty is more necessary, in maintaining this conflict, than watchfulness. Unceasing vigilance is indispensable. "Watch and pray that ye enter not into temptation." "What I say unto you, I say unto all, Watch." (AA-TRE)

-Victory or Defeat?

The issue of the conflict is not uncertain. Christ has bruised Satan under our feet. If we resist. in the strength of the Lord and in the use of his armor, we shall conquer. If we do not resist, or if this resistance is in our own strength or with our own weapons, we shall perish. (CH-CP)

WATCHMEN

The reason for which woe is denounced on ministers who fail to preach the gospel is that men cannot be saved without it. All men are exposed to eternal death. There is but one way of deliverance from that death, and woe to him who, although officially called and dedicated to the work, fails to make that way known. If any man knows of a certain preventive of the cholera, which now threatens our land, he would be a murderer if he did not make it known. So, the blood of souls, the Scriptures assure us, will be required of those watchmen who fail to warn their fellowmen of their danger. (CH-CP)

WATER

Water represents purity, and the washing with water the purification of the soul. (AA-PT)

WEALTH

Worldly prosperity has ever been found an unfavorable soil for the growth of piety. It blinds the minds to spiritual and eternal things, dries up the spirit of prayer, fosters pride and ambition, furnishes the appropriate food to covetousness, and leads to a sinful conformity to the spirit, maxims, and fashions of the world. (AA-TRE)

Neglect not while you live, to do good and communicate. Remember that you are but the stewards of the wealth you possess, and therefore it is required of you to be faithful in the distribution of what is put into your hands. If you have tried the plan of parsimony, lest you should lessen your estate, now try the plan of wise liberality, and see whether that saying of Christ is not verified by experience, "It is more blessed to give than to receive". (AA-TRE)

WILL

The moral condition of the heart determines the act of the will, but the act of the will cannot change the moral condition of the heart. (AAH-CF)

WISDOM

What is wisdom? The fact is plain that religion is in the Scriptures often called wisdom, and wickedness, folly. The good are the wise; the wicked are fools. But why is this? Because it implies the selection of the best means and the use of the best ends. The highest end is God's glory, the best means, obedience to his will. It is the height of folly to select any creature good or temporary attainment as the chief end. This all but the righteous do, and therefore all but the righteous are fools. (CH-CP)

-Of the World

Other masters enough will demand your attention; other teachers essay your guidance. The wisdom of the world will laugh at your narrowness and point you to other ways of approach to God. I charge you, by the welfare of your own souls—and what should a man give in exchange for his soul? To bear steadily in mind that the world by its wisdom has never attained to the knowledge of God. (BBW-TSW)

WITNESSING FOR CHRIST

In one sense it is every man's duty, provided he has received the knowledge of the gospel, to preach it, i.e., to make it known to others. The commission and command, "Go ye into all the world and preach the gospel to every creature," was given not to the apostles exclusively, nor to the ministry exclusively, but to the whole Church and to all its members. Every member has the right and is under obligation to make known this great salvation to his fellowmen. (CH-CP)

WORDS

The great truth here presented (Matt. 12: 36) is that the words of men reveal their character and shall furnish the criterion by which that character is to be determined. (CH-CP)

Words reveal the character because they are determined by it. Words of blasphemy or irreverence; words of malice, of satire, of contempt; words of pride and vain-glory; words of impurity; words of falsehood and treachery; words of folly and nonsense; - all these reveal what the man is. They determine his character. They are to the man what foliage, flowers, fragrance, and fruit are to plants. (CH-CP)

THE WORD OF GOD

-Its Authority

If the Bible has no more authority than is due to the writings of pious men, then our faith is vain, and we are yet in our sins. We have no sure foundation for our hopes of salvation. (CH-STA)

-Its Design

The design of all the revelations contained in the Word of God is the salvation of men. God does not make known His being and attributes to teach men science, but to bring them to the saving knowledge of Himself. (CH-STA)

-And Truth

When our Lord says, "Thy word is truth," he says that all that God has revealed may be confided in as exactly corresponding to what really is or is to be. His Word can never fail, though heaven and earth pass away. (CH-STA)

-And the Holy Spirit

Although the truths of the Bible have this transforming and saving power, the minds of men because of the fall are not in a condition to receive it. Therefore, it is necessary, to render the Word of God an effectual means of salvation, that it be attended by the supernatural power of the Holy Spirit. (CCH-STA)

-Answers Life's Great Questions

The Bible being the Word of God, all the great questions which for ages have agitated the minds of men are settled with infallible certainty. Human reason has never been able to answer to its own satisfaction, or to the assurance of others, the vital questions, what is God? What is man? What lies beyond the grave? If there is a future state of being, what is it? How may future blessedness be secured? Without the Bible we are, on all these subjects, in utter darkness. (CH-STA)

-Essential to the Christian

The Bible, therefore, is essential to the conscious existence of the divine life in the soul and to all its rational exercises. The Christian can no more live without the Bible than his body can live without food. The Word of God is milk and strong meat; it is water to the thirsty; it is honey and the honeycomb. (CH-STA)

THE WORK OF THE LORD

The work of the Lord is the work in which the Lord is engaged, the work of instructing, correcting, and saving men. It is not any secular or worldly work, in which we are engaged, but the work which the Lord came down from heaven to accomplish, which he is now carrying on by his providence, by the ministry of angels, by the Church, and which is to be consummated in the kingdom of heaven. We are co-workers with God, with Christ, and with the Spirit. It is a great and glorious work in comparison with which everything else is insignificant. (CH-CP)

WORKS (GOOD)

-Defined

A profoundly good work is one which springs from a principle of divine love and has the glory of God as its object and the revealed will of God as its rule. None of the actions of an unregenerate man are of this character. (AAH-CF)

-Not Perfect but Accepted

The best works of believers, instead of mer i ting pardon of sin and eternal life, cannot endure the scrutiny of God's holy judgment. Nevertheless, the good works of sincere believers are, like their persons, despite their imperfections, accepted, because of their union with Christ Jesus, and rewarded for his sake. (AAH-CF)

-Evidences of Salvation

A saved soul is a holy soul, and a holy soul is one whose faculties are all engaged in works of loving obedience. Grace in the heart cannot exist without good works as their consequent. (AAH-CF)

Although not the ground of our acceptance, good works are essential to salvation, as the necessary consequences of a gracious state of soul and perpetual requirements of the divine law. Gal. 5:22; Eph. 2:10; John 14:21. (AAH-CF)

WORLD

Let the worldings have the world and make the most of it. I will never envy their prosperity, for it is but for a moment, and then, like a passing scene in a drama, disappears forever. Their feet stand on slippery places, and in due time their steps will slide, and all their music, their mirth, and their wine will cease forever. And when they sink, they will rise no more. They plunge into a horrible abyss, where no ray of hope ever enters. Oh, their end, their dreadful end! (AA-PT)

You must not fancy, then, that God sits helplessly by while the world, which He created for Himself, hurdles hopelessly to destruction, and He is able only to snatch with difficulty here and there a brand from the universal burning. The world does not govern Him in one of His acts: He governs it and leads it steadily onward to the end which, from the beginning, or ever a beam of it had been laid, He had determined for it. (BBW-TSW)

WORLDLINESS

(Conformity to the world) is destructive to spirituality. It is impossible to live near to God, and yet be conformed to the world. (CH-CP)

WORSHIP

-Regulated by God's Word

Since God has prescribed the mode in which we are acceptably to worship and serve him, it must be an offence to him and a sin in us for us either to neglect his way, or in preference to practice our own. (AAH-CF)

As shown from Scripture, not only all teaching for doctrine the commandments of men, but all manner of will-worship, of self-chosen acts and forms of worship, are an abomination to God. (AAH-CF)

-In Homes

A company thinly scattered over a large house always appears cold and uncomfortable; while the same persons brought near together, in a small house, have an entirely different appearance; and we see why social meetings in private houses are felt by sincere Christians to be more profitable, often, than the more solemn assemblies of the Church. And, upon the same principle, all worshippers feel more animated when surrounded by a multitude. (AA-TRE)

WRESTLING

-As Spiritual Warfare

Paul says, "For we wrestle not against flesh and blood, but against principalities, against powers, against the rulers of the darkness of this world, against spiritual wickedness in high places." From this message it is evident that our spiritual foes are numerous and powerful, and that the believer's conflict with them is violent: it is a "wrestling", or a contention which requires them to put forth all their strength, and to exercise all their skill. (AA-TRE)

WRITING

When we consider how much good has been done by the published works of such men as Baxter, Owen, Doddridge, Alleine, Boston, Edwards, etc., we wonder that men gifted with a talent for writing attractively and power fully, do not devote more of their time to the preparation of good books. (AA-PT)

The man who is enabled to write a truly evangelical and useful book, or even a single tract of first-rate excellence, may convey the saving truth of the gospel to a thousand more persons than the living preacher can ever instruct by his voice. (AA-PT)

YOUTH

-Concerning Habits

Be careful to form good habits. Almost all permanent habits are contracted in youth, and these do in fact form the character of the man through life. (AA-TRE)

-Concerning Friendships

Be particular and select in the company which you keep, and the friendships which you form. "Tell me," says the proverb, "what company you keep, and I will tell you what you are." Evil communications corrupt good manners. Vice is more easily and extensively diffused by improper companions, than by all other means. As one infected sheep communicates disease to a whole flock, so one sinner often destroys much good, by corrupting all the youth who fall under his influence. We would entreat you, dear young friends, to form an intimacy with no one whose principles are suspicious. The friendship of profligate men is exceedingly dangerous. Listen not to their fair speeches, and warm professions of attachment. Fly from contact with them, as from one infected with the plague. (AA-TRE)

ZEAL

-True and False

True or false zeal is not determined either by its energy, or by the self-denial and exertions which it leads. Many unholy men are exceedingly fervid in their zeal, and many such make the greatest sacrifices for their ends. (CH-CP)

True zeal relates to a holy life. It is remarkable how often the greatest zealots for God, the Church, and sound doctrine (as they regard it), have been unholy and even immoral in their lives. (CH-CP)

-And Spiritual Power

Zeal is the chief source, or one of the chief sources of spiritual power. God employs living souls to communicate. In all ages, men of zeal have produced great results. This qualification, in the absence of others, can accomplish wonders. (CH-CP).

-A Gift from God

Remember that zeal is a gift of the Holy Spirit; that whatever grieves the Spirit quenches our zeal, and that the more we are filled with the Holy Ghost, the more we be filled with godly zeal. (CH-CP)

Appendix One

Thoughts on Archibald Alexander, Charles Hodge, and AA Hodge

by the late Dr. David C. Calhoun

Dr. David Calhoun, the late Professor of Church History at Covenant Seminary, intricately created the most researched and fascinating history of the old Princeton Seminary ever attempted. Its appendices and footnotes, alone, are invaluable resources on, not only Princetoniana, but Americana from 1812-1921.

So, when I (ENG) was told by my publisher that he thought it was a good project to publish this anthology on the 100th anniversary of the death of Dr. B. B. Warfield, I began thinking of who might enhance the work biographically. I found Dr. Calhoun's email address, and wrote to see if he would be willing to do so. The response that follows was quickly sent to me about one month ago:

Dear Dr. Gross,

> This is David's wife, Anne. I am sad to tell you that David is in hospice at home and very near the end of his life. He would be so sorry to know that he could not provide the Afterward for your lovely book. You have had such an interesting life and ministry, and I know David would have so much enjoyed fellowship with you.

Sincerely,

Anne Calhoun

The following remarks on the lives of these three great Princeton theologians come, in their entirety, from Dr. David Calhoun's thoroughly researched two volumes entitled, Princeton Seminary, and published by The Banner of Truth Trust.[24] I pray that both the quoted words that follow and the original volumes of Dr. Calhoun may prove as inspiring to the readers as they have been to me and many others. And, so soon after his death, may they also bear witness of Dr Calhoun's life as a great scholar, missionary, and man of

---

[24] David Calhoun, Princeton Seminary, two vols, Banner of Truth Trust, 1994, 1996, 1050+ pages

godliness who exemplified in his life and ministry both the loveliness of Jesus Christ and His undying love for the world. So, it is especially fitting to share with you the lives of three incredibly impactful men in the words of one who will always be remembered as one of their true heirs.

In his preface, Dr. Calhoun wrote, "The study of the history of Old Princeton Seminary has been to me an intellectual challenge and a spiritual blessing. And it is my hope that this book may challenge those who read it to seek 'solid learning' in the truth of God and that it may be - in the words of Princeton's first professor (Archibald Alexander) in his book on the Log College - 'conducive to piety.'"[25]

Archibald Alexander (1772-1851)

"Early in 1850, revival came again to Princeton. On that communion Sunday a few weeks before revival began, not a single new member was added to First Presbyterian Church. Dr. Alexander spoke to the congregation that day. The pastor later wrote, 'I have always believed that those remarks were instrumental, under God, of bringing believers to the throne of grace, to supplicate more earnestly for a revival of religion.' ...Prayer meetings were held throughout the campus and at First Presbyterian Church. Students met in their rooms for intercessory prayer.... Dr. Archibald Alexander, whose preaching had been a major factor in the earlier awakening (1815), was a vital part of this revival. For six or seven weeks, services were conducted every evening except Saturday; and Dr. Alexander, although he was nearly eighty years old, preached repeatedly.

"He preached his last sermon to the students in the seminary chapel on Sept 7, 1851. The next Sunday, at Princeton's First Presbyterian Church, he took his place at the communion table by the side of the pastor and spoke to the congregation, urging them as pilgrims to a faithful and hopeful life. It was his last public service.

"There were last visits with Charles Hodge, who later said that 'he never saw and never imagined a deathbed where there was so little of death.' He told how Dr. Alexander, with a smile, handed him 'a white bone walking-stick, carved and presented to him by one of the chiefs of the Sandwich Islands,

---

[25] David Calhoun, PS, vol 1, xxvi, Banner of Truth Trust

and said, 'You must leave this to your successor in office, that it may be handed down as a kind of symbol of orthodoxy.'[26]

"When relieved from pain, Dr. Alexander said that it was due to the ministration of angels and added, 'They are always around the dying beds of God's people.' He acknowledged … 'All my theology is reduced to this narrow compass: Jesus Christ came into the world to save sinners' …. On Oct 22, Archibald Alexander died peacefully.

"Alexander's students, almost two thousand now scattered around the world, mourned the death of their beloved teacher…. When David Wilson – who had just opened the Archibald Alexander High School in Liberia - heard of Dr. Alexander's death, he wrote from Africa … 'Other good men there are, but there is no other Archibald Alexander.'

"About five feet, seven inches tall, Alexander was a small, slender man. He was never arrogant or domineering, but he was an outstanding leader. Contemporaries, such as Henry Boardman, often placed the 'secret of his power' in the 'combination of excellencies which his character presented – in his blended piety and wisdom; his simplicity and consistency; his sound sense and spirituality; and his heart sympathy with everything good, and kind, and useful.' …A. A. Hodge wrote that Archibald Alexander, 'more than any man of his generation, appeared to those who heard him to be endued with the knowledge, and clothed with the authority of a prophet.'

"Dr. Alexander created and shaped Princeton Seminary. He impressed his viewpoint and personality upon it as few men have ever stamped an institution. He modeled both 'piety' and 'solid learning' – and he would not let the seminary lose sight of either. From him came all the motifs of of the Princeton theology, but Dr. Alexander was not content to teach Bible and doctrine. 'He aimed to send out warriors of the cross.' The students sometimes playfully called him 'the pope.' They had 'unbounded confidence,' as one of them wrote, 'in his sanctified common sense.' Another commented on 'his wonderful sagacity and acquaintance with the human heart.' Adding, 'his powers of managing and trimming into shape all sorts of characters, as

---

[26] It was a moment of great personal excitement when I (ENG) was shown this very walking stick in the archives at Princeton Seminary, by my friend and then Archivist at the Seminary library, William Harris. Knowing my devotion to the Princeton theology, he wryly remarked, "I thought this might be of some interest to you." As a missionary-educator my mind imagined the scenes of a converted animist giving this to Dr. Alexander, and his then passing it on to my great mentor-over-the-ages, Charles Hodge. As I held it in my hands, I prayed that I would be a faithful defender of biblical Augustinianism and missiological devotion-as were the great Princeton theologians.

come here, are remarkable.' Another, Elijah Lovejoy, spoke for many when he wrote his father soon after he began his studies at Princeton, 'Come here, and I will introduce you to one of the best men in the world – Dr. Alexander.'

"At the re-opening of the seminary chapel on Sept. 27, 4, Charles Hodge said (when reminiscing about Dr. Alexander and Dr. Samuel Miller – the first two professors of the seminary): 'The first signal manifestation of the divine favor to this Institution was the selection of Dr. Archibald Alexander and Dr. Samuel Miller as its professors, and their being spared for nearly forty years to devote themselves to its service....'

"They were in the first place eminently holy men. They exerted that indescribably but powerful influence which always emanates from those who live near to God....

"It often happens, however, that men are very pious without being very good. Their religion expends itself in developing feelings and services, while the evil passions of their nature remain unsubdued. It was not so with our fathers. They were as good as they were pious. I was intimately associated with them, as pupil and colleague, between thirty (Dr Miller) and forty (Dr Alexander) years. In all that time I never saw in either of them any indication of vanity, of pride, of envy, of jealousy, of insincerity, of uncharitableness, or of disingenuousness. I know that what I say is incredible. Nevertheless, it is true. And it is my right and duty to scatter these withered flowers upon their graves.

"Archibald Alexander Hodge saw his father standing in his study weeping, exclaiming, 'It is all past, the glory of our Seminary has departed.'"[27]

Charles Hodge (1797-1878)

"Except for a year in Philadelphia (the city of his birth), and two years in Europe (for advanced studies), Charles Hodge had lived in Princeton since his college days. He loved the town – its seminary, its college, and its people.

"B.B. Warfield, a student in Hodge's later years, wrote that he had 'sat under many noted teachers' and that Dr. Hodge was 'superior to them all. He was in fact my ideal of a teacher. Best of all men I have ever known, he knew how to make a young man think.' Warfield commented in detail concerning his course in exegesis with Charles Hodge:

---

[27] **David** Calhoun, Princeton Sermons, vol. 2, pp 340-349, Banner of Truth Trust

"He taught exegesis only to the juniors, and although five years have elapsed, the impressions made at that time remain as vivid as though it were yesterday…. After his always strikingly appropriate opening prayer had been offered, and we had been settled back into our seats, he would open his well-thumbed Greek Testament – on which it was plain that there was not a single marginal note – look at the passage for a second, and then throwing his head back, and closing his eyes, begin his exposition. He scarcely again glanced at the Testament during the hour, the text was evidently before his mind, verbally, and the matter of his exposition thoroughly at his command. In an unbroken stream it flowed from subject to subject, simple, clear, cogent, unfailingly reverent. Now and then he would pause a moment to insert an illustrative anecdote – now and then lean forward and suddenly with tearful, wide-opened eyes, to press home a quick-risen inference of the love of God to lost sinners…. This then was how he taught us exegesis.[28]

"In 1872 Princeton celebrated the fiftieth year of Charles Hodge's professorship, an event at that time without precedent in American academic life…. On April 24 the shops in Princeton were closed and people came from far and near to fill the First Presbyterian Church. Charles Hodge's wife, Mary, his eight children, his beloved brother Hugh – now blind – and the great company of Hodge grandchildren were there. Also present were four hundred former students from almost every year of the seminary's history….

"Charles Hodge had taught 2,700 students – more than had attended any other seminary in the country. Now scattered across America and the world, these men honor him, said Henry Boardman, for the great mind God has given him and 'love him for his still greater heart'….

"As Dr. Hodge came to the platform to reply to the addresses of the morning (15 speeches following Boardman's), the audience rose to welcome him, and many remained standing while he spoke.

"There was a public dinner and an afternoon meeting … for the reading of letters of congratulations from friends not present. Afterwards Henry Boardman said to Dr. Hodge, 'How did you stand all that?' 'Why,' Hodge replied smiling, 'very quietly. It didn't seem at all to be me they were talking about. I heard it all as some other man.' [29]

"In early Oct 1873 Charles Hodge, James McCosh, and others from Princeton were in New York City, for the Sixth General Conference of the Evangelical Alliance. One observer described Hodge as 'the most impressive personality f the Alliance,' a picture of 'strength lying in repose,' with a face

---

[28] David Calhoun, Princeton Seminary, vol 1, p 195, Banner of Truth Trust
[29] David Calhoun, Princeton Seminary, vol 2, pp 36-39, Banner of Truth Trust

both 'radiant' and 'serene' .... Dr. Hodge gave the opening prayer, saying in a voice softened by old age:

> "Come Holy Spirit, come! Descend in all thy plenitude of grace. Come as the Spirit of reverence and love .... We have come to confess Thee before men; to avow our faith that God is, and that He is the Creator, Preserver, and Governor of the World.... We are here to confess Christ as God manifest in the flesh, and as our only and all-sufficient Savior ... and who, having died for our offenses, has risen again for our justification. We acknowledge Him as now seated at the right hand of God of the Majesty on high, all power in heaven and on earth having been committed to His hands. Thanks be to God, thanks be to God that He has put on us, unworthy as we are, the honor to make this confession, and to bear this testimony to God and to His Son. O God, look down from heaven upon us. Shed abroad in our hearts the Holy Spirit, that we may be truly one in Christ Jesus.
>
> "O Thou blessed Spirit of the living God, without whom the universe were dead, Thou art the source of all life, of all holiness, of all power. O Thou perfect Spirit, Thou precious gift of God, come we pray, and dwell in every heart, and touch every lip. We invoke the blessing of Father, Son and Holy Ghost on this Evangelical Alliance...."

"Later in the conference, Charles Hodge addressed the delegates on the 'Unity of the Church Based on Personal Union with Christ' – a moving call to Christians and churches to manifest real unity in spite of their manifest and real differences. Dr. Hodge said:

> "If all Christians really believed that they constitute the mystical body of Christ on earth, they would sympathize with each other, as readily as the hands sympathize with feet, or th feet with the hands. If all churches, whether local or denominational, believed that they are one body in Christ Jesus, then instead of conflict we should have concord; instead of mutual criminations, we should have mutual respect and confidence; instead of rivalry and opposition we should have cordial cooperation. The whole visible Church would then present an undivided front against infidelity qnd every form of Anti-Christian error, and the sacramental host of God, though divided into different corps, would constitute one army glorious and invincible.'" [30]

---

[30] David Calhoun, Princeton Seminary, vol 2 pp 40-41, Banner of Truth Trust

"Charles Hodge's theology, according to the Lutheran Charles Krauth, was 'a Calvinism so gentle in its spirit toward other forms of evangelical Christianity.' William Paxton wrote, ... 'There is not one point of the Calvinistic system that he obscures, but he lets in upon it the full light of God's love and mercy.'"

"Charles Hodge ... usually sought to find the largest amount of common ground between his position and that of those with whom he differed. He was praised not only by those closest to him but also by many who took other theological positions. Charles Krauth said of him, 'Next to having Dr. Hodge on one's side is the pleasure of having him as an antagonist....' [31]

"John Kennedy, pastor of the Free Church in Dingall, Scotland, visited the United States in 1873. On his return home he is reported to have said that there were two things he saw in America that exceeded his expectation – Niagara Falls and Dr. Hodge! [32]

"On the last New Year's day of Charles Hodge's life, a seminary student visited him in his study and asked for a motto. The old man wrote in a firm hand 'Thy word is truth.' This motto was the strength of Charles Hodge's theology and his bequest to the next generation. [33]

"On April 14, 8, he spoke at the Sabbath Afternoon Conference in the old oratory in Alexander Hall. His topic was, 'Fight the Good Fight of Faith' (1 Tim 6:12) .... A week later he preached in the seminary chapel at the communion service for the graduating class. 'We cannot commemorate Christ as Savior without thereby acknowledging ourselves to be His, the purchase of His blood and devoted to His service,' Dr. Hodge told the seminary seniors. In May he went to Washington for his annual visit with his brother-in-law. There, on May 16, he attended church for the last time, leading in prayer at the funeral of his old friend Professor Joseph Henry of the Smithsonian Institute.

"Charles Hodge returned home to Princeton and began to rapidly to decline in strength. He sat in his beloved chair in his study, talking about the grandchildren, whose tiniest concerns he cherished, and about the General Assembly, the Berlin Conference, the affairs of the town that had been his home since boyhood, and especially about the seminary in which he had taught for over fifty years.... He died on June 19th, repeating to himself the hymn,

---

[31] David Calhoun, Princeton Seminary, vol 2, pp 58-59, Banner of Truth Trust
[32] David Calhoun, Princeton Seminary, vol 2, pp 60-61, Banner of Truth Trust
[33] David Calhoun, PS, vol 2, p 65, Banner of Truth Trust

Jesus, I am never weary, when upon the bed of pain;

If thy presence only cheers me, all my loss I count but gain,

Ever near me, ever near me, Lord remain.

"The funeral was on June 22, 8, at the end of the college's commencement week. It was a beautiful afternoon in the little town. All the stores were closed and all business suspended.... William Paxton gave the funeral address, paying heartfelt tribute to their teacher and friend:

"To sum up all, when due allowance is made for his intellect and his learning, after all his chief power was in his goodness. Christ enshrined in his heart was the center of his theology and his life. The world will write upon his monument GREAT; but we, his students, will write upon it GOOD."

"The Princeton students and faculty were lavish in their praise of their beloved teacher and friend. James P. Boyce said, 'He is one of the most excellent of men; so modest and yet so wise, so kind and fatherly in his manner, and yet so giant an intellect, he is a man who deserves a world of praise.' William Paxton said, 'His was not a dead theology .... What he gave us was bread from our Father's table.' John Macmillan remembered 'the marvelous manner in which he brought [God's] love and life down into our lives.' Charles Aiken told the Princeton students, 'To him more than to any other man I ever knew had the grace been given not only to bring captivity every thought to the obedience of Christ, but to draw the motives of life from Christ, and to find the daily strength and joy of life in Christ.'

"Despite the praise and acclaim he received as a great theologian and churchman, Charles Hodge was humble. About a year before his death, Dr. Boardman said to him, 'You ought to be a very happy man. Consider what you have accomplished, and the universal feelings toward you.' 'Now, stop! said Hodge, with a wave of his hand. 'All that can be said is, that God has been pleased to take up a *poor little stick* and do something with it. What I have done is as nothing compared with what is done by a man who goes to Africa, and labors among a heathen tribe, and reduces their language to writing. I am not worthy to stoop down and *unloose the shoes* of such a man.' [34]

---

[34] David Calhoun, PS, vol 2, pp 61-62, Banner of Truth Trust

Archibald Alexander Hodge (1823-1886)

"Charles and Sarah Hodge's children enjoyed living in their large house and playing on the seminary campus. A student of this time described the oldest son, Archibald Alexander Hodge. As he ran 'about the Seminary grounds, a flaxen-haired, blue-eyed. Rosy-cheeked little boy of seven or eight summers, and one or tow of his little brothers with him.' AA Hodge later remembered his life ... in a home 'all radiant with love, with unwavering faith, and with unclouded hope.' The children were Dr. Hodge's pride and joy. '...He prayed for us at family prayers, and singly, and taught us to pray at his knees with such soul-felt tenderness, that however bad we were our hearts all melted to his touch.'

'Ten-year-old Archibald and his sister Mary Elizabeth gave a letter on June 23, 33, to Princeton graduate James R. Eckard, who was soon to set sail for Ceylon. It read:

> 'Dear Heathen: The Lord Jesus Christ has promised that the time shall come when all the ends of the earth shall be His kingdom... And if this was promised by a Being who cannot lie, why do you not help it to come Soon there will not be a nation, no not a space of ground as large as a footstep, that will lack a missionary. My sister and myself have, by small self-denials, procured two dollars which are enclosed in this letter to buy tracts and Bibles to teach you.
>
> Archibald Alexander Hodge, Mary Eliz. Hodge
>
> Friends of the Heathen [35]

"A.A. Hodge and his wife ... had served at the Presbyterian mission in Allahabad, India, for nearly three years, until serious physical problems forced them – with their two children – to return to the United States in 1850. He became 'a living missionary force' at the seminary. According to Francis L. Patton: 'His experience in the mission field enhanced his zeal for the mission cause, gave him a grasp of the missionary problem, and an interest in missionaries that made him always the trusted counsellor of all those among his pupils who contemplated a missionary career.

"In 1877 he came home to Princeton ... 'His large heart embraced the world, but no one could mistake the special place that Princeton had in his affections.' For one session father and son shared the teaching of theology at

---

[35] David Calhoun, Princeton Seminary, vol,1, pp 192-193, Banner of Truth Trust

Princeton, and the Charles Hodge turned over to AA Hodge the entire work of the department." [36]

"In 1886 the seminary faculty was made up of seven teachers …. Although he was not the senior professor, the real power at Princeton Seminary was Archibald Alexander Hodge. Charles Hodge's son and successor was known as a theologian who could preach and a preacher who could teach theology. During his first year at Princeton College Robert Speer went to the old beer hall on Nassau Street to evangelistic meetings…. He never forgot the sermon by 'the little round, redheaded man who preached with tears coursing down his cheeks.' Years later Speer said, 'I can still hear the message Dr Archie Hodge gave on that platform. If ever there was a man who could plead for Christ with a clear and intellectual presentation of the Gospel, but with all the fervor and tenderness of a Christian apostle, it was Archie Hodge.'

"Although AA Hodge's voice was weak and his speech often labored, Francis Patton declared that 'to hear him when he was at his best was something never to be forgotten.' Patton, himself a gifted speaker, thought that AA Hodge was 'one of the greatest preachers' in America.

"Hodge believed that the most important issue of his time was the defense of historic Christianity and especially of the doctrine of the inspiration of the Bible. In all his later writings he affirmed 'with ever increasing warmth' that the Scriptures are 'the very word of God, and the only infallible rule of faith and practice.'

"A shock of personal bereavement was felt by everyone in Princeton when word went out on the morning of November 12, 1886, that Dr. Archibald Alexander Hodge was dead. 'His death was sudden, but never was one more ready for it. He preached with great power and persuasiveness in the college chapel on Sunday morning … and after a period of great suffering found rest in the sleep of death about midnight Thursday.'

"'His heart, like his intellect, moved in vast circles, and encompassed the world,' Dr. Paxton said. 'While God had created him with a giant intellect, grace had made him a child, in the simple, sincere, undoubting exercises of piety.'

"AA Hodge was sixty-three when he died; only seven years earlier he had taken over the chair of theology from his father. B.B. Warfield, who would soon join the faculty as Hodge's successor, wrote, 'Nothing can give the faintest conception of the beauty of his Christian character, or of the astounding greatness of his ordinary conversation. His intimate

---

[36] David Calhoun, Princeton Seminary, vol 2, pp 51-52, Banner of Truth Trust

acquaintances feel that a great light has gone from their lives in his departure. No one can enter in where he entered into our hearts, and no one can rule as he ruled by our firesides and at our tables.'" 37

---

[37] David Calhoun, Princeton, Seminary, vol 2, pp 100-103, Banner of Truth Trust

www.ingramcontent.com/pod-product-compliance
Lightning Source LLC
Chambersburg PA
CBHW071430070526
44578CB00001B/59